FG

D0487991

Leab.
GARRISTOWN LIBRARY
Inv/07 : 07/FG7   Price €28.87
Title: Riding the storm: my
Class: 798.45Murphy

CHARLANNA CHONTAE FHINE GALL

WITHDRAWN FROM STOCK

TIMMY MURPHY

Riding the Storm
My Autobiography

TIMMY MURPHY

Riding the Storm
My Autobiography

with Donn McClean

A **RACING POST** COMPANY

Published in 2006 by Highdown
an imprint of Raceform Ltd
Compton, Newbury, Berkshire, RG20 6NL
Raceform Ltd is a wholly-owned subsidiary of Trinity Mirror plc

Copyright © Timmy Murphy and Donn McClean 2006

The right of Timmy Murphy and Donn McClean to be identified as the authors of this work
has been asserted by them in accordance with the Copyright, Designs and Patents Act 1988.

All rights reserved. No part of this publication may be reproduced, stored in a retrieval system,
or transmitted in any form or by any means, electronic, mechanical, photocopying, recording
or otherwise, without the prior written permission of the publishers.

A CIP catalogue record for this book is available from the British Library.

ISBN 1-905156-27-8

Cover designed by Tracey Scarlett

Interiors designed by Fiona Pike

Printed in Great Britain by William Clowes Ltd, Beccles, Suffolk

DEDICATION

To Mam and everyone who gave me a leg up in life and in racing.

ACKNOWLEDGEMENTS

I would like to thank everyone who helped me tell my story. To all those people, too numerous to name, who willingly gave their time in order that I could re-live the distant and recent past, a big thank you. Without you I would have not been able to piece my story together. Thanks also to Brough Scott of the *Racing Post* and Jonathan Taylor of Highdown for their energy and drive and to Donn McClean for his attention to detail.

CONTENTS

CHAPTER ONE

CONVICTED

Leabharlanna Fhine Gall

Garristown Library
Ph: 8355020

I could see that Judge John Crocker's lips were moving and I could tell that there was noise coming from his mouth, but I couldn't hear his words. My mind was too busy dealing with my own thoughts. I would know my fate in a matter of moments.

I stared straight ahead, straight at the judge, straight through him, my head doing somersaults. They had told me to prepare for the worst, so I had. But how do you prepare yourself for prison? I mean, how do you truly prepare for something when you don't have a clue what it's like? I began to focus on the judge, and tried to listen to his words.

'It is a tragedy to see a successful young man from any profession standing in the dock of a crown court having pleaded guilty to being drunk on an aircraft and, more seriously, indecently assaulting a member of the crew.'

There is nothing attractive about Isleworth Crown Court. The darkness just adds to the general feeling of gloom. I was standing in the dock, facing the judge, with the barristers in between us and my friends and family over to the left. I didn't need to look; I knew they were there: Seanie Curran, Jim Old, David Gandolfo, Mark Pitman and my three uncles who had come over from Cork. I appreciated their presence, I really did, but there was nothing they could do for me. Not now. It's amazing how you can be in a small room that is full of your closest friends and still feel as if you're alone.

For the previous three hours, the legal teams had been discussing the happenings on Virgin Atlantic flight VS901 from Narita airport, Tokyo, to Heathrow airport, London, just over three months earlier, 14 April 2002. That was the day my life changed. I faced two charges as a result of my behaviour on that flight, one of being drunk on board an aeroplane and another of indecently assaulting an air stewardess. Simon Connolly, prosecuting, had said that as the air stewardess walked past my seat I grabbed her leg and quickly moved my hand up her skirt.

It was difficult to just stand there and listen. I couldn't refute it. I had no right of reply. I couldn't remember what had happened on flight VS901. An alcohol-induced haze had drawn a shroud over the ten hours following take-off. Ten hours from hell, by all accounts. I didn't disbelieve it.

I was ashamed. I am ashamed. Ashamed and embarrassed. Accounts of what happened on the plane were diluted somewhat in the courtroom by character references from Mark Pitman, Mick Fitzgerald and others, but not even they could undo what had happened. They couldn't turn back the clock.

'It seems clear to me that you must have known you had a problem with drink.'

Alcohol had certainly got me into some poor situations in the past, but this was different. This was a whole different league. I had never made national headlines before; I had never been ashamed enough to cut myself off from the rest of the world for days before; I had never sought counselling before; I had never been staring down both barrels of a prison sentence before. All those other situations were gentle sea breezes compared to this hurricane.

So many thoughts went through my head. If only I hadn't gone to Japan. If only Cenkos hadn't been invited by the Japan Racing Association to run in the Nakayama Grand Jump. If only I hadn't been first rider for his trainer, Paul Nicholls, at the time. If only I hadn't drunk so much the night before the flight. If only I hadn't been drinking on board the plane. If only I had listened to my mother when she told me to go easy on the drink in Japan.

My mother. She was the big loser in all of this, probably even bigger than me. I had committed the act so it was right that I should suffer the penalty, but she had done no wrong. She and my father had to go about their daily lives in the small community of Kilcullen in County Kildare, where everybody knows everybody and everybody talks about everybody. There was no doubt that she felt the shame and the embarrassment even more acutely than I did. Mam wasn't in court. She was too ill to travel. I had been difficult to manage when I was growing up, but now, as an adult, I had probably caused my parents more heartache with this one act than I had during my entire childhood.

'We have your drunken loutish behaviour on 14 April, when even you can recollect drinking a vast amount, both on the plane and before you got on it.'

The three and a half months between the plane journey and the court case had been hell. I had decided that I wasn't going to ride again until after the court case, but five weeks at The Priory rehabilitation centre gave me the confidence to go and try to live my life again. Stop being a recluse. It was difficult going to Stratford on 1 June; it was difficult facing the press and other people, even my weigh-room colleagues. But, even though it was only for one ride, it was worth it. The support I got from the other jockeys and from the public that day – shouts of encouragement as I walked into the parade ring, wishing me well – was incredible, and it meant an awful lot. Khatani, my ride, wasn't a world beater, but he had won a couple of races. It didn't matter anyway. He was my first ride since Cenkos in the Nakayama Grand Jump, and I was hugely indebted to David Gandolfo for putting me up. When I was riding I was free; it didn't matter if it was at Cheltenham, Stratford or Kilmuckridge, or even on my pony Bluebell around the fields at home. For those five minutes and two miles and five furlongs at Stratford, I escaped. My sole focus was the horse, getting him travelling, keeping him interested, getting him positioned, presenting him at every fence. My only concern was what was happening on the racecourse within my immediate environment. My worries flowed out through my boots on to the ground. I was race-riding again.

'I accept that there are great pressures on jump jockeys, but there are also great pressures on cabin staff on long-distance flights.'

My solicitors had advised me to plead guilty. I didn't feel comfortable pleading guilty to something of which I had no recollection, but that was the advice, so that was what I did. They were the experts. Plead guilty and hope for leniency.

'I accept that you were a loud drunk, not a nasty drunk, on the aircraft. However ...'

I didn't hear any more. I was expecting a custodial sentence and I was just waiting to hear how long. How many days? How many weeks? I hadn't a clue. It was as if everything went into slow motion except for my heart. I felt dazed. I forgot to breathe. I went light in the head. And then he said it. Six months. Six months in prison.

Half a year? I didn't expect to get half a year. What now? How would I cope with prison? Would I survive? What would I do then? My riding career was over, that was for sure. Nobody would want an ex-con riding their horses. My head was spinning. Maybe I could go to America, just be a work rider, forget about all this. So many quick-fire thoughts. But I wouldn't get a visa, not with a record.

And the memories came tripping over one another. Jumping over Becher's Brook at home with my brother Brian and getting grass stains on our trousers. Riding around the field with my Dad, him tightening me up on the rail, teaching me how to race-ride, me coming home in a huff, hopping my helmet off the kitchen floor and declaring to my Mam that I would never ride with Dad again. Riding out at Mick Halford's, riding point-to-point winners for Michael Hourigan. Winning the Mildmay of Flete on Terao. Winning the Hennessy on Ever Blessed, the Irish National on Davids Lad, the Pillar Property on See More Business. All for nothing. Only memories. I was back to zero now, probably below it. No future, no prospects. Just six months of incarceration.

'Take him away.'

CHAPTER TWO

EARLY DAYS

I was born on Newberry Stud, just outside Kilcullen in County Kildare, on 20 August 1974, the first of two sons of Jimmy and Helen Murphy. My Mam and Dad both came from Cork, Dad from Watergrass Hill, halfway between Cork City and Fermoy, and Mam from Canteen Cross, just outside Shanballymore, a little village that lies between Mallow and Mitchelstown about ten miles from Doneraile and deep in the heart of racing and point-to-point country. Indeed, the first ever steeplechase race – a match between two prominent landowners, Mr O'Callaghan and Edmund Blake – was run in 1752 from Buttevant church across four and a half miles of country and the Awbeg river to the steeple of the St Leger church in Doneraile. It is from that race that steeplechasing derives its name, and Corkmen have been riding horses at racing pace over obstacles ever since.

My Dad was one of those Corkmen. Still is. He began just by riding this old donkey they had at home, progressing from there to ponies, and then to point-to-points. Point-to-points in those days were very different to the ones we have now. Back then they used to jump stone walls and banks and ditches. It was literally cross-country. They'd just get legged up and off they'd go in their peaked caps. And there were things that went on in those days that you can only look back on now in wonder. Like the time this fellow came up the inside of Dad going to the final fence. Dad shouted over to him 'Watch your inner!', and when the other guy looked over his shoulder, Dad reached over and pulled the bridle off his horse. The other fellow was so incensed – quite understandably – that he whacked Dad over the back with his whip. The net result was that they

13

were both disqualified and the horse that finished third was awarded the race. Or the foggy day when Dad knew the steward who was policing one of the markers. It was just an old bale left lying on the ground, and you had to go round it to the right. But the marker couldn't be seen through the fog from the enclosures, so Dad told the steward that if he said he went round it he wouldn't have to buy a drink that evening. Sure enough, every time they came to the bale the whole field went right and Dad went left, saving about a hundred yards each time. Of course Dad won doing handsprings, and that evening in the pub the steward's glass was always full.

Dad was a good rider, by all accounts. The fact that I was his son was a huge help to me when I set out to make my way, especially in point-to-points. People down that end of the country knew Dad well, and once I started to get a few rides I was known as Jimmy Murphy's son. You still had to go and prove yourself of course, and once you got a little bit more success you were known in your own right, but it was great to get a little bit of a leg up.

Dad loved the training side as well. He just loves horses and has always been interested in different training methods. Getting horses fit and keeping them healthy. He worked and rode for the trainer Jack Keefe, who was based just outside Shanballymore, but he didn't have horses of his own until he and Mam moved to Kildare.

My mother is the eldest of seven children. Her father was a blacksmith and had a small farm, and my father used to go up to the farm with Jack Keefe's horses to get them shod. That was how my Mam and Dad met. They got married in Cork and my Dad gave up riding – or, he said he gave up riding – and got a job as a stud groom in Castle Hyde Stud just outside Fermoy. A little while later he got a job at Newberry Stud, which was owned by Mr and Mrs Hexter at the time – it was bought by Lady Clague in 1975 – and they moved to Kilcullen to live on the farm.

Dad got a horse of his own on the day that I was born. I'm not sure Mam was best pleased. He would do his day's work at Newberry Stud and then he'd be off with his horse in the evenings. Mam says she hardly ever saw him in those days. When they got married he'd agreed he wouldn't ride again, but I guess he just couldn't stay away in the end. About two years after I was born, Jack Keefe was having a problem with this horse and he asked Dad if he would go down and ride it in a point-to-point one Sunday. Mam was pregnant with my brother Brian at the time, and Dad headed off down to ride the horse without telling her. He would have been in his late forties or early fifties at the time. Anyway, the horse won, the embers were rekindled, and it all started off again.

It was always my Dad's intention that I would ride. It was he who named me Timothy James, Timothy after his father and James after himself. I'm not sure my Mam really had a say. His thinking was that I would ride in point-to-points as Mr T. J. Murphy, just as he rode as Mr J. J. Murphy. I don't think he ever really considered the possibility that I wouldn't be interested in horses, or that I wouldn't be good enough to ride. I don't suppose either of those were options. There are photos of me at home sitting up in front of my Dad on his horse. I was probably too young to sit up on a chair on my own, never mind sit up on a horse, but that's the way it was. I don't really remember any time in my life when I couldn't ride. Dad bought me a rocking horse when I was ten months old. Grundy won the Derby that year, so the rocking horse was always called Grundy.

I don't remember the day when Dad came home with a pony for me. I was only three years old and apparently he was all excited about putting me up on my new pony and seeing how I would react. But kids are funny. We had a kind of a sandpit at the time which Dad used to fill up every so often by bringing a bucket of sand down on the tractor. The day my pony arrived – and Dad really was so excited about it, dying to see my face when I got this new pony, a pony of my own – I showed no interest in the animal at all and headed off to play in the sand for the day. Mam was sorry for my Dad, she saw how disappointed he was, but deep down she was secretly delighted and harboured some hope for me pursuing a life that wouldn't be dominated by horses. Alas, some hope.

There were always horses around when I was growing up. There were horses out in the stables and there were horses around the house. You'd go from the house to the stables and from the stables to the house. That was the routine. Dad always had a racehorse of his own that he'd be messing around with, and he would have a mare or two as well. Christmas Leaf, Wild Surmise and Snuggledown. Dad did a bit of breeding as well. The first thoroughbred foal I remember him having was this tiny filly. She wasn't big enough or good enough to race, but she was perfect for me. I broke her in with my Dad, and she was handy enough for me to ride. She was the first real thoroughbred racehorse that I rode.

It was great living on a stud farm. It wasn't until I left home that my Mam and Dad left the house on the farm and moved to their own house just across the road from the main gate. Funny thing, the house on the farm was always home to me, even though we never actually owned it. That is probably the main reason why I want to have my own place with a bit of land around it. That way you can do what you like, have a couple of horses, pre-train, break, whatever you want. We Irish have a thing about property anyway, but I think my desire to own some land is stronger than most people's, and that is probably where it stems from. But growing up on a stud farm was really great. I suppose, as a child, you feel like you own the whole lot anyway

I used to help Dad a bit on the stud. I wouldn't go off to the sales with him or anything, to Newmarket, or even Goffs or Ballsbridge, as Tattersalls (Ireland) was then, but I used to help him out at weekends, just leading horses in and out, and feeding. All the lads up there were great, Mick Doran and Mick Clifford in particular. They all seemed to be really happy doing what they were doing. But even then, my main interest was in racehorses. I liked looking after the yearlings and the mares a bit, but it was the horses who were back at the farm for a break from racing that interested me most. They would be mainly fillies out of training, or racehorses having a break. I loved the look of them. They were completely different to the racehorses my Dad had. They were leaner and looked fitter. Perhaps it was because the horses coming back to Newberry

Stud were Flat-bred whereas my Dad's horses were all bred to be three-mile chasers. Or perhaps it was because they had been trained harder and were simply fitter. Dad always liked a horse to carry a bit of condition. He'd always favour a big strong horse over a lean fit one. He would do loads of slow work with his horses but would never gallop the brains out of them. I remember thinking that the horses on the stud were very skinny and wondering if that was what racehorses were supposed to look like. But as I grew older I realised that just because they are fit doesn't mean they can gallop any faster. They have to be strong as well. Jumping is basically a stamina game, and there is a fine line between getting them fit and keeping them strong.

In fairness to my Dad, he never pushed me into riding, even though he was a great horseman and horses was all he did. He's in his late seventies now and he still rides. And all he ever wanted for me was horses. He would travel the length of the country to see me ride, but he wouldn't walk across the road to watch me play a game of football. I remember him saying to me one day, 'Where are you going with that ould Gaelic football? You'll never get paid for playing Gaelic football.' I suppose Dad was one of the reasons why I had such an interest in riding in the beginning. Horses were my father's life, and if I hadn't been into horses I probably wouldn't have got to spend much time with him. He made it easy for me to ride if I wanted to, but it was never a case of having to do it. I always wanted to get up in the morning and go riding out. I wasn't too fond of the mucking out and the grooming, mind you, but I'm sure that most kids are the same. Do as little of the work and as much of the riding as you can get away with.

So we'd go riding out, me and Dad, he on his horse and me on my pony, Bluebell. (I'm not sure at what point I began to prefer Bluebell to the sandpit. Neither am I sure why we called him Bluebell at home, because his registered name for racing was Canteen Cross, after my Mam's homeland outside Shanballymore.) Dad taught me an awful lot about riding, although we used to have terrible rows. Hands down, stirrups down. I just wanted to be a jockey straight away. I wanted to hook up my irons as short as they would go and perch like a jockey. But my Dad was from the old-school method of training. Lots of slow work and walking the roads. We'd walk up the road and down around the field. We had this big hill and we'd walk up and down it for hours, walk into the river and out again. I'd be bored out of my head. I just wanted to gallop. I'd be riding a finish on my pony, walking behind my Dad on his horse, but there are only so many finishes you can ride when you're walking. Then we'd walk around this island in the middle of the river where the water would be right up to your boots, and out again into the field.

Then we'd get to gallop. Yaahhhh! I would just point Bluebell in the right direction, give him a kick in the belly and cling on. The poor pony would be flat out, his tongue hanging out, and Dad on the horse would be just cantering beside me. There was a bend in the field, and Dad used to tighten me up going around it. Of course he did it just to try to teach me a little about race-riding, but I used to hate it when he did it. My mother always knew when he tightened me up because when I got home I'd blast into the kitchen and hop my helmet off the floor. 'I'm never riding with him again!' I'd shout, almost in tears. My mother wouldn't say too much. She knew that the next day I'd be out riding with him again, for certain. She'd just let me get over it on my own. I have no doubt that it stood me in good stead in the long run.

It was just my father's way. Instead of sitting me down and telling me how it would be in a race, he'd just try to show me. He communicated through horses. I rarely talked about anything else with Dad. He was a poor communicator, as was I really. I never remember Dad telling me that he loved me when I was young, or me telling him that I loved him, but that's the way he was brought up, I suppose. Different generation. Of course I had my falls, and when I did, my Dad would just sit there laughing at me. It was his way of trying to toughen me up, and it worked. Whenever he sat there laughing, I just wanted to get up again and get back on the horse, just to prove to him that I could do it.

I had a fairly scary moment, though, one day when I was about six. I never used to be able to hold Bluebell. I'd just get up on him and he'd go wherever he wanted to go. That was our agreement. I'd just kick him on to try to make him get there faster. This time he ran round the house and under the clothes line. He was small enough to get under it, but I wasn't. My neck got caught in the line. When the pony felt me stopping, he stopped, turned round and started to come back in the opposite direction, with the result that the clothes line got wrapped around my neck. Then the pony galloped off. Luckily it was an old clothes line and eventually it snapped. It scarred me all around my neck though, and I got a bit of a fright, but it happened so quickly and was over so quickly that I didn't think about it too much. When you're that age, you don't. Maybe it was only when I got older that I realised I'd been lucky to get away with that one. But at the time, it didn't stop me getting up on Bluebell the following day.

Sometimes my father and our next-door neighbour, Ray Nolan, who has since passed away, used to go up to the Curragh with the horses. I loved going to the Curragh, with its vast expanses stretching all the way to the horizon. Ray had this big horsebox, bigger than a double box, and we'd load the two horses into it with Bluebell up the front and get the tractor to pull it up to the Curragh. We'd be up and out at around five in the morning. I remember the pony used to get fierce excited. He'd be pulling my arms out as we walked around looking for a nice bit of ground, and then we'd be off. I'd set off on my pony behind the two horses. I couldn't hold one side of him, so I'd just let him go. I had no goggles, so I used to go the whole way with my eyes closed. It was a great buzz. I think Bluebell got as big a kick out of it as I did.

I went up to Punchestown one day with Dad and Joe and Des O'Brien, friends of Mam and Dad's, and friends of mine now. They were schooling two horses after racing, Dad on one and Joe on another, and Joe took a terrible fall. He broke his shoulder and, I think, his arm as well. I remember thinking that Joe was cool, having a fall and breaking an arm, like a real jockey. Poor Joe was in bits in the ambulance and I was thinking, 'Jeez he's a great lad. This is good stuff. This is the life of a jockey and it's brilliant.' I'm sure he wasn't thinking the same at the time. I remember seeing Dad have a fall in a point-to-point and going into the ambulance room afterwards and saying, 'Go on, Dad, fair play to you.' When you're a kid, you get a great kick out of fallers. When we went up to Punchestown we'd go to stand at the big double out in the country, hoping for fallers. The more carnage the better. The banks looked bigger then than they do now, but maybe that's because we were smaller. When you're a kid, jockeys are like gladiators, going out and coming home full of muck and sweat and blood. It all added to the buzz.

We built our own fences on the hill out in the field beside our house, and Brian and I used to jump them. The harder you fell and the more grass stains you got on your jeans, the better it was. We'd make the frame ourselves and we'd pick out birch and branches and stuff them in. Then we would jump over it and turn somersaults. We'd make the spread wider so that it was more difficult to jump, and so that you would almost definitely fall. Brian wasn't always so keen, but I had the authority that goes with being the elder brother. When he broke his collar bone after one particularly innocuous-looking fall, he was even less keen.

Dad had an old book in the house on riding style which I used to read a lot, checking out what was the right way to fall. I'd practise curling up and rolling and making myself as small as possible. I used to strap my saddle to a chair in my room and ride it. Use my whip. Switch my whip. I would spend hours in my room doing that. There was nothing I wanted more than to be a good rider. I'd say I rode at least a million finishes and switched my whip two million times on that chair, and I always just got up on the line. I won 32 Gold Cups and 48 Grand Nationals one season. I'm sure it all helped in the long run.

Like every kid who had an interest in horses and in racing, the Grand National was the biggest day of the year. We'd be out building fences for days afterwards. Every year our Christmas tree and as many neighbours' Christmas trees as we could muster would go into our Becher's Brook, and around Grand National time we used to go down on the Curragh and chop furze bushes to make fences. Then the poor pony used to get it. My poor pony. I'm sure Bluebell dreaded Grand National day. He'd be marking the days off in his calendar every year. We'd build the fences as high as we could, and we had a drop over the far side, steeper than any brook, that I'm sure he could have managed without. Of course, the more often you fell the better it was.

I used to love watching the racing on telly. Strange thing, but even then I watched races through jockeys. I had my favourite horses through the years all right, but the jockey was the most important thing to me, even then. If you listen to a jockey commenting on a race these days, you will notice that they comment by jockey as opposed to by horse. Comments like 'I could see AP travelling well at that point', or 'Mick asked him for a big one there'. It's almost always all about the jockey.

Frank Berry was my jockey in Ireland, and Jonjo O'Neill was my jockey in England. I remember watching Frank winning the Sun Alliance Chase on Antarctic Bay and the Champion Chase on Drumgora. But the best of all was when he rode Bobsline to win the Arkle, getting the better of the English horse Noddy's Ryde. Frank was from Kilcullen and was the local hero. He was the main reason why you didn't really mind being dragged to mass on a Sunday. You'd see Frank at mass. Frank Berry went to mass. We'd be all chuffed to bits.

Jonjo O'Neill is a distant relative of mine on my mother's side. That was probably the reason why I first started to follow him, but I loved watching him. I remember watching him ride Dawn Run to victory in the 1986 Cheltenham Gold Cup. We were all there in the sitting room, Dad, Mam, Brian and me, just glued to the telly, watching as she led, then as she was passed by Run and Skip, then when she looked cooked going to the second last. We cheered like hell when she found reserves of energy from somewhere on the run-in. Afterwards all four of us were out of breath and we just danced around with joy. We had no bets or anything. But this was beyond betting, beyond money. It was as if Ireland had beaten England in the World Cup final. We are getting a bit used to Irish horses winning the Gold Cup these days, but back then it was a rarity. In fact, bar Tied Cottage's win in 1980, from which he was subsequently disqualified, you had to go back to Davy Lad in 1977 for the last Irish winner before Dawn Run. I wasn't even three years old at the time, so Dawn Run is the first one I remember. It was just unbelievable. We always watched racing together, as a family.

I used to have pictures up on my wall of horses and jockeys in the same way as normal kids would have pictures of football players or pop stars. Dawn Run, Bobsline, Buck House and Corbiere. It didn't really matter if they were English or Irish. As long as they were good horses and the pictures were good, with the jockey looking stylish, they had a good chance of making it on to the wall.

One of my friends at school, Robert Byrne, son of the vet John Byrne and now married to Amber O'Grady, Edward O'Grady's daughter, was a John Francome fan. We used to have wicked rows over who was the best rider, Jonjo or Francome. It was almost like a Manchester United versus Liverpool rivalry among football fans. It was bizarre in a way: there were Francome and Jonjo riding away in England, completely oblivious to these two young lads in Twomilehouse fighting over which of them was the better rider. Though I suppose it's no more bizarre than Irish kids supporting English soccer teams. Robert and I shared this common desperate desire to be a jockey. In fact, Robert's nickname at school was, and still is, Jockey. He is now the manager of Millgrove Stud.

I remember getting Jonjo's autograph in Punchestown one year. That was amazing, and it had a profound effect on me. It took me ages to pluck up the courage to go up to him and ask him for his autograph, but I was delighted when I did. It would be like a kid who was into football trying to pluck up the courage to ask David Beckham or Michael Owen for his autograph. That's how big a hero Jonjo was to me. I didn't know what to say to him. Just 'Jonjo, can I have your autograph?' I suppose. But he was so nice about it. He could have refused, or said he was too busy, or just ignored me. Who was I? Just some young kid who was completely irrelevant to him. It would have been nothing to him to just walk on past and ignore me, but it would have had a huge impact on me if he had, just as it had a huge impact on me when he stopped and took the time to sign my racecard.

When people ask me for my autograph now I always do my best to take the time to give it to them. You don't always have a lot of time between races, but I really do try. You only have to be nice and have a quick few words. I can see it from the other side. It's nothing to me to take a few seconds. I'm grateful that someone thinks enough of me to ask for my autograph. I'm just an ordinary person. I'm just lucky to be able to make a living doing what I love.

In the summer they used to make hay in some of the fields around us on Newberry Stud. They'd make the hay and keep all the bales in one place. We'd be in heaven – a ready-made racecourse. We'd use the bales as fences and wings and rails, and race all the way around the field. I'm not sure if we were supposed to gallop around the fields in Newberry Stud, but nothing was ever said. It was the summer and the ground was firm anyway, so we probably didn't do too much damage. We'd be going for hours. Poor Bluebell would be exhausted.

But he was a great little pony. He was only 13.2 hands and grey when I got him, though he went white after a couple of years, probably from the stress I put him through. He was a huge part of my life. I went to gymkhanas with him and I went hunting and pony racing on him. I remember the first time I took him to a pony race meeting. Dad wasn't able to go because he was away at sales with Newberry Stud, so Mam drove me there with Bluebell in the box attached to the back of the car. We weren't sure what to do, so we put all the gear on the pony, blinkers and bandages and whatever else we could find. We just thought it was the thing to do. I met a fellow recently, Tom Butler, who was telling me, twenty years on, how he remembers us and our pony that day. We must have looked a state. My Dad went mad afterwards when he heard. We knew no better though.

Bluebell much preferred hunting to racing. It was different to racing, and you'd get a different type of kick out of it. You'd get all decked out in your hunting gear and we'd all meet just down the road from our house at Carnalway Cross, so we could ride down. There weren't too many kids my age who used to hunt with us. Robert Byrne, Elizabeth Charlton and Jane Hickey, daughter of Michael Hickey, who would later breed Kicking King – that was about it. They used to tease me like hell about not being that good a rider. That's what kids do. They find your weak spot and pummel it. The girls in particular were desperate for teasing. They'd often tell me that they were talking to someone who told them that that Timmy Murphy fellow, he'd never make it as a rider. Nice chap and all, but he'd better study hard because he's not good enough to be a jockey. One February evening when I was about nine or ten, my Mam was down at the bottom of the lane when she spotted a bit of paper attached to the gate. She picked it off, saw that it had my name on it, and brought it into the house to dry it off by the fire. She didn't give it to me until the following day – Valentine's Day. It was a Valentine's card from one of the girls saying something like, 'Well, you'll probably never make it as a rider, but anyway, Happy Valentine's Day'.

Bluebell was stronger than me when he was hunting and I wouldn't be able to hold him at all, so we would be up front with the redcoats most of the time. In fact, I'd often be ahead of them. They didn't seem to mind. They'd just leave me off. Once the hounds started hunting, Bluebell would be off. He'd jump anything. He used to frighten the life out of me with the things he'd take on, ditches and dykes some of the hunters would be baulking at. They'd be going down to another part of the ditch, or going for a gap, but Bluebell would just barge up through the middle of them, full steam ahead. He'd jump anything that got in his way. All 13.2 hands of him, and me on his back. I had a good few falls off him, but he was bombproof, to be fair to him. And I only really had two scary incidents, the clothes-line one and one other fall when I got hung up in a stirrup and was dragged down the road for a short while. That was all. I suppose you'd be a bit shook up for a little while afterwards, but all you wanted to do was go and ride again. I can never remember a time when I got up in the morning thinking that I didn't want to ride.

Mam was always a little nervous when we went out to ride, and she'd always tell us to be careful before we left. She rode when she was younger, but she had a bad fall one day and that was it. Even now, she finds it difficult to watch me riding. She prefers watching the video in the evening after racing when she knows I have come home safe. Dad was different. He'd just fire you up and let you off. I probably gravitated towards my Dad's idea more than my Mam's, but at the same time you'd always have a little bit of care about you. A fearless man is not necessarily a brave man.

My brother Brian wasn't as big into it as I was. He was two years younger than me, and he didn't get the same kick out of horses as I did. He was more into machinery when we were kids. When we'd go down to my Mam's folks in Shanballymore during the summer, Brian would spend more time on the tractors and the machines than he would with the horses. But we had great craic down there. We'd go down for three or four weeks every summer. Grandad had set up his own forge, and there were always horses about. Uncle Mick was there – Mick Welsh, my Mam's brother. He took over the shoeing when Grandad died. And Uncle Pat, his wife Patsy and their children Sheila, Trisha and Jimmy. They ran the local shop and Post Office – the regular supplier of sweets for the holiday. And Uncle Tommy – well, we used to call him Uncle Tommy, although he wasn't really our uncle, he just lived there with Grandad and Granny, but he was always Uncle Tommy to us. My cousins, Tim and Colm Noonan, used to live just down the road, and we'd all hang out together for the summer. Tim was round about my age and Colm was Brian's age, so the four of us used to have great craic together with the horses, the cattle and the tractors. Uncle Tommy was great with all the kids. He'd take us round the farm and show us how to milk the cows and drive the tractor. When we got a bit older Brian used to go over to the Noonans' because they were contract farmers and had all the machinery. He'd go off with them to cut silage or hay while I stayed with the horses.

Tim and Colm also used to come up to us from Shanballymore for a couple of weeks during the summer, and I'd take Tim riding. Tim wasn't that big into riding either, but I used to put him on the pony anyway and I'd ride the racehorse, and we'd head on down the fields. Of course, Tim wouldn't be able to hold the pony – few could – so he'd just be clinging on for dear life with the pony running as fast as his little legs could carry him, trying to keep up with the racehorse. I remember I used to have a pain in my stomach laughing at him. When he eventually pulled him up – or rather when the pony stopped from exhaustion – he'd have this big red face on him. I'd have tears of laughter streaming down my cheeks. But Tim got a great buzz out of it. When you don't ride that often and you're on a horse, or even a pony, that is galloping flat out, you think you're going a million miles an hour. I'm sure he wouldn't have done it if he didn't get a kick out of it. And, of course, it was great entertainment for me.

We did a lot of messing as well. One day we were at a loss for something to do so we decided we'd dam the stream that ran through the woods. We just thought it would be a good idea. Turns out it wasn't. We flooded half the fields on the farm and my Dad came down. Big trouble.

There were always horses around at Shanballymore, young ones and old ones, and they had a couple of mares in training with Jonjo Harding (Brian and Richard Harding's dad). I used to help in the breaking of the youngsters. There were these things being lunged, and I'd be put up on their backs. They'd be jumping all over the place and plunging, and I'd be on them. I think I was being used a bit as cheap labour, but I loved it, and it was all good experience for me at the end of the day.

I'd go around with Grandad and Uncle Mick to the different yards around the place when they'd be called out to do some shoeing. They'd shoe anything, from racehorses to point-to-pointers to old donkeys. They used to have a donkey on the farm at home that we'd ride, and we'd have bets with each other to see who could stay on it the longest. It's not easy staying on a donkey's back when he doesn't want you there. He'd just put his head down and you'd have nothing in front of you to hang on to, so you'd just kind of slide off. We used to ride the cows as well when they came down to be milked. We'd be waiting for them on top of the wall and we'd jump on them and, again, see how long we could stay on. We had a few spills from the cows as well. You'd get a bit cute and try to identify the older ones, the ones that wouldn't be as frisky. I'm not sure if we were really supposed to be riding the cows, but I don't remember ever getting told off for it. Maybe the adults just never knew we did it. And maybe the cows enjoyed it. It was something different for them to be doing, trying to get these mad kids off their backs. They'd have long enough during the winter to be trying to make chewing grass seem interesting.

All my Mam's family were really great to us. We had such freedom there. We were on our summer holidays and we had the run of the place. We never had cows up in Kilcullen, and they added an extra dimension. On the stud farm at home everything had to be fairly prim and proper, but down in Shanballymore on the farm it was just pure fun. And they had a video recorder. Heaven.

Uncle Mick used to tell me that I'd make a great jockey. He used to tell me that he'd get me going in pony races, and that I would progress from there. He was probably just talking in general, but it had a huge impact on me. I'd ride my socks off all summer down there, and I hated leaving. I'm sure I wasn't much fun for a day or two after I came home at the end of the summer. And, true to his word, Uncle Mick did do a lot to get me going on the pony racing circuit. He used to do the shoeing for Jonjo Harding, and Jonjo put me up on a lot of his ponies. That was the first experience I had of a real racing yard. Even though it was a point-to-point yard, it was a real racing yard to me. I also used to ride a mare on which Jonjo's son Brian learnt to ride. When he went off riding ponies that could race, I got to ride her. She was great and all, a great mare for a young fellow to be starting off on, but she just wasn't fast enough to win a race. I also got Brian's cast-off clothes. I had a pair of his boots with the sole falling out of one of them, but it was a big thing to have your own pair of riding boots, so I was delighted to have them.

I loved pony racing. I loved the buzz. I loved the smell of the grass and the horses and the chip vans. I got the same sort of sensation when I went back to the point-to-point scene from the Curragh. You felt like a real jockey, getting into your boots and colours, and feeling the tension beforehand. I wouldn't be able to sleep for days before a ride. I had most of my rides for Jonjo Harding, but I also had a couple for Con Horgan. He had a mare called Blue Nun. I remember I was due to ride her at Monasterevin one day. Dad was bringing me to the meeting, but he was faffing around at home on the day, doing something that was probably hugely important to him but seemed like a complete irrelevance to a ten-year-old who had been looking forward to this ride for weeks. I had a real chance of breaking my duck on Blue Nun. Anyway, we left too late, I missed the ride, and of course the mare won. There was uproar. I didn't talk to my Dad for days. Turns out it was my best chance of having a winner on the pony racing circuit. I had plenty of seconds and thirds, but I never rode a winner.

I remember doing gymkhanas too. Lead rein and that kind of thing. I remember Dad used to lead me round over these little poles, and I'd be decked out in my jodhpurs, jacket and boots. I remember winning rosettes – not for riding or anything, just for being there and being able to stay on as I was led round, and for looking cute in all my gear.

We probably couldn't really afford to have horses as we did, but there was no way my Dad was going to give them up. Mam and Dad worked hard to give us what they could. Ireland wasn't a well-off country back in the late 1970s and early 1980s, and everyone else was the same as us, just working to make ends meet. I remember Mam scrimping and saving to get me a pair of football boots, then buying them a couple of sizes too big so that I'd get value out of them.

I liked football, but I was too small and light for Gaelic football, and that was all they played in Twomilehouse, where I had the majority of my primary schooling. I played Under-11, but wasn't really that good. I loved soccer though. We played soccer in the school yard, but there was no soccer team in the school or the parish. There was once a one-off game between Twomilehouse and Killashee. Killashee had a soccer team and we had put together a team to play them. We were in training for the game, and I was dying to play, but a couple of days before the game I got a bit of a cold. My mother got worried and decided to take me to the doctor, telling me that I could have pneumonia. Of course I protested. There was no way it was pneumonia. It was hardly even a head cold.

Anyway, she dragged me kicking and screaming to the doctor's and he diagnosed me with pneumonia. She was right. It took me a long time to realise it, but Mam was rarely wrong.

I did a bit of swimming, a bit of running and a bit of boxing too. Mam didn't really approve of boxing, but she wanted to give me every opportunity to have a go at different things before I committed to a life with horses. She had had a lifetime of it with Dad, the danger and the injuries and the worry. I don't think she really wanted to go through it again with me. But all I really wanted to do was ride horses. From the time I first learnt to talk, when people asked me what I wanted to be when I grew up, the answer was always a jockey, even though I could hardly say the word. Before I left primary school I had modified that answer – to champion jockey.

CHAPTER THREE

GROWING PAINS

Primary school began for me in Killashee, just outside Naas, about ten miles from our house. It was a private, fee-paying school, and we probably couldn't afford it, but my Mam thought it would be the best school for me. She always put us before herself. Whatever she thought was best for us, she would do, even if it meant doing without something herself. If it wasn't about horses, Dad wouldn't have much to do with it, so everything else was down to Mam.

But I got into awful trouble in Killashee. There was this fish pond there, and we used to jump into the pond and try to catch the fish. What else were you to do when you were five? That always resulted in a caning. Sister Jarlath was the head sister, very handy with the cane, she was. Robert Byrne was in Killashee at the time as well, and we got each other into trouble. They used to take us for nature walks, but Robert and I would hang around out the back and, when nobody was looking, we'd veer off and head on up into the woods. We thought it would be fine. We'd just join them at the end and nobody would notice. Actually it rarely worked out like that. They used to have to send search parties out looking for us. We'd get into terrible trouble for that as well. More canings. The funny thing was, it didn't seem to make much difference. We knew we'd get into trouble if we went against the rules, we knew that getting into trouble meant a caning, and we knew exactly what was within the rules and what wasn't. And we didn't like the canings. Yet it didn't stop us getting into trouble. I suppose we didn't really stop to think about it before trying to catch the fish or leaving the nature trail. It was only afterwards, before the canings, that we would think, 'Uh oh ...' Boys will be boys.

I was only a year in Killashee, although it seemed like longer. My mother realised fairly quickly that it wasn't working out, so she moved me back to school in Twomilehouse. That was much better for everyone. It was closer to home and therefore easier for me to get to, it was cheaper for Mam and Dad – no fees – and ultimately I was happier there. In fact, I had some great times there. Robert Byrne and Jane Hickey were the only other two racing kids there really. Jane is a daughter of Michael and Sheelagh Hickey, who stand Old Vic at their Sunnyhill Stud and who bred Kicking King. Jane got engaged to Joe Foley, owner of Ballyhane Stud in County Carlow, just a couple of weeks before Robert got married to Amber O'Grady. There must have been something in the air around about that time! Rossa Fahey and Tiernan Conroy were my other friends at school in Twomilehouse, and the Colberts, Donal and Declan. They were the football family. Their dad used to train the football team.

Twomilehouse was a very small village, and you'd know everybody and everybody's family. Father Byrne was the parish priest. He was a big racing man. He got involved in a horse called Teach Dha Mhile (Twomilehouse in Irish) when I was older, which was trained by Dermot Weld. He won a couple of races, including a Group 3 race up the Curragh. We were scared of Father Byrne. He had these big bushy eyebrows and he always had a frown on his face. We still all became altar boys though. Anything to get out of actually going to class.

I didn't really have any interest in the lessons side of school. I enjoyed it because the craic was good, but I wasn't really that interested in learning anything. I struggled at most subjects because I didn't have that interest. You have to be interested in something if you want to be good at it. I wasn't stupid though, and I'm sure if Dad had been a doctor or a solicitor then I would have taken school more seriously and done better. But my Dad was a horseman, and that's what I was interested in.

Mr Carr was the headmaster at Twomilehouse. He was all right. He was a bit scary, but you could still have a bit of a laugh with him. Although everything was very black and white. There was no testing the water with Mr Carr, no pushing the boundaries. If you broke the rules you were in trouble, full stop.

In secondary school you quickly got to know which teachers you could mess about with and which teachers you couldn't. Kids can suss people out fairly quickly. Our Irish teacher, Mrs Stewart, was big into racing, which was quite a help for me. Not that I had any more interest in Irish than I had in other subjects, but I didn't get into so much trouble in Irish class. Actually, I got away with murder in Irish class, to the extent that after a while I actually behaved myself better in Irish class than I did in any other class. It was a funny thing. I kind of felt responsible, like I didn't want to abuse her niceness or something. Is that what they call reverse psychology? I'm not sure. Whatever it is, it is a potent weapon that is at a teacher's disposal.

I'll never forget our geography teacher. Batman we used to call him. He used to have this big cape like teachers wear in those old movies. He'd walk the corridors with his big cape flowing along behind him and everyone would disappear, like rabbits into burrows, in order to keep out of his way. He was a bit scary too, and he was a great shot with a piece of chalk. Rarely missed. Then there was Mr O'Brien for woodwork, and Mr Whelan for PE. I liked woodwork, even though I wasn't really that good at it, and I loved PE. Anything sporting. Miss Ryan was our English teacher. The Romeo and Juliet thing didn't really do it for me. I couldn't figure out why Shakespeare couldn't just come out and say what he meant. What was it with all these riddles? What was his problem? We'd spend a whole class figuring out what he was trying to say. Why didn't he just say it in the first place? He would have saved us all a lot of time, which we could have spent riding horses or doing something useful.

But I didn't sit in class day-dreaming about riding horses all the time. I wouldn't be bursting out the school door to get home in order that I could go and ride out. Not all the time. It depended on what was going on. If there was racing on telly we'd go home and watch that, and then go riding. If there wasn't any racing on I could have taken it or left it. It wasn't until I got older and started riding racehorses that I had to ride out every morning. And we played a lot of football, my brother Brian and me, or if there was rugby on telly we would have a go at that. Or play on the bikes, usually racing each other. Or head down into the woods and play there, or down by the river. We weren't really allowed to play down by the river, but kids will often go where they're not supposed to go. But before we could do anything after school, we had to do our homework. Mam's rule. We just accepted that that was the way it was, and it was a good rule. The later you left it the more tired you were and the more difficult it was to do it. I can see it now with my own son, Shane, who is five years old. If he does his homework straight away, he flies through it. If he leaves it until later he can't get through it at all.

I was quite a restless child. I didn't have patience for much and I didn't sleep well at night when I was young. Mam taught me to knit and to sew when I was about five. She thought that knitting or sewing would help me to relax, and it did. I would do some knitting before going to bed at night when I was small. When I got a little bit older, I used to sew jockeys' colours, white spots on maroon polo necks, so that I could ride for Lady Clague, the owner of Newberry Stud. I made tassels for hats and whips from scraps of leather, and I used to sell them to the lads on the Curragh.

We didn't really have that many friends around us at home when I was at primary school, which is why I used to have to play with my brother Brian quite a lot. The school was about six or seven miles away, Robert Byrne was on the Curragh, which was about ten miles away, and we didn't know anyone in the town at that stage. We never really had anything to do with the town. But when I was in secondary school we had a few friends who used to come out to us – Justin Walsh, Shane Lamb and Martin Fanning – and we used to try to teach them how to ride. I remember bringing one of the girls out one day, Hazel Lawlor, and trying to impress her. I hadn't a car or a motorbike, but I had a horse – and here's how to use one. It was a bit cheesy but, as I recall, it wasn't without success.

Hazel's father was in charge of the boxing club. I did a bit of boxing, but Mam wasn't gone on the idea of me, a little whippet of a fellow, presenting myself as a punch bag, even though it was something that might have diverted my attention away from horses. I did a bit of swimming as well, but nothing could compete with riding. As I got older, I got more difficult. I wanted to be a jockey, and I wanted to be a jockey now. I lost any interest I had in school, and I acted the maggot a lot in class. Mam was being called up and down to the school every other day. She spent more time in the building than some of the kids.

I was only about twelve or thirteen when I first seriously began to think about giving up school. I had no idea how to go about becoming a jockey, but, as I said, I could see no point in this school business. What use is Pythagoras's Theorem to you when you're meeting a fence wrong in a three-mile chase? But at the same time, I was growing. That's what you do when you're that age, but it wasn't good news for an aspiring champion jockey.

I began to skip meals. When Mam began to make dinner, I would invent something I needed to do just so that I wouldn't be around for the meal. It wasn't good. I wasn't healthy. You can't fight nature, but I was going to give it a good shot. Mam used to think that my teeth were beginning to look big in my head. Not a good sign. I was often hungry, but weren't the top jockeys always hungry?

I became a bit of a handful at home. I used to sneak out my bedroom window regularly in the evening. Mam would come into my bedroom to find me gone, the window open and the curtain flapping away in the wind. I remember one evening asking her if I could go to the teenage disco Nijinsky's on the Curragh, right beside Robert Byrne's house.

'No, you can't.'

Kicking and screaming.

'No way. Definitely no.'

'Right, I'm going to bed early then.'

I went into my room, put on my glad rags, jumped out the window and cycled up to the Curragh.

I had made two mistakes, schoolboy errors. The first was asking for permission to go to the disco in the first place. If you don't ask, you can't be told that you're not allowed to go. The second was telling Mam where the disco was.

There I was, thirteen years old, in Nijinsky's, a great lad. All my mates were there, so it wasn't like I was doing something unusual or rebellious. I was dancing with a girl and making significant progress, I thought, when suddenly she stopped.

'What's up?'

'Is that your dad?'

Sure was. I was dragged out by the ear. The embarrassment. It took me a long time to make up the street-cred deficit for that one.

I made a couple of attempts to run away from home. The first time I left, I packed my bag and stayed in my friend Justin Walsh's shed. His parents didn't know I was there. I wasn't sure what I was going to do; I just wanted to be away from home, to be independent. When I woke up the following morning, cold, tired and hungry, I thought, 'Ah look, this homeless craic isn't for me.' I was dreading going home though, because I knew I'd lost and I knew I'd be in huge trouble. Mam and Dad had probably been out looking for me all night. But I figured I'd face it anyway. Getting a bollicking was a far more attractive proposition than spending another night in Justin Walsh's shed.

So I went home and walked into the kitchen. Dad was there, reading his newspaper. He looked up at me when I walked in. I braced myself.

'All right?' he asked.

'All right,' I muttered, and carried on through the kitchen and into my room.

I wondered if they had even realised I was missing. What a wasted effort.

The longer I stayed in school, the more I wanted to get out. I knew what I wanted to do, what I wanted to be, but I was just too young to know the best way to get there. If I had known then what I know now, I would have paid more attention. Mam knew that the best thing for me was to finish school, that there would be time enough then. Of course she was right. She tried everything to keep me in school, to drill into me the importance of going to school, of having an education behind me just in case I didn't make it as a jockey. Not many people can make a living out of riding horses you know. But I couldn't countenance that. I was going to make it as a jockey and that was that. I couldn't not.

What I didn't know then, though, is that there is so much more to racing than just riding horses. There is so much more you need to know about, even if you are successful.

You have to think of the day when you stop riding. You can't be a jockey all your life. More than that, the career of a jump jockey is one of the shortest careers you can choose, so you have to try to have some sort of a plan for when you stop. You won't have the same salary. Whatever I do after I stop riding, it is unlikely that I will earn the same money as I'm earning now. That's why I think it's important to have an education behind you, even if you are hell-bent on being a jockey.

I don't think Dad was really bothered; he wanted me to be a rider and he didn't really seem to mind how I got there. So it came down to a battle between me and Mam, and before long she relented. I suppose she figured it was going to be impossible to stop me pursuing a career as a rider. Actually, she never really wanted to stop me riding, she just wanted to make sure I did it the right way. But my lack of patience and my restlessness dominated my every move.

I was fourteen when I got a job with Noel Chance on the Curragh. Or rather, I was fourteen when Des O'Brien got me a job with Noel Chance on the Curragh. Des, remember, was a brother of Joe O'Brien, who used to come down to ride out with my Dad – the fellow who broke his shoulder at Punchestown that day. Des knew Noel and he asked him if he would take me on at weekends. So every Saturday and Sunday morning I would get up on my bike, saddle over the handlebars and bridle over the saddle, and head off to the Curragh, happy to be out. It was about six miles from Newberry Stud to Noel's place on the edge of the Curragh, but it didn't matter. It could have been 56. I think my mother thought the cycle might be too much for me after a while. There's your bike now, and there's a job in a racing yard, so off with you. If you want it badly enough you'll do the cycle. I did, and I did. The cycle home was a bit tough all right. You'd be after riding out four or five lots in the morning and you'd be knackered getting on to your bike to cycle those six miles home. But this was a real racing yard, with real lads and real craic. This was the big time, and it was worth it.

Noel had moved from the Phoenix Park to the Curragh. Ireland was in the middle of a recession at the time, and most trainers were finding it difficult to make ends meet. Noel was no different. It is amazing the way things turn out though. If you had told Noel then that he would train two Gold Cup winners by the year 2000, I doubt he would have believed you. But even back in the late eighties he had racehorses. Real racehorses. Completely different to the racehorses we had at home. Or at least I thought they were. I probably didn't fully appreciate what I had at home at the time.

I used to get to ride all the lunatic horses. I'm not sure if that was because they thought I was a good rider or because I was the new young kid and they thought they'd have a bit of fun with me. Whatever the reason, I used to have these lunatics and they'd be plunging and bucking and pulling me all over the place. I wasn't very strong so I wasn't great on these things, but it was all part of my learning experience. Actually, I'm sure the lads altered the riding arrangements after Noel had sorted them. They would be clever like that – give the young lad the difficult horses. John Kennedy was there at the time, and Peter Burke and Paddy McLoughlin. I'm still in contact with Paddy. He was at Noel's with me and he was at Dermot Weld's when I was there. He's still there actually. They were all older than me so I guess I was kind of influenced by them.

I rode out at Noel's on those weekends and I rode out there as often as I could during the following summer. It took over my life. Everything else went by the wayside. Football, swimming, boxing. Nothing else mattered. It wasn't all a bed of roses, though. I was the new kid, the weekend rider, the social rider, and as I said, the lads used to give me all the crap jobs. More than that, they'd try to knock the cheekiness out of me. You'd get a hiding or you'd get hung upside down in the barn just for giving cheek to the older lads. If you were really bad, or if they just felt like it, they'd give you an oiling or a blistering. An oiling was when they pulled your trousers down, oiled your bollocks, put a load of feed on top of you and hung you upside down in the barn. A blistering was when they put a bit of blister in the oil. Neither was very pleasant. I don't think that sort of thing goes on any more, but it toughened me up, that was for sure. I probably gave a lot of cheek, so I was often in for a dead leg or a dead arm, or an oiling or blistering. It could have turned me off racing for life, but I learnt. I learnt to give my cheek from a distance, often while running.

It was a small yard, predominantly a Flat yard – Warren O'Connor used to ride the Flat horses – with about ten or twelve Flat horses and only two or three jumpers. Noel didn't really have a National Hunt jockey as there just weren't enough jump horses, and I didn't have a licence at the time, so obviously there was no chance I would get a ride for Noel. I had no experience either, so even if I had had a licence it would have been highly unlikely.

Dad was adamant that I take out an amateur licence, not a Flat licence, not an apprentice licence. You can only ride in point-to-points and bumpers if you are an amateur, and he wanted me to get experience that way, riding against fellow amateurs. Of course he was right. Also, as I have mentioned before, from the day I was born he wanted me to ride as Mr T. J. Murphy. If you are not an amateur, you are not a gentleman, not a Mr.

But things weren't happening quickly enough for me. I couldn't get rides without experience and I couldn't get experience without rides. How was I going to get rides? It was like I was standing at the bottom of a mountain, looking up towards the summit and knowing that I could get there. But I couldn't see how I was going to get up to the first ledge. If I could only get on to the first ledge, the rest of the mountain looked easy. And I thought I had the ability. Of course I had the ability. Wasn't I going to be champion jockey?

Some of the lads in Chance's yard were talking about going to England. I was intrigued. Ireland was too small, they said. England is bigger. There's more racing in England and more opportunities. They have 59 racecourses and they race every day, which sounded bountiful compared to the 27 racecourses in Ireland and the staccato racing, especially during the winter. One of the lads, Peter Burke, was going to England, and I thought it would be a good idea if I went with him. It made complete sense to me. Here was I, a fifteen-year-old champion jockey in the making whose light was under this bushel on the Curragh where nobody would ever be able to see me. England, in contrast, was the land of opportunity. There was loads of racing and they needed loads of jockeys. I'd have to start off at the small tracks of course, but after a while they'd notice me and I'd be able to ride for one of the big yards. A move to England was really the only way to go. Why hadn't I thought of it earlier?

Actually, the idea was bananas. I had no licence, no money and no contacts. I wasn't even sure if I had somewhere to stay on my first night there. My intention was to go to Nigel Tinkler's. I'd looked him up in the *Racing Post* and saw that he was doing quite well. He had plenty of runners and a few winners. Truth was, I didn't think about the details. I thought I'd be a jockey in no time.

I went into my room one evening and had a look around it for the last time. I packed my suitcase, made my bed and vacuumed the room. I considered taking with me the framed photos of Jonjo O'Neill and Dawn Run hanging on my wall, but there wasn't enough room in my suitcase and I needed to travel light. So I took the pictures down from the wall, wrapped them up and just left them on my bed. Once I was happy that I had everything, I jumped out the window, strapped my suitcase to my bike and headed off to the Curragh. There was a bus that left Newbridge for Dublin at six o'clock the following morning, and I was going to be on it. Get to Dublin, go to the airport, and get a flight to England. What could be simpler? I figured I'd stay in Noel Chance's barn for the night so that I'd be close to Newbridge and wouldn't miss the bus.

What strikes me now, looking back, is the innocence of it all. I wanted to be a jockey, all the good jockeys were in England, ergo I would go to England. It was a no-brainer. Nothing else mattered. Family, friends, home, Ireland, health, money. I was just heading over so that I could be a jockey. I hadn't thought about how it was going to happen, where I was going to stay, how I was going to eat. All I knew was that in a little while I'd be riding in those races at Newbury, Cheltenham and Aintree that I used to watch on the television.

Somewhat unsurprisingly, then, I hadn't stopped to consider how Mam and Dad would react to my departure. It wasn't that I thought it wasn't important, it was simply that I didn't stop to consider them. When it came, their reaction was swift and decisive. I can imagine my Mam going into my room and seeing the curtain flapping in the wind. Oh no, he's gone again, off to Nijinsky's or something. Honestly. Another little piece of her heart broken. But hold on a second. This is different. Bed made, photos on the bed, room sparkling, suitcase gone, wardrobe half-empty. This is for real. Jimmy! Jimmy!

Mam contacted everyone, including the local gardaí, who might have had an idea where I was or where I was going. Someone told her about the six o'clock bus from Newbridge and my intention to be on it, so she got to Newbridge for 5.30 to intercept me. But I never made it to Newbridge that morning: Mam had also contacted Noel Chance, who checked his barn and found me there, all packed up and ready to make it in the world as a jockey. Noel dissuaded me from going. He made me see a little bit of reason. So I had to shuffle my way home with my tail between my legs. 'I'll never get going now,' I thought.

It is fairly scary to think what might have happened if I had managed to get myself to England that day. I give a little shudder every now and then when I think of it, knowing what I know now. There is no way I would have made it. I would probably never have been heard of again. Of course at the time I couldn't see it. I wouldn't listen. I wouldn't be guided by people I should have listened to. People who knew much better than me. People with experience. Because I knew it all. At fifteen, I knew it all.

The reality is that I am only where I am today because of the people who have been around me. People who went out of their way to help me, people who looked after me better than I have looked after myself. I have been very lucky to have been surrounded by people who cared about me enough to stick by me, advise me, suffer me and protect me from myself. Without them, my story would be totally different.

People like my Mam. The battle to ride was one I ultimately won, though I'm not sure if I really was the winner in the end. One day, she met with the school vice-principal, John Kinane, and he said to her, 'Helen, you know, take him away. His heart isn't here. His heart is on the Curragh. He's gazing out the window and he just wants to be there. And you know, if you let him go, he won't look back.'

CHAPTER FOUR

GOING IT ALONE

Ileft school and moved out of home, in the summer of 1990. I turned sixteen that August, and they both just happened at the same time. The cycle from home to the Curragh and back again was getting to be a real pain and I just saw it as a waste of time. My Mam wasn't too happy about the riding or the leaving home. She was pretty upset about the whole thing actually, but I was doing it. It was a fairly major step in my life, moving out of home, and it must have been fairly traumatic for my Mam and Dad, but it wasn't for me. I wasn't sad about leaving home, which is pretty surprising looking back now. I just wanted to get on with life, get on with riding. It was all happening too slowly for me. I was sixteen. If I didn't get going as a rider soon, I'd be past it before I knew it.

I moved in with Paddy McLoughlin's granny in Newbridge. It was great to be so close to the Curragh. I could practically see it from my bedroom window. I still got there on my bike, but it was a one-mile cycle as opposed to a six-mile cycle. That was much more manageable. But, as I said, Noel had only a few National Hunt horses, and I needed National Hunt horses if I was going to get National Hunt rides.

Paddy got a job in Dermot Weld's later that year. There wasn't a lot happening for me at Noel's – I didn't even have a licence – so I figured I'd go with him. The way I looked at it, Dermot had bumper horses. Flat yard, bumper horses. I figured there wouldn't be too many amateurs at Weld's at the time and I should be in line to ride some of the bumper horses if I took out an amateur licence, as had always been the plan. And I was right: there weren't too many amateurs at Weld's. But James

Nash arrived after I got there and he began to ride the bumper horses. That was understandable, as James had experience riding in point-to-points at the time and I had none. But that didn't stop me feeling frustrated as hell that he was getting rides and I wasn't.

I took out my amateur licence when I was at Weld's. It was one of the few sensible things I did while I was there. I remember getting all the forms together and going up to the boss in the office to get them signed. That was more daunting than presenting a young horse to a schooling fence. It was a lot easier to get a licence then than it is now. You just had to get a couple of trainers to say that you could ride a bit. You didn't have to do any Turf Club courses. Dermot and Noel were willing to say that I could ride, so I got my licence OK.

The craic was good at Weld's. There were loads of apprentices there at the time – Shambo, Farmer and Gremlin; Paddy, Jeff Byrne, Willie Walsh and Daragh O'Donohoe; about ten young lads – and we all used to hang out together. Paddy McLoughlin was always a good friend to me. His Dad used to work in the Rathbride yard at Weld's, and Paddy used to work over there with him. Sometimes, instead of going home at weekends I'd go to Paddy's family's house with him and have dinner there. They were a really nice family. There was always a nice atmosphere in their house. Willie Walsh went to Hourigan's around the same time as me, and he was also at Kim Bailey's with me. He is now with Godolphin out in Dubai, and he remains a good friend to this day.

We all lived in Newbridge, and we all used to cycle to Weld's. There'd be a big mad rush out of the gate every day after work. There is a big downhill run as soon as you come out of the gate at Weld's place, Rosewell House, and head towards Newbridge, and we all used to race down it. Everything was always a race. Lads used to get serious falls off their bikes coming down that hill, but you just laughed and kicked on. The more carnage there was the more craic we had.

I'd moved out of Paddy McLoughlin's granny's house after going to Weld's, and into digs with Bob and Sheila Kelly in Newbridge. The Kellys were great. They had three kids, Teresa, Siobhan and Robert. James Nash lived there as well with them, and Gerry Leech. They looked after us all very well. But as far as being a jockey, or even getting a ride, was concerned, I still wasn't going anywhere quickly. I hadn't had a ride at Weld's and there was no sign that I was going to get one, so I started to ring round different trainers. I'd just get the *Irish Field* and start ringing trainers. 'I'm Timmy Murphy, and I'm just wondering, do you have anyone to ride your horse for you on Thursday?' It was always a maybe or a flat-out no.

The no's you didn't mind so much. You'd be disappointed at the time, but the no's were much better than the maybe's. Maybe you can ride this or maybe you can ride that for me at the weekend – I'll get back to you. The trainers probably didn't appreciate it at the time, but you'd be almost holding your breath waiting for them to call you back. You'd be waiting by the phone on Wednesday – no call. Thursday – still nothing. They have to call by Friday if they're going to give me a ride. Nothing. Not a word. They didn't even call to say sorry, but Ted Walsh is riding, or Tony Martin, or James Nash. They just didn't call, and that was the frustrating thing. Chances are they forgot about me as soon as they put the phone down. Who was this young fellow anyway? This whipper-snapper phoning me up looking for a ride? Tommy Murtagh or something. Says he works for Weld. Why doesn't Weld give him a ride? Anyway, where's that farrier? They didn't think of a young fellow on the other end of the phone hoping with all his energy that they would call. At least call him back to say sorry, no ride. Waiting by the phone. It's like when your child asks you if you can go to McDonald's for dinner on Sunday. Can we, Dad? If we have time? 'We'll see, son,' you say as you turn the next page of your newspaper. The child spends the entire week longing for Sunday while you just wonder how they make up those sudoku puzzles. Sunday arrives, roast beef again, heartache. The ones who just laughed and said 'No way – are you kidding me?' were actually better. At least you knew where you stood. It was the empty promises that were the most annoying. The maybe's.

It was killing me. Here I was, a young fellow whose burning desire to be a jockey left no room for any other desire, hawking his wares round every door he could think of and having each one systematically closed in his face. But it is difficult for a young person trying to get going in any profession. Roy Keane was passed over a number of times because he was considered to be too small. Dick Rowe turned down The Beatles in order to sign Brian Poole and the Tremeloes. 'Too guitar-ish,' I think he said. I'm not sure what I was. Too inexperienced, perhaps. Not well known enough. Or maybe just plain not good enough.

It was my dad who gave me my first ride on a racecourse, Red Hugh in a bumper at Dundalk on 11 July 1991. He had bred him himself, out of his mare Another Mary, who had bred the little filly that I broke in with him. I hardly slept a wink the night before. I couldn't wait. This was it, my first ride, my first real ride, my name on the racecard and everything. Mr T. J. Murphy, claiming seven, on the same page as Mr T. M. Walsh, Mr C. P. Magnier and Mr A. J. Martin. I remember the smell of leather in the weigh room and the banter between the older lads beforehand. I didn't join in. I was too sick in the pit of my stomach, and I was too shy anyway. I remember the feel of the breeches on my legs and on the saddle. Racing breeches. They were just kind of thin and sleek and cool. All my riding-out gear was thick and bulky by comparison. And my boots, shiny and real tight around my legs. I felt like a million dollars getting on Red Hugh in the paddock. I looked well and I felt great. Like a gladiator. I just didn't know that I was going out into the Coliseum to have my head ripped off by a lion.

I don't remember too much about the actual race. The saddle was a bit slippery under my breeches. Slippery and sleek, but it felt good. My Dad didn't discuss tactics with me too much, which was just as well as I was a passenger for most of the race. We finished fifth out of the sixteen runners, which was respectable given that both I and the horse were debutants, and that we were sent off at 25–1, almost the outsider of the entire field.

My first ride in a point-to-point was also for my Dad, on a horse of his called Snuggledown, at Gowran Park on 1 March 1992. I had never jumped a proper steeplechase fence before I jumped the first on

Snuggledown that day, though I had done loads of schooling at home over poles and artificial fences that we made up. We had a big log up in the field with bushes thrown over the middle of it. That was the closest I got to a real fence. I was brilliant at jumping that. Dad did, of course, give me some instructions. I'm sure it was as big a moment for him as it was for me. He just told me to jump off out the back and try to settle him, hang on to his neck-strap, and have fun.

I was left a mile at the start. The others were lining up, the starter was saying 'No, I won't start you', so I was waiting, then suddenly he let us go. By the time I got Snuggledown moving forward, the other eight runners were almost at the first fence. As I approached the first myself, I remember thinking, 'Jesus, this is massive. We'll never get over this. How are we supposed to jump this? We must have strayed off the track. This can't be right.' I wasn't entirely sure what to do, so I just let the horse do what he wanted. In fairness to old Snuggledown, he was bombproof. He stood off way further than I expected him to, but I wasn't arguing. I was just trying to stay on. Hup!

We seemed to spend an age in the air. Soaring. I could almost feel my ears pop. This was very different to scooting over a couple of poles at home, where you'd hardly leave the ground. This was for real. We were like a kestrel looking for prey. I was up there, on top of his back, higher than anything else in the world. I could have fallen off the back of him. I didn't feel relaxed. All I wanted was to come back down. The underside of the horse's belly brushed over the top of the fence. I hardly noticed. I had placed my trust in Snuggledown. It was his responsibility to get us safely to ground on the other side. I readied myself, bracing my body for the impact when the horse's forelegs would come into contact with the ground again. The descent lasted an age. And then, thud. The impact went up through the horse's forelegs, through his body, right through my legs and out through the top of my head. I'm sure I wavered, I'm sure I didn't look too steady, but I stayed on. Snuggledown hardly broke stride and galloped on towards the next obstacle. I let out a sigh. I hadn't even realised that I'd been holding my breath.

The second fence wasn't so daunting. It was the same size as the first, but we had done it once, so why not again? The fences passed by underneath us. Two, three, four, five. We were back around by the stands again and heading out on another circuit. My confidence grew with each passing fence. I began to think that I could see strides, and I began to ask Snuggledown to jump when I thought he should. More often than not, however, he didn't. He knew when he needed to take off. Who was this youngster on his back trying to teach him how to suck eggs?

We were getting further and further behind the rest of the field though, and old Snuggledown was losing interest. He was slow over the sixth and that was it, he'd had enough. I couldn't make him go forward any more. This was no fun for him, the others had gone, so he just slowed to a canter, then a trot, then a walk. The power drained away from underneath me. There was nothing I could do; it was like being in a car running out of petrol. When we stopped, the adrenalin seeped out of my body and I realised I ached. God, I ached. My calves, thighs, forearms and biceps. But as I sat there on Snuggledown, a smile came over my face. Here was I, sitting on a horse on a racecourse, in my boots and silks and helmet, a jockey. A real jockey. A real, beaming jockey.

And I thought I was good. I thought I knew horses, I thought I was stylish, and I thought I had the talent to succeed, which made it all the more frustrating that I couldn't get going at Weld's. I just needed a break there. Just one break. One mount on a good horse that would allow me to show everyone how good I was. Then they would see. Then they would want me to ride their horses. There were a lot of good horses at Weld's at the time, like Kiichi and Rare Holiday, and Vintage Crop was just getting going. But I didn't have anything to do with them. Brendan Sheridan rode them, and that's just the way it was. I was glad to be living with James Nash, who had ridden in lots of point-to-points. He seemed to know what he was doing. There were plenty of bumper horses at Weld's, and James used to ride them all, in bumpers and in the big amateur handicaps. He tried to put me in for a couple of spare rides, but it never really happened. To tell the truth, I never really got close to getting a ride at Weld's. It wasn't really a yard that was known for giving a young amateur an opportunity.

Looking back on it now, you can see the naivety of it all. I was just seventeen, going on champion jockey. How many seventeen-year-olds get to ride regularly? But patience was not something I possessed in bucketloads. I wanted it all to happen yesterday.

I'd had my first drink at Noel Chance's. It was nothing too serious. The lads would have a little flask of whiskey that they'd pass around on cold mornings so that they could warm up their insides. I would have a little sip, like everybody else. The fact that I was fifteen at the time – not like everybody else – was neither here nor there. And it usually did the trick.

I began to drink properly when I was at Weld's. It was easy to get into a routine. Work hard during the week, get paid on Friday, go out all weekend. Friday, Saturday and Sunday, every weekend. That was what you did, what everybody did. Work, get locked for the weekend, work. That was the scene. If I had been hanging around with lads who didn't drink when I started working on the Curragh, I have no doubt I wouldn't have drunk. But everybody drank. Drink was everything, and Saturday was the big night. Everyone had work on Saturday morning, so we probably shouldn't really have been going out at all on Friday night, but it was the weekend, and Friday was pay day, so we invariably did. But there wasn't as much Sunday racing back then as there is now, so Saturday was usually the big night.

It started off that all the boys were drinking and I was trying to get in with them, trying to be the big fellow, but I wasn't able to drink. I remember thinking early on that not drinking was probably the way forward, that if I could manage not to go out drinking I would have a better chance of making it as a jockey than if I couldn't. That was probably a fairly mature observation for a young fellow, but I didn't act on it. I didn't have the balls to follow it through. Everybody was drinking, so I suppose there was a little bit of pressure there on me to drink as well, to be a part of the gang. Not in a bad way, but just because everybody else was doing it. If you weren't drinking it was like arriving at a black-tie ball wearing an open-neck shirt and a pair of chinos.

When you're young, you start off just having a few pints because it's all you can manage. But then it gets progressively worse because you're able to handle more and you just drink more as a result. But we only really drank at weekends. Unless there was a birthday party, a big winner or a festival meeting or something, you didn't go out during the week. You just couldn't afford it. I was on £80 per week. My digs were about £35, and I put a little bit into the Credit Union every week. My Mam had drilled the importance of saving into me from an early age. If you wanted something, you saved up for it; if you didn't have the money, you couldn't buy it. So I'd get paid on a Friday, I'd put a little aside for the Credit Union, I'd pay Bob and Sheila their digs money, and I'd spend the rest on drink. Twenty pounds would get you through a whole night. I used to drink pints because there was more value in them than in anything else. Pints of Budweiser. You got more for your money.

I didn't drink more than anybody else, though. I wasn't able to. My difficulty was keeping up. My idea was, if I could drink four or five pints, that would be a good night. But I'd be trying to lie up with the other lads. They were bigger and older and more used to it than I was. I was the youngest in the group and I was fierce green. You tried to be the big man. You'd fall home on Saturday night – great night – and you'd be dying the following day. Always. The morning after a night's drinking was always a disaster. But I didn't think I was doing anything wrong. I was just doing what everyone else was doing. The difference was that everyone else was able to get up for work the following morning. I wasn't.

I just couldn't handle it. It didn't suit me. I couldn't wake up. I wouldn't hear the alarm, or I'd ignore it, or I'd switch it off without really waking up. If I could have gone out and just had a pint or two, I would have been grand, but I couldn't. I had to do the dog on it every time I went out. Be the big man. If I could have stood back then and saw where I was heading – because it was obvious where I was heading – I might have stopped. But when you are in it you can't see it. It's like when you are in a bad relationship: everyone else can see it except you. Everyone else can see that you would be better off out of it. Crucially, though, only your very good friends will say it to you.

Mick Halford would say it to me later. Kay Hourigan, Michael Hourigan's daughter, would say it to me. Adrian Maguire would say it to me. Chris Broad, my agent, would say it to me. In fact, years later Chris got me to give up drink for four months. He actually wanted me to give it up for a year, just to prove that I could do it. He thought I was drinking too much at the time and he said that it would do me good to give it up. I said I'd give it up for four months, from September to Christmas. I managed it, but it wasn't easy. I couldn't wait for Christmas to come that year so that I could drink again.

People say, 'Just give it up. It's easy. Where's your will power?' But it's not just about will power. Will power doesn't work if you have diarrhoea. You have to get to the source of the problem and sort that out first. There are reasons why you drink, and you have to understand them. You drink when you're happy, you drink when you're sad, you drink to celebrate, you drink to commiserate. I didn't understand this at the time, so I just drank. Of course, as far as I was concerned I didn't have a problem. Not me. I wasn't sitting on a park bench with a bottle in a brown paper bag. I didn't drink every day. I could go for ages without having a drink. No problem. It wasn't until I got to The Priory years later that I got to fully understand my relationship with drink.

Nights out would be great craic. Everyone would be in great form and you'd be buzzing. You wouldn't think of the big picture. All that mattered was the night, the here and now, the craic. When you were on a night out, it was easy to forget that you were about as far removed from being champion jockey as *Mr Happy Goes to Town* was from winning the Pulitzer Prize. We'd go out in Newbridge or Kildare town, depending on who was out. Willie Walsh and Paddy, and Terry Finn. Spider, we called him. You'd basically go out with the lads in the yard, but even later, when I was working at Halford's, I still kept in touch with a lot of the lads at Weld's.

We'd usually end up in Snaffles nightclub in Newbridge. Or rather, more often than not, we'd end up outside it. There was this bouncer on the door, George, who would never let us in. I never knew George's surname. You talked about 'George' and everyone knew who you were talking about. He must have had something against our group. I'm not sure why, but he would never allow any of us in. You'd try to sneak in past him, but he'd always remember you and he'd always cop you. You'd try everything. Shirts and ties, suits, fake IDs, even fake moustaches. Nothing worked. Even when we were legal he wouldn't let us in. 'Where d'you think you're going?' There were lads who used to stand and argue with George for ages, but it was a waste of time. George would just keep shaking his head. Eventually you'd just have to turn round and walk away. So we took to sneaking in through the fire exits. We came up with this idea that if any one of us got in, that person would go round and open the fire exit to let the rest of us in. It turned into a bit of a game in the end. There was as much craic in actually getting into the nightclub as there was in being there. The bouncers used to stand there scratching their heads. How are these lads getting in? And once you were in, you'd just be waiting for a bouncer to grab you and kick you out. 'I thought I kicked you out earlier?' You'd just feel a hand on the back of your neck and you'd be marched to the door. You wouldn't even argue. There was no point. You'd just walk out calmly with them, before turning back and heading for the fire exit again.

But in the meantime things weren't going so well for me at Weld's. I was ticking along, riding out, mucking out, having the craic, living from day to day and week to week, but all the while the realisation of my ambition to be a jockey was getting further and further away. I was losing sight of it in a haze of drink, laziness and indifference. I wasn't even close to getting a ride, but the more time went on the less concerned I was about it. I probably could have continued happily at Weld's, earning my £80 a week, working during the week and drinking at weekends, having the craic. In fact, if nothing had happened outside my control, I could easily still be there today. But, thankfully, something did happen. I was sacked.

I'm sure the drinking was a factor, and my timekeeping wouldn't have been exemplary, but I was sacked mainly for being hard on the horses. If a horse wouldn't do what I wanted it to do, I was a bit quick with the stick. Even though I loved horses, I lacked patience. I wouldn't give them a chance. If they weren't cooperating with me my first recourse was to the stick, not the carrot. You will do what I want you to do and you will do it now. That continued on to the racecourse when I got older. Horses who weren't trying for me, I'd just beat them. My record with the stewards testifies to that. It was the same in yards when I was younger. It was something that was just in me, and it took a long time for it to register.

Dermot wasn't happy with this. He gave me a few warnings, but they had very little effect on me: instead of coaxing a horse, I kept on trying to bully him. He had expensive horses and he couldn't have this young upstart abusing them just because he had a short fuse. He was right, but I was devastated. James Nash and Paddy McLoughlin were staying and I was on my way. I was going nowhere. All I was doing was moving around yards without giving myself enough of an opportunity to get going in one.

I got a job with Declan Gillespie on the Curragh shortly afterwards. Fortunately for me, there was plenty of work going at the time for a young fellow who was willing to roll his sleeves up and get stuck in. I didn't mind working. I was a good worker when I was actually there. I didn't mind doing whatever needed to be done in order to get rides on the track. And I was promised rides at Gillespie's. 'You should be able to ride this next week' – the usual. But they never materialised. It was like going back to the days of ringing around trainers looking for rides. Next week. Empty promises.

Like at Weld's, it was mainly Flat horses at Gillespie's. He had a couple of bumper horses, but I never got to ride any of them. Niall McCullagh was there at the time, and Willie Supple. He had a really good team of lads. Mr Gillespie and I never really saw eye to eye. He was so pernickety. Everything had to be done with near military precision. You couldn't trot on to the gallop in the morning. If you trotted on to it, you had to turn round, go back to the start and walk on to it. I suppose it was long odds against me making a go of it there at the time in that kind of environment, and sure enough I never settled at all. I suppose, again, I didn't really give myself much of a chance. I lasted about a month before I was fired.

Things didn't look good. Here I was, a teenage wannabe jockey who had been fired from two of the top yards on the Curragh in the space of a month or so. And when you can see no prospect of getting a ride or getting going, you tend to throw your hat at it. I was becoming more interested in having the craic and less interested in working on getting going as a rider. If you don't try to get rides, you can't fail. And how bad would it be to continue as I was going anyway? Wasn't I having a ball at the weekends?

I learnt very little in my first three years on the Curragh. I learnt how to drink and where the best pubs were, but very little else. At Weld's you didn't even get to ride work. You were just riding out and mucking out, and that got boring after a while, so you diverted your attentions elsewhere. It was better craic to go out and get drunk.

I couldn't go home, or at least I felt I couldn't. Not because I wouldn't have been welcome – I know I would have been – but because I'd decided that once I left home I was going to paddle my own canoe. I wasn't going to go back looking for help from Mam or Dad. I had made the decision to leave against their wishes, and I couldn't go back now, cap in hand. Everything I did later, I more or less did myself. My first car, my first house, even my first motorbike. I just got a loan out from the Credit Union and paid it back every week.

I wouldn't open up to Mam. She was always trying to get me to talk to her, but I just wouldn't. I was a bad communicator. And Dad was just Dad. I'd go home, I'd ride out with him and we'd chat about horses and all, but there was no real depth to our conversations. I would ask for a bit of advice about riding, and he'd try to help, but I was short-tempered and not really prepared to listen. I thought I knew everything when actually I didn't really know that much at all. I wasn't close to my brother Brian either, which is fairly surprising, I suppose, given that we were the only children in the family, both boys, and there were only two years between us. When I left home I probably severed a lot of ties with my family. I had no rock, no soulmate. Nobody in my corner except me and my pint of Budweiser.

All in all, it was turning into a fairly sad story. A young fellow with a latent talent for riding who was throwing it all away in the pubs of Newbridge and Kildare. If you have a talent for anything, you need experience in order to develop it. You think you know it all when you are starting out, that all you really need is an opportunity so that people will notice you, but you don't know it all. Actually, you know very little. As an aspiring jockey you need experience to hone your race-riding skills, your sense of position, your timing, your balance, your strength. And I was getting no experience. I was in grave danger of becoming just another rider who was never going to fulfil his potential, and there are plenty of those. One more wasted talent would hardly be significant.

Then I heard that a small trainer at the other end of the Curragh was looking for riders, and I decided to give him a call.

CHAPTER FIVE

FIRST WINNER, FIRST CLASS

Mick Halford hadn't been training that long when I first came into contact with him. He had ridden as an amateur with Frank Ennis and he had been assistant trainer to Noel Meade before he set up on his own at Birdcatcher Stables, on the far side of the Curragh. I just rang him one day and told him who I was and that I had heard he was looking for lads. I also told him I had worked for Noel Chance, Dermot Weld and Declan Gillespie. He didn't ask why I wasn't working for any of them any more, and I didn't tell him. I'm sure he knew that I wouldn't be coming with glowing references. But Mick's dad worked as a farrier at Newberry Stud, where my father was stud groom, so he knew of me. He just told me to come down and that we'd have a chat.

In the meantime he rang Dermot Weld and Declan Gillespie to ask them about me. I'm not sure what either of them said, but neither of them was jumping up and down about me. Neither told him how lucky he was to be getting me. My Dad told Mick to keep an eye on me and to make sure I worked hard. That's what dads do, I suppose. Mick had heard that I had been late for work once or twice in my previous jobs and that I had been hard on one or two horses. The word coming from Weld's was that I could be a bit of a brat around the yard, and that I didn't like horses. The late Anthony Powell, who had ridden Maid of Money to win the 1989 Irish National and who was tragically killed in a car crash four years later, apparently told Mick to watch me, in the 'keep an eye on that fellow' sense. I didn't know this until much later, but apparently he told him that I could burst a horse as quickly as you could look at one.

Mick didn't hold any of this against me. He sat me down when I arrived the first day and told me I was starting with a clean slate. He says he does that with all new lads who come into the yard, but it was very relevant and very important for me. 'I don't care where you have come from, or what you did in Weld's or Gillespie's, you're starting afresh here,' he said. 'But the first time you're late for work, or the first time you vent your anger on one of my horses, you're out the gate.'

I thought I knew what it was like to work on the Curragh, but it was different at Halford's. I'm not sure what it was. It was a smaller yard, more close-knit. Mick was one of the lads. It wasn't a case of 'I'm the boss and you do what I tell you', it was more a case of all hands on deck. These are the things that need to be done; it doesn't matter who does them as long as they get done.

And I knew from the start that I had a much better chance of getting rides at Halford's than I'd had at Weld's. Actually I would have had as good a chance of getting a ride on the track if I'd been working in a sweet shop as I had at Weld's, so that was hardly surprising. Nevertheless, things were looking up. There was a definite route opening up for me and my ilk to get a ride at Halford's. If you got on well with something at home, especially if it was a bit tricky, then there was a great chance you would get to ride it on the racecourse. I could see that.

Mick always was and still is a great man to give a young fellow a chance. It is not a coincidence that so many young riders had their first rides on the track for Mick. Lads like Tadhg O'Shea, Jason Maguire, Emmet Butterly, Rory Cleary, Adrian Lane. They all had their first rides on the track for Mick. As well as that, there were more jumpers at Halford's than there were at any of the other places I had been. He had more bumper horses, and he had hurdlers and chasers for the winter and a few Flat horses for the summer. So I could see real prospects of getting a ride or two.

But still it wasn't easy. Philip Dempsey was the yard's main amateur at the time, and you ended up riding a lot of the horses he didn't want to ride, or one of the difficult ones that had his own ideas about the game. But I kept my head down and worked hard. I was quite meticulous about my work, in the same way that I was meticulous about my shoes and my clothes. When I was raking the yard, I'd rake it in my own way, taking pride in making sure it was done properly. And when one of the horses I looked after was going racing, I'd take great care to make sure he looked his best. In fact, the best-turned-out prize came to be a bit of a thing with me. I used to try to win it with all my horses. If I had two or three going racing, I'd be disappointed if I didn't win at least one.

We brought Nilousha to Tramore in August 1992. She was a quirky old mare who didn't really like to be alone in her box, so I decided to stay with her during the day. While I was there I noticed a girl across the way plaiting the tail of her horse, so, at a loss for something to do, I decided to plait Nilousha's tail. I remember Mick coming in to saddle the mare before her race.

'Who plaited her tail, Timmy?' he asked.

'I did.'

'And who taught you how to do that?'

'Nobody. I just saw that girl over there doing it, so I figured I'd give it a go.'

Nilousha won her race that evening, a two-mile handicap, and finished second in a handicap hurdle the following evening. The hypothesis that her plaited tail made her run faster has yet to be disproved.

I was with Mick a while before I had my first ride for him. I was no different to anybody else. I had to bide my time. There was one mare I used to ride all the time at home. Lisdowney Lass was her name, a mare by Law Society out of a Tap On Wood mare who was bred and owned by Seamus Burns, whose Lodge Park Stud bred and raced a whole host of top-class fillies, including Park Appeal. She used to spend the whole time bucking, so nobody would want to ride her. But she was a well-bred mare who was related to a couple of winners, so I said I'd ride her at home in the hope that I'd get to ride her on the track. From the moment you got on her until the moment you got off her, she'd just buck and buck and buck. I got on with her OK though. Well, better than any of the other lads who tried to ride her anyway, which probably wasn't saying a lot. I used to just leave her off and let her buck as much as she wanted. There was no point in doing anything else. If you tried to correct her at all she'd just go absolutely mental. So I would just sit up in the saddle and let her buck away under me. She'd be fine when we cantered, but then we'd pull up and she'd start bucking again.

I was asked to ride her in her first race on the track, a bumper at Naas in January 1993. I was ecstatic. Here was a big owner and he was happy for me to ride his mare in her first ever race. Mick's thinking was that she was a fairly difficult filly and that I got on well with her, so why not? They thought she would win that bumper, so they were disappointed when she only finished fifth. She was grand during the race, no signs of temperament at all, but she just wasn't good enough on the day. That was hardly unsurprising, however. That bumper was won by a little-known once-raced gelding from a small stable called Danoli.

Lisdowney Lass ran twice more that spring, I rode her both times, and she finished well down the field both times. Her debut was her best run. It was a pity. She worked like a good horse at home, as far as I could tell, and I always thought she had plenty of ability. She just never chose to show it on the track.

There was another horse at Halford's, Bens Buck, a six-year-old gelding who had had his problems and therefore hadn't run before I got to Halford's. Even though I looked after him at home, it wasn't certain that I was going to get to ride him in his first race. He was Philip Dempsey's to get off. Thankfully, he did. He decided to ride a horse for Mick Munnelly in the bumper at Leopardstown on St Patrick's Day 1993, so I was given the leg up on Bens Buck.

Mick wasn't at Leopardstown himself on the day. He was at Cheltenham, busy watching Deep Sensation win the Champion Chase and Rhythm Section, under five-pound claimer Paul Carberry, get the better of Charlie Swan and Heist in the bumper. That was a hell of a year for Irish-trained horses. We are used to having eight or nine winners at the Cheltenham Festival these days, but we were more used to one or two then. In 1993 we had six: Rhythm Section, Montelado, Shawiya, Fissure Seal, Shuil Ar Aghaidh and Second Schedual. The Irish were back.

I can't say I was too bothered, mind you. My main concern, indeed my only concern, on Champion Chase day 1993 was the 5.20 at Leopardstown. Bens Buck was an unconsidered 16–1 shot, but he belied those odds to carry me into fourth place, just seven lengths behind the winner, Abbey Monarch. Mick's father was there looking after things in his son's absence, and he seemed thrilled. He told Mick afterwards that I could ride. That young Murphy fellow can ride.

Mick always said that I was a better rider on the track than I was at home. I wouldn't stand out riding work, but when I got on to the track he said you could see it. I wouldn't panic, wouldn't get excited. Even in my first couple of races, when most young fellows would be excited as hell, he said that I wouldn't be. He was wrong. Deep down, my insides would be like a gaggle of geese. He said that I just got on and did it, that nothing seemed to faze me. I wasn't too sure about that one. I just felt I was there to do a job. Although I would be as nervous as a kitten, I would always try not to let it show. I was never given to over-exuberance. I'm still not. So I just tried to get on and do the job as well as I could with minimum fuss.

Mick thought I got on well with horses, too. It was a long way from the message that came from Weld's about me not liking horses. I'm not sure why or how those different perceptions of me came about. Maybe when I was at Weld's I didn't really like myself. I didn't like where I was in my life or where I was going, with the result that I probably took it out on whatever I could, mainly the people closest to me and the horses with which I was working. It was different at Halford's. I felt different there, more comfortable. I felt I could talk to Mick. He was just one of the staff. He'd drive the jeep to the races and I'd often travel with him, just the two of us in the jeep. The conversation wouldn't be riveting or anything, we wouldn't solve the problems of the world and we wouldn't have great belly-laughing craic, but it was good for me. I felt he was listening to me. The conversation was almost always driven by him, but I would answer his questions as honestly as I could. He would ask and I would answer – that was the way it worked. We could drive for miles and miles without exchanging one word, but I felt comfortable with that. I didn't volunteer that much information, and I'm sure I didn't ask him much about himself, but I felt at ease with him. I would listen to whatever advice he gave me, be it on riding, on working or on life, and I would try to take it on board. I wouldn't always succeed, but I would be sincere in my efforts.

I was jocked off Bens Buck for his next race, a bumper at Navan, but I wasn't too put out about it. Philip Dempsey was available and he was the stable's amateur, so he was offered the ride. I still felt I was making progress. At last, I was learning. I got into a good routine at Halford's. I'd get up in the morning in the Kellys' house in Newbridge at about six o'clock and cycle to Halford's for about 6.30. I'd muck out my five or six horses, then tack up and go and ride out, three or four proper lots. After that there might be breakers or young horses to do. I did a little bit of schooling at Halford's, but not too much as John Shortt used to come to do most of it. I might get to school a youngster that was just getting off the ground, or ride a lead horse or something, but not too often. I'd be just working away, riding one here and one there. I wasn't that well recognised.

During the summer there was lots of racing. You'd go racing two or three times a week to lead up the horses that you'd be doing. I liked going racing. As I said, I used to go all out to win the best-turned-out prizes. It was something on which to focus my attention, and it was a few quid extra for me if I won one. I used to do nice small plaits in their manes. It would only take about half an hour to plait a mane, and then I'd do their tails. I was an expert after Nilousha in Tramore. Some people didn't like plaited tails, but it worked for me and it made my horse stand out. It showed that you had put the effort in. I used to use baby oil and give them a good grooming. I'd put baby oil on the dandy brush and that would bring up a lovely shine on their coats, then I'd do my quarter marks. There was a prize for nearly every race: £25 usually, maybe £50 for a big race. That was a lot of money when you were earning £80 a week and nearly half of that was going on your keep. As well as that, I took pride in it. I liked to have my horses looking well. And it was good for my relationship with Mick as it showed him I was making an effort, and that was important.

So I was tipping away at Halford's, working hard and getting the odd ride. I was still going out at weekends, still drinking plenty of pints of Budweiser, still trying to get into Snaffles, but the difference between my time at Halford's and my time at Weld's was that I felt I was progressing. It wasn't all about the drink and the craic. There was a part of me now that said, 'Timmy, just keep this thing together and you might just be going somewhere.' I wasn't getting a ride every week or anything, but I would get to ride in a bumper every three weeks or every month or so. Compared to not race-riding at all, and not even riding work, it was huge progress.

George Halford, Mick's uncle, had a couple of point-to-pointers he used to be messing around with. In fact, Mick himself rode his first winner for George on a horse called For Going. George had this young point-to-pointer, a four-year-old called Gayloire, that he used to bring down to Mick's sometimes so that he could work with some of Mick's horses. Dyser Molloy, father of National Hunt jockey Bobby Molloy, used to look after Gayloire for George. He was kind of his little project. George was running the horse in a maiden point-to-point in Cashel in May 1993. I'm sure Philip Dempsey was offered the ride, given that he was the stable amateur, but he wasn't going to the meeting, so Dyser asked me if I would ride him. I was blown away. This was the big time.

I had ridden in six point-to-points up to that time. All six rides had been for my Dad, and I hadn't got around on any of them. I had either fallen off or pulled up on all six. This was a chance to ride a horse that might have a bit of ability, for a real point-to-point trainer. This was a real ride. And, while riding in bumpers was brilliant, riding over fences was just in a different league.

But I didn't excel on Gayloire. Actually, I was awful. I left it too late on him. With the horses I rode for Dad, my primary objective was to get

61

round. I'd hold on to them for as long as I could just to try to make sure they conserved sufficient energy to complete the course. Tactics were irrelevant. Just get him to complete and you'll have done your job. As I've said, in six attempts I had a 100 per cent failure rate, so I didn't know what it was like to ride a horse who had a real chance of winning. And Gayloire did. I hunted him around, hung on to him, hunted some more, and hung on to him again. Gayloire jumped well and was travelling the whole way, but I wanted to make sure that we got round so I never really put him into the race. I remember letting him go at the second last once I was happy that we would complete the course, and I remember being surprised by the way he picked up. We finished strongly in third place, an unlucky loser.

I was thrilled afterwards. I had got round, my first completion in a point-to-point, but in reality I could have won. I should have won. If I'd had a little more experience I would have won. If I'd had just one ride beforehand on a horse that was capable of seeing out the distance, I would have had an idea about tactics. It wasn't really even tactics. It was just a case of not leaving him with too much to do.

The scenes afterwards were not scenes of jubilation. George wasn't happy. While I was thinking there was a chance I could have won if I had allowed the horse to go on sooner, George was convinced that I would have. Bloody jockeys! These youngsters who don't know the game. He'd get Philip Dempsey to ride him next time, and he'd win. He'd get his money back. But Dyser stuck up for me. He asked George to give me another chance. It was my first time ever completing the course and it would be a bit harsh to jock me off. I would learn from the experience. And crucially, if Dempsey rode him next time, his odds would be a lot shorter than they would be if Mr T J Murphy was on board.

Fair play to Dyser, and fair play to George for giving me another chance. I didn't have to wait too long for it either. Gayloire was entered a few weeks later at Kilmuckridge, and George asked me to ride him again. I was under pressure to perform, but I didn't really feel it. All I felt was the nervous excitement of another ride with a good chance. I'd do it differently this time. I knew that this horse had ability. I knew he was fit enough to get round and I knew I didn't have to hold on to him in order to make sure he would had enough energy to get over the last. I'd be able to ride a race this time. And if the cards fell right …

I was preparing for a week. I made sure my saddle was OK, the same saddle I'd slung over the handlebars of the bike when I cycled down to Noel Chance's, the same saddle I still ride with today, my favourite saddle. It was the first saddle I ever bought. I have about ten saddles today, different saddles when I am doing different weights, a couple in the north of England and a couple in Ireland, but the first saddle I ever bought is still my favourite. It was made in Australia, a Bates saddle. It's just really comfortable. It moulds to the horse, like it's a part of the horse; there is nothing that sticks out or sticks into you. It's dead flat so that if a horse makes a mistake there is nothing to hit you up the backside and send you flying. I have only ever seen one other like it, and that was just this year, so I bought it. I now have two. I couldn't use it when I was at Hourigan's because he reckoned I was too light and I needed a heavier saddle. He gave me this thing, the most awkward yoke you've ever seen, full of lead, and just plonked it on top of the horse. It was like riding off a fish box. Adrian Maguire used to use it when he was at Hourigan's, and if it was good enough for Adrian, Mike used to tell me, it's damn well good enough for you.

Anyway, I was getting ready for this ride on Gayloire for about a week. I got my boots polished, my breeches gleaming, my lead, whip and helmet ready. I hardly slept I was so excited. On the day, the smell of the tent was the first thing that hit me when I walked in. The weigh room at a point-to-point is nothing like the weigh room at the races. For weigh room at Kilmuckridge, read big tent with bales of hay. Tent, grass, muck and leather all rolled into one beautiful smell. And the second sweetest smell of all, anticipation.

I moved a bit gingerly into the tent, not knowing if I should make eye contact with anyone, not knowing if I knew anyone or if I should know anyone, or if I should say anything to anyone. I took up a vacant spot on a bale, didn't look left or right, just mumbled a kind of hello to nobody in particular. I wasn't riding in the next, but everyone else was getting ready. There was craic and banter but a lot of nerves, which curtailed the banter somewhat. Lads were getting caps tied and boots zipped, and suddenly nearly everyone was gone. It was an eerie feeling, like when everyone has gone out to play in the school yard and you are still there in the classroom – silent, quiet, lonely, but nice. You can hear them all outside, but you are happy to be there on your own, in your own little cocoon. Time enough.

I got myself ready – tights, breeches, silks, boots – and got on the weighing scales, just a little set of bathroom scales in the corner with a makeshift curtain around it. Put some lead into my saddle. Helmet and whip. Dyser came to get the saddle. Suddenly everyone was back after the previous race, mad rush, people shouting and slagging and changing, and then it was my turn. We were called out. I strode into the parade ring with the other jocks, looking a million dollars and feeling a million dollars, my heart doing five-furlong pace. George gave me a leg up and I was off down to the start.

The cards could hardly have fallen better in the race itself. Gayloire jumped and travelled like a dream throughout. We arrived upsides something else going to the last. I didn't know what it was; it didn't matter. When we touched down over the last I rode for all I was worth. I punched and kicked and smacked and punched and kicked some more. I thought I was edging ahead, but I wasn't sure. I didn't stop riding until we were well past the winning post. I turned round to look at the other horse and rider. John Berry on the favourite, Brandy Cross. My heart sank. This was his local track. They'd hardly give it to me.

There were no photo finishes at point-to-points at the time. When there was a close finish, the judge would use his, well, judgement, and call the winner. Dyser came to get me and Gayloire as we pulled up, delighted with himself and delighted for me. I still wasn't sure if we had won or not, but Dyser had no doubt. 'There'll be trouble if they don't call us the winner,' he said. When we got to the unsaddling area, John Berry and Brandy Cross were already there in the spot reserved for the winner, even though the judge hadn't called the result. My heart sank, but Dyser wasn't having any of it. He dragged me and Gayloire straight in and barged past everyone, saying something about where they could go if they didn't like it. 'They're only chancing their arms going into the winner's enclosure,' he told me. 'They know who's won as well as we do.'

This was all new to me, an eighteen-year-old rider who had just completed the course for only the second time in his life. Even though I was dismounting in the winner's enclosure, I was still unsure. I really had no idea who had won, but Dyser was fairly convincing. I would have been disappointed all right if I hadn't won, but I didn't dare to think about the possibility that I might have. I just repeated the words 'Please let me have won, please let me have won'. I'm not sure to whom I was saying the words. Probably to some higher authority who has much more of a say in these things than me, or even the judge. Then they announced the result over the public address system. Gayloire had won. Gayloire and Mr T. J. Murphy.

Dyser jumped up in the air. He'd had two weeks' wages on Gayloire, and probably wouldn't have been able to eat until the end of the month if he had got beaten. George was thrilled too. I couldn't believe it. I really couldn't. It was just the best feeling you could ever imagine. My first winner. I don't know what it can compare to. I imagine it is fairly exciting to score your first point in Croke Park, or to score a goal in an FA Cup final, so it might have been something like that. I had certainly never experienced a feeling like it before.

You spend all your days as a child riding around a field, racing against your dad or your brother or your cousin, or against yourself. You are usually winning the Grand National, but sometimes you're just winning a novice hurdle at Tramore or a point-to-point at Punchestown. Just racing against yourself, imagining winning and being led back into the winner's enclosure with the small crowd applauding politely. Well, this was it. Try to think of something you dreamt of when you were a child. Something that was so far removed from your reality as a child that you thought it almost unattainable. It could be driving a truck, or getting married, or playing at Anfield, or kicking a ball with your child. Now imagine how you would feel, or remember how you felt, upon attaining that goal. That was me at Kilmuckridge.

I didn't have one overriding emotion. Euphoria, pride, ecstasy, pure excitement, absolute happiness, a sense of achievement, a sense of vindication, of not letting people down – they were all there. Suddenly I was the centre of attention, and I surprised myself by liking that. Suddenly I was someone. I wasn't just a nobody, unsaddling somewhere away from the public eye, or making my way back to the jockeys' tent with my saddle while the assembled racegoers and media encircled the winner. Someone like Philip Dempsey or Enda Bolger or Tony Martin. Now I was that winner. I was Enda Bolger. For now, it was me they wanted. I imagine it's a bit like when you get a little bit of recognition in a job. You're nobody for years. You're the gofer. None of the management team knows your name. Then you do something good. You solve a problem or you get a good review from a customer or you set up a system that works. Suddenly people in the company know you, your boss's boss knows your name, people say hello to you at the water cooler, you gain a little bit of recognition. Ah, he is doing a good job after all. That was what this winner afforded me. A little bit of recognition.

I couldn't wait to tell everybody. We stopped at a phone box on the way home so that I could phone Mam and Dad to tell them, but they weren't in. We stopped a couple of times, but there was nobody home all evening. I was bursting to tell them. I ended up phoning Uncle Mick and talking to my granny and telling her. Ah, that's great, Timmy. Your first winner was it? That's lovely.

If there had been no horsebox going home that evening, I would have just floated home anyway. Dyser was happy too. Having put his wages on at 8–1 he had guaranteed his solvency for as far into the future as he could see. I kept thinking back on my ride. On how easily Gayloire did it for me, how little I had to do, how easily he travelled throughout the race, and how I rode him out on the run-in. I wondered how stylish I'd looked, how I'd compared to John Berry. I fancied myself as a bit of a stylist, irons up as far as I dared, more Lester Piggott than Ted Walsh. I was sure that I'd looked good, and I knew it was effective. Didn't I get up in a photo from John Berry on the favourite? And I thought, 'Imagine, you could do this for a living! Imagine going home from work every day feeling like this!' This was what I wanted to do.

I floated into the yard the next day as well. Mucking out and raking yards was no problem. Indeed, I'd say I floated about for a couple of weeks on the back of Gayloire's win. I just kept on remembering it, remembering the feeling, recalling the finish, the announcement of the result, Dyser's face.

Gayloire's win helped me get on at Halford's as well. No longer was I just another lad in the yard. I was now the lad who had won on Gayloire at Kilmuckridge. Philip Dempsey still had the pick of the bumper horses – one winner wasn't going to change any of that – but Mick started to put me up on a few more.

I basically got to ride a lot of the horses Philip Dempsey was unable to ride. Don't get me wrong, though, I was delighted to be riding them. I was delighted to be getting into the breeches and the silks and going out riding. I really was. But I remember thinking, 'Jesus, it's still not happening for me. I'm not getting anywhere. If I keep on riding crap I'll keep on finishing down the field, or not finishing at all. I'll never get noticed.' I'd had a whiff of success, and I wanted more; riding these horses wasn't doing my confidence any good. You'd only be riding every three or four weeks, so you weren't really building on your previous experience. Every time I went out to ride it was like my first ride all over again. I'd be expecting to finish down the field. It was almost like when I rode one of my Dad's point-to-pointers. I'd just be trying to get round. I never expected to get in the shake-up. And then, of course, when I rode Gayloire the first time, a horse that had the ability to win, I didn't know what to do and I ended up making a mess of it.

Riding racehorses is a lot about confidence. It's like any sport really, or most things in life. If you stand over a putt and expect to knock it into the back of the hole, the chances are you will knock it into the back of the hole. Or if you go for an interview and you really don't expect to get the job, in all likelihood you won't get it. And success breeds success. If you have holed the last three putts, you will expect to hole the next one; if you have missed the last three, you will approach the next one more in hope than in genuine confidence. When you are riding horses without much of a chance you are all the while finishing down the field, and you don't really expect to win on the next one. You push them out, but they can't go any faster. You think it's you. You think you should be able to make them go faster. You don't realise that it's not you, it's them. They have a maximum speed and no jockey can make them exceed it. You didn't often see Tony Martin or Tom Mullins pushing one down the back straight. In the back of your mind you think it's because they are top-class riders, and they were, but the reality was that they also had the engine underneath them. They didn't ride bad horses. They didn't need to.

I gained a better appreciation for all this when I began running myself. I started running initially in order to keep fit, but it also had the effect of enabling me to learn how a horse feels in a race. There is a maximum speed at which you can go for a given period of time. It doesn't matter what someone does or says in order to try to encourage you to go faster. 'I'll whack you on the arse if you don't go half a stride faster. You don't believe me? There. I'll do it again.' But you simply can't if you don't have the engine. You physically can't. In a long-distance race, if you force yourself to go faster than the pace at which you are comfortable, you will have nothing left for the end. You possibly won't even finish. It's exactly the same with a horse. Every horse has a maximum pace at which he is comfortable. You hear a lot of talk these days about this horse or that horse who has a high cruising speed. The trick is to find a horse's cruising speed and let him go at that speed. Cruise control. The less you do on his back the better. If you push him along and go faster early in the race, he will be a spent force at the business end. That is why it is so difficult for horses when they go up a grade. They often can't cope with the faster pace in the early part of the higher-class race. They'll go a fast pace for a certain amount of time, but they won't be able to keep it up. So when you ride a bad horse in a good race, you have to allow him to travel at his own pace, with the result that you often get behind. You just try to make sure he finishes. It annoys me to hear pundits say, 'Oh, if he had been handier earlier he probably would have won.' Often if the jockey had had the horse handier earlier he probably wouldn't have finished as close as he did.

So there was I in the summer of 1993 riding ordinary horses at Halford's, but riding nonetheless. It was much better than at Weld's where I wasn't race-riding at all, and I appreciated that in the beginning. I really did. After a while, however, I began to want more. It's like anything. When you don't have food or shelter, all you want is food and shelter. When you have a big house and a well-stocked larder, though, all you want is a Ferrari.

I began to wonder where it would end. Philip Dempsey would always ride the good ones, and Halford only had about four or five bumper horses, so how was I going to get a chance to win again? It wasn't like I was going to get an outside ride or anything. Who would use me? And why would they? They didn't know me. And if they knew anything about me they knew that I rode the horses Dempsey didn't ride and couldn't get one of them to finish better than mid-division.

Then, just as Gayloire's win at Kilmuckridge was becoming a bit of a distant memory, George decided that he would allow him to run in a bumper. I held my breath for about six days before I got the news I desperately wanted to hear. Three days before Gayloire was to run I learnt that I would ride. Exhale. My insides did the can-can while my outsides remained largely nonplussed. That's great. Thanks.

Gayloire finished third at Kilbeggan on 21 June, Mr T. J. Murphy up. Everyone was happy. Mick was happy, George was happy, I was happy. Actually, I was thrilled. I got a real kick out of riding a horse with ability. They said they'd go back to Kilbeggan with Gayloire for another bumper three weeks later. He seemed to act on the track, he handled the ground, and it seemed to make sense to go back again. He could go even better with the experience under his girth. Again I held my breath. In truth, I would have been desperately disappointed if I had lost the ride. I wasn't. Mick was great like that. He was always loyal. As I've said, if you proved that you could do a job, or if you got on well with a horse, he tended to leave you on it. And George was great as well. He seemed to have forgotten the ride I gave Gayloire in Cashel.

So they left me on Gayloire, and we went and won that bumper at Kilbeggan three weeks later, ironically again beating John Berry into second place on Queen Kam. That was amazing. It fell just a little bit short of the thrill I got when I rode him to win at Kilmuckridge – it's never as good as the first time – but only a little bit. My first winner at the track was another landmark. More centre of attention, more feelings of 'this is cool, imagine doing this for a living'. When you ride your first winner on the track, you know what all the mucking out, the riding out, the getting up at six o'clock in the morning and all the cycling through the rain to get to work is for. It's all worth it.

I rode Gayloire on the track once more, in a maiden hurdle at Tramore later that summer, in which we finished third behind Enda Bolger on Merry People and Ken Whelan on Taylors Quay. Of course, Merry People went on to be a really decent handicap chaser. Somewhat incredibly, John Berry finished fourth that day on a horse called Mountain Sky, just a length behind me and Gayloire. John must have been sick of the sight of Gayloire's tail.

I ticked along from then until the end of the summer. Mick had quite a few horses who had a bit of ability. Some decent handicappers rather than graded race performers perhaps, but they were not without some talent. I worked hard during the week, played hard at weekends, and had a few rides in between. I was riding quite well given the limited opportunities I was getting, I was getting noticed a little bit, and I was, I thought, worth my seven-pound claim. It was getting to the point where I was outgrowing Mick's yard. Although I couldn't really see it at the time, Mick simply didn't have the raw material that would give me the opportunity to get to the next level in my career. His yard was more Flat than National Hunt at that stage. He only had four or five bumper horses, and I was an amateur rider who needed to ride bumper horses. Riding what Philip Dempsey didn't ride was brilliant in the beginning, but it was getting to the point where it wasn't enough. I needed something more.

Mick was friendly with Michael Hourigan, and Hourigan had loads of bumper horses. Truck loads of them. Mick also thought it might be a good idea for me to get away from the Curragh. He thought it wasn't doing me any good, and that I was in danger of throwing it all away. He was right. So Mick rang Michael Hourigan to ask him if he could take me. There usually was space down in Lisaleen for a young lad who could use a shovel and who could spell 'horse', but Mick wanted to be sure. 'This lad can ride,' he told him. 'You'll just need to keep a bit of an eye on him. And he takes direction OK. You can eat the head off him and five minutes later he'll be back talking to you as if nothing has happened.'

Then Mick put it to me: how about going down to Michael Hourigan's? Give it a try, see how it goes, and if it doesn't work out you can always come back here. And I thought, 'Here we go again, someone else who doesn't want me working for him. Another excuse, another sacking.' But this was different. Mick explained that he was happy to keep me during the winter. I could break yearlings or look after the young horses, but it would be better for me if I were to go to Hourigan's. He said I would learn a lot more. 'Go down for the winter, and there'll be a place for you here next spring if you want it.'

I wasn't too keen in the beginning. Hourigan had a reputation for being tough to work for. There was no question that I would have to work harder than I had done on the Curragh, and for less money. And I was happy enough ticking along from day to day at Halford's. Still, the case Mick presented was compelling. He didn't have the horses for me, but Mike did. As I said, I couldn't really see it at the time, but he was right. I wasn't promised any rides at Hourigan's, but I was promised schooling. Loads of schooling. I loved schooling. It wasn't too far behind riding in point-to-points for me, and I hardly got to do any schooling on the

TIMMY MURPHY: RIDING THE STORM

Curragh. Hourigan's was a real National Hunt yard. I'd only just turned nineteen and my idea of long-term planning was deciding where I was going to go out on Saturday night, but even I could see that it was probably the thing to do.

I rang Uncle Mick to ask him what he thought. 'What do you know about Hourigan?'

His response was emphatic. 'You should go there. You'll ride loads and you'll learn loads.' I wouldn't have known how big Mike was in the point-to-point scene in the south. You didn't really talk about the point-to-point scene on the Curragh as very few of the lads would have had any interest, and those who did didn't know that much about what went on on the far side of Nenagh. But Mick Welsh was adamant. 'Hourigan will have loads of point-to-pointers for you to ride,' he said. 'He has loads of runners every weekend. Lorry loads.'

So I said I would go to Hourigan's. I'd give it the winter and I'd be back at Halford's by the following summer if things didn't work out. If you had told me then that I wouldn't work at Mick Halford's again, however, you would have had some job getting me to believe you.

CHAPTER SIX

SUCCESS BREEDS SUCCESS

My Mam and Dad drove me down to Michael Hourigan's. I was
fairly well presented, well groomed, my suitcase neatly packed.
I always liked to have my shoes well polished. My Mam said that she
could see her face in them.

I left my stuff in the car and went into the house with my Dad. We
walked up to the first house on the left as you went into the yard and just
knocked on the door. A girl opened it, probably a stable lass; this was
probably the lads' and lasses' accommodation. Well, it looked like the
lads' accommodation. Fairly basic, spartan even. 'I'll have to fend for
myself here,' I thought. I wondered how many lads actually lived in the
house. Four maybe, five tops. Surely you couldn't fit any more than five
lads in this house? And me, that would be six. I'd probably have to share
a room with somebody. Hope he's tidy. It wasn't anything like Bob and
Sheila Kelly's place, but it didn't look too bad and I suppose we were in
real rural Ireland. I could probably manage to live here all right.

'Hello, I'm Timmy Murphy.'

The girl showed me and my Dad around. The yard, the feed room, the
equine swimming pool and the fields where they galloped, although you
couldn't really see the fields through the darkness. Then she brought us
back to the feed room and told me that I could leave my stuff there. It took
a few seconds for the realisation to dawn. This wasn't the feed room at all.

I walked nonchalantly out to the car to get my stuff.

'Mam, givvus the keys for the boot, will you?' I called out abruptly.

'But your suitcase is on the back seat, Timmy.'

'Just give me the keys!'

I took a black bag out of the boot, emptied the contents of my suitcase into it, scuffed up my shoes a bit and handed the suitcase back to Mam to take home. There was no way I was walking into that house carrying a suitcase.

It had all fallen into place. This building, what looked like the feed room, was to be my home. The house was the Hourigans' own home. A little cottage, where Mike and Anne lived with their children Paul, Laura and Kay. Young Michael was in England at the time and Mark wasn't yet born. The stable lass who'd shown us around was Kay, Mike's daughter.

Mam got out of the car and came in to see where I was going to be living. It didn't get any better as you went upstairs. In fact, the higher you went the worse it got. The dirt and the damp and a crowd of lads in one big house. It was like a cross between *Only Fools and Horses* and *The Waltons*. Mam wasn't happy to leave me there. She didn't articulate as much, but I could tell she wasn't impressed. Dad just kept nodding his head and saying that I would be fine. They knew that Hourigan's was fairly rough and ready, and we had spoken about it a little going down in the car, insofar as we spoke going down in the car, but I don't think they were quite expecting what turned out to be the reality. I had mixed feelings about it myself. I can't say I was thrilled with the facilities, that was for sure. Nor was I over the moon about the rising damp. But it was exciting all the same. Lots of horses, lots of schooling, a whole new vista.

Mike was exactly the same then as he is now. A scary little man. Everything was full on with Mike. Run hard, work hard, gallop hard. When we'd be loading horses, it would be 'Yah! Yah! Yah!' When we'd be working it would be flat out. Everything in a mad rush. No let-up.

Hourigan's was totally different to anything I had ever experienced before, a real shock to the system. You come from Weld's, where everything is neat and tidy, and everybody has their shiny boots, all pretty, where nobody gets to ride any work except Kinane and Sheridan and the jockeys, and you go down to Hourigan's. Yah! Yah! Yah! You get a pair of wellies thrown on to your feet, you get thrown into a load of muck, and you get roared at and abused. We used to load the horses on to these big lorries when we were bringing them away to work. You'd be leading them up and Mike would give them a slap and they'd jump up on top of you. It would just keep you sharp. You'd be half asleep going about on the Curragh. You'd do your three lots, routine, and you'd just try to look good. It could even get boring on the Curragh sometimes. It sure wasn't boring at Hourigan's.

It was usually cold and often wet, and it was always hard work, but it was great. A brilliant experience. You were learning all the time, and there was a great bunch of lads there. And Mike was always one to keep your feet on the ground. He'd always bawl you out of it before he'd praise you. But when you saw him coming down the yard you'd be scared out of your wits. It was like the sensation I used to get in school when I'd see Batman coming with his cape. You'd know by Mike's walk that he was in bad form. Head down, peaked cap obscuring his face, wellies going 90 miles an hour like little propellers. He was small, but God he could walk quickly when he wanted to. And when he did, it was time to beware. There'd be a scattering of lads when he was coming. I'm not joking – it was quite incredible. You wouldn't be able to find anyone. The last one to cop that he was coming was the first one to get it. There was a bollicking in him, and someone was going to get it. You were just unlucky if you were the last one left standing when he arrived. But Mike was always one of us. Up at Weld's, the boss was always the boss. He'd act like the boss and be treated like the boss. But Mike was always Mike. One of the lads.

Ros Easom was travelling head lass when I arrived. She was always roaring and shouting as well, and most of the lads were afraid of their lives of her, but I used to get on OK with her. I think you just had to *plamás* her a little. But when she said jump, you had to jump. How high exactly? Once you did, she was OK.

Ros would be roaring at you, Mike would be roaring at you, and lads would be roaring at other lads – loads of roaring. If you weren't roaring or being roared at you might as well be at home in your bed. There was an urgency about everything. Horses off, get down, get into the field, bring them in, bring them out. It was a bit manic because everyone was mad busy. You had to have one lot done by a certain time so that you could get back and bring the next lot out and start working.

Of course Mike didn't have all the gallops and schooling grounds that he has now. He just had his small circle gallop and a load of fields. Twice a week we used to bring the horses away to a stubble field to work. We'd wreck that after a couple of days, and then it would be on to the next field. You'd push and push horses, and you'd be learning all the time without actually race-riding. There'd be about ten horses and lads riding out together, and we used to race against each other. We'd push them out at the end and everything. It was great craic, and it was as close to race-riding as you were going to get.

We'd put all the horses on to the walker and get the next ones. More roaring and shouting, flat out, up into the lorry, get up, get down, get your next two horses, put them on to the lorry and get off out of the yard. And that was just with the horses who were working that morning. There would be other horses who weren't working, who were just going to have a bit of a canter at home, but they needed to be done as well. You'd ride two lots per lorry. There'd be about ten horses on the lorry and five lads, so you'd take two off the lorry at the same time, you'd lead them round the field in twos, then you'd split up, so that half the lads would be leading them round in twos at the bottom of the field and the other half would ride work. Once you were finished riding work you'd bring them back, get down, get up on the next horse and ride work on him. It didn't matter if it was Dorans Pride or some thing that couldn't lie up in a point-to-point, they were all treated the same. You'd get into the lorry after work and it would be like a sauna. There'd be sweat and steam and muck everywhere. Then it was everyone and everything back to the yard to hose down. The lorry, the horses, the lads, everything. You just had to make sure that you were in your waterproofs.

We did a lot of loose schooling in the indoor school as well. One lad would go down to the bottom of the school with a plastic bag, one fellow would go up to the top end, and Mike would stand in the middle with a Long Tom. You'd have about five or six loose things schooling at the same time. There was a thin line between shaking the plastic bag enough to get them to move on and shaking it too much so that they'd stop or jink. Then there'd be more roaring and Mike would be going mad, and you had to be on your toes anyway to mind you didn't get hit by a loose one. You're going too fast, too slow, keep your hands down, your heels down, your legs down, leave down your irons. And all this while getting a smack from a Long Tom just to make sure you were awake and paying attention. It was brilliant. I don't regret a single moment of the time I spent at Hourigan's.

I got to school horses almost as soon as I arrived. That was the promise I got. No rides, but lots of schooling. As a result, I didn't expect to get rides. If I got one or two, all well and good, but I didn't expect it. That was a huge difference between Hourigan's and other places I had been before. No empty promises. I'd had enough disappointments. At Hourigan's I was able to enjoy what I was doing without waiting and wishing and hoping for rides. It was probably the main reason why I was so content there.

And I was learning lots. It was like I was learning how to ride all over again. Mike kept telling me to drop my irons from the first day he saw me ride out. I'd just nod my head. 'Yeah, I must, I'll get around to that next.' I had no intention of dropping my irons. I was a stylist. All the stylish jockeys rode short. Short irons, so that they could tuck up nice and neatly in the saddle.

Then, one morning, on my way off the gallop, Mike stopped me. 'Here, cummere.' I knew he wasn't calling me over to tell me how well I was doing, or to tell me he was going to increase my wages from £60 a week to £80. That was, after all, what I was on when I worked on the Curragh, but it didn't seem to be Mike's primary concern. 'Look,' he said, 'if we're going to get on, you're going to have to drop your irons at least six holes. If you don't want to do that now, you can fuck off. I have a pain in my arse asking you to drop your irons. It's up to you now. It makes no difference to me. I don't care what you do, but you have to care if you want to stay here.' He grabbed my left leg, got the iron and literally pulled it down. He dragged my heel down and pushed my knee in. 'There,' he said. 'That's the way I want you to ride. It's up to you though. It's your career. The way you're riding now, you're depending on your arms to hold you, and I'm fucked if I'm going to put up with it. You walk down that passage now and decide for yourself what you want to do.'

This was serious. This wasn't, 'Ah now, Timmy, would you ever drop those old irons there like a good fellow?' This was, 'Drop your irons or drop out of here.' So I did think about it. I really did. There was very little upside to keeping going the way I was going. I'd have no job in the morning and no accommodation. And what if he was right? What if I was doing it all wrong just so that I could think I looked good? What if I really was relying on my arms to hold me in place? That wouldn't be good. And there was every chance that Mike was right. Although I thought I knew it all, I was gradually coming around to the realisation that maybe I didn't. Mike had a wealth of experience in the game. He had started riding out for Charlie Weld when he was fourteen. He was one of the top apprentices in Ireland in the 1960s and he'd had some top jockeys through his 'academy' at Lisaleen, most notably Adrian Maguire. All things considered, there wasn't really a choice to be made.

So I went around for about two weeks with my irons down, my heels down and my knees tucked in, feeling like a fool. Of course I could ride, but this was totally alien to me. It was like being right-handed and trying to write or throw darts or use a mouse with your left. You know how to do all those things, but you're not used to doing them with your left hand. After a while, though, I got used to it. I did sneak them up one or two holes until I got to a height with which I was comfortable, but after that it felt good.

Adrian Maguire had left Hourigan's a couple of years earlier, but he was still a hero there. I remember watching on television as he drove and kicked Omerta home in the 1991 Irish Grand National, getting the better of Charlie Swan on Cahervillahow, with the third horse, Cool Ground, a distance back in third. It was a strange turn of events that led to Maguire winning the Cheltenham Gold Cup on the same Cool Ground the following year. Everybody in the yard was a huge fan of Adrian. There were photos of him up in the boys' hostel. He was probably one of the major reasons why there were so many good young riders at Hourigan's at the time. They had seen the grounding and the opportunities that Maguire had had, and how successful he was afterwards. His success was definitely an influencing factor on me agreeing to go there. He was the A. P. McCoy of his time. It was a shame that he never was champion jockey, because he deserved to be champion jockey. He came so close in the 1993/94 season, when he and Richard Dunwoody were neck and neck for the title from a long way out. Adrian was 42 winners ahead of Dunwoody in January, yet it went down to the wire, Dunwoody winning by three in the end. The title actually wasn't decided until the final day of the season at Market Rasen. Their battle brought National Hunt racing into the limelight, but it must have nearly killed the pair of them.

The first time I met Adrian was in the Cú Chulainn bar after a point-to-point in Patrickswell, not too long after I started getting going with Hourigan. He was riding for David Nicholson, The Duke, in the UK at the time. He was suspended, so he came over to Ireland to do some hunting with the show jumper Nick Skelton, who owned a couple of horses who were in training with The Duke. He was down with Mike, so he just came along to the point-to-point for the day. I had ridden a couple of winners at that point-to-point, but there were two others on whom Adrian thought I should have won. I wouldn't usually be one to make conversation with somebody just because he is famous. I never have been. I don't know why, it's just something I've never done. Even if there was someone I really admired, I still wouldn't go up to talk to him just because of who he was. Just like I wouldn't expect somebody to come up to talk to me just because they have seen me riding on the television. So when I was introduced to Adrian I just said, 'How are you?' and went on about my business. I would have loved to quiz him. I would have had so much to ask him, about horses, about riding, about England, about how he got a break there and would it be worthwhile giving it a shot. But I didn't. I just had a drink and left. I became good friends with Adrian later, however, after I moved to England. We had a lot in common when I moved over, and we are still good friends today.

There were some very good horses at Hourigan's when I first went there. There were always good horses around Hourigan's. Deep Bramble was there. He won the Ericsson Chase in 1993 in a real thriller with Flashing Steel. Ultra Flutter was there – won three on the bounce in the spring of 1994 including a valuable handicap hurdle at the Punchestown Festival in which he beat that year's Coral Cup winner, Time For A Run. Tropical Lake was there, winner of the Glenlivet Hurdle at Aintree in 1994, in which she beat Mysilv and Pridwell. I actually got to ride her at the Galway Festival that summer. Anusha was there, winner of the Ladbroke Hurdle in January 1995. And, of course, there was Dorans Pride, who won five times and was second three times in his first eight races. On his ninth race, the 1994 Sun Alliance Hurdle at Cheltenham, he fell at the final flight when just about to tackle Danoli. Mike maintains to this day that he was staying on and would have given Danoli something to think about. We will just never know.

And there were loads of horses, too, that needed to be done all the time. Like I said, everything was full on at Hourigan's; everything had to be done quickly because we didn't have the staff. It was exactly the same later when I'd be going to a point-to-point. I couldn't tell you how to get to most of the point-to-point tracks I've been to because I used to sleep most of the time in the back of the lorry on the way there. You'd just be knackered. I wouldn't even know which way you should turn out of Hourigan's gate. You'd just load up and off you'd go. At the point-to-point you'd lead up maybe two or three, and maybe ride one. As time went on, you'd lead up one and ride two or three. But there were no airs or graces about it. Everybody mucked in. There were horses that needed to be led up, and whoever was there would do it. That was the way it worked. You'd often be leading up in your breeches and boots with just a jacket thrown over your shoulders.

It was a great grounding for me. And the fact that you were riding for a top yard meant that you got noticed. I hadn't fully appreciated how big

Hourigan was or how well his horses were regarded on the point-to-point circuit down south before I got there. But it was a huge help to me. There was also the fact that the horses were well schooled. Even if they weren't that good, at least they'd had a lot of practice at jumping at home and they had some idea of how to get from one side of a fence to the other. That's why riding on the point-to-point circuit was such good experience for me. It can be a bad experience, and it is for many. If you were relying on spare rides from small yards that wouldn't have had their horses fit or schooled, you could get into bad habits yourself. Riding dodgy ones is no good to anybody. I was very lucky that way. And when you'd be riding good horses, you'd get a name for being able to ride good horses, and people who had good horses would be ringing you up, asking you to ride theirs. It is self-fulfilling. As I said, nothing succeeds like success.

But my breakthrough didn't look likely at the start, and it took a while. I wasn't too anxious about it in the beginning because I knew it was going to take an unusual set of circumstances for me to get rides. There were a lot of riders there when I got to Hourigan's, all of whom would have been ahead of me in the pecking order when it came to getting rides. Kevin O'Brien was riding most of them at the time, Shane Broderick was the stable's conditional, David Casey was there, John Cullen; then there was Peter Henley, Aidan Fitzgerald, Robbie Byrnes, all amateurs and all of whom were ahead of me in the queue for point-to-point or bumper rides. And, of course, there was Enda Bolger, who would ride just about whatever he wanted to ride. Bolger would just come in the odd morning. You'd never see him around the yard. No way. He wouldn't be mucking out or grooming horses, not Enda. He had served his time. But you'd see him at the races or at a point-to-point if we had something going that was expected to win, and you might see him on a schooling morning.

But he was cute out. One day he came down to school after the local point-to-point at Patrickswell in the lashing rain. We were all there, about ten of us, there to school together, but it was so misty and wet that you could hardly see your hand in front of your face. We all set off

81

anyway, through the rain, battering and driving these horses up over these fences as Enda just hacked along behind on the inside, bypassing the fences. Every now and then you'd hear him laughing. 'Ye're some eejits, boys!' We didn't mind. It was all good craic, and it was our chance to race. But it was probably a bit dangerous, and it wasn't for Enda. Then, as we came up the straight he pulled back on to the course and jumped the last two fences beside Mike.

'How did you go, Enda?'

'Ah, I went grand, now, just grand.'

Most of the eight or nine lads ahead of me who were looking for rides, were really only looking for the second string as Enda would generally ride anything that was well fancied. If I had been promised rides, I probably wouldn't have lasted too long there. It was hard to see a way in which I would get a ride. Hourigan would have to have plenty of runners at a meeting on a day, and runners at a different meeting as well, in order for the other lads to be off riding them so that I could get an opportunity. But because I wasn't promised rides, I was in a different frame of mind to the one I'd been in on the Curragh. I was happy just to be there, to ride work and school. I wasn't tearing my hair out in frustration at not getting rides.

Then, a break. You need a lot of them if you are to make it in this game, and I got a huge one one night in November 1993 when Gerry Stack rang me out of the blue to ask if I would ride a horse for him in a bumper at Clonmel. Gerry was a friend of my Dad's who was keen to give me an opportunity. Fair play to him, because he probably could have got any amateur to ride. Of course I was delighted. An outside ride! The horse was called The Real Article, a big, unfurnished four-year-old grey, white even, who had never run before. Gerry told me that he was no world-beater but could be all right, and he would give me a good spin. He hung like a gate out to his left that day, which isn't a great deal of use at Clonmel, which is like a right-handed Chester. In spite of that, however, we managed to finish second behind a mare of Pat Flynn's called Aries Girl, who would go on to win two more bumpers that winter, finish second to Mucklemeg in the Cheltenham Bumper, and win the Punchestown Champion Bumper the following April.

As it happened, Mike had a mare in the same race, Shannon Amber, who had run about six times before in bumpers and maiden hurdles but hadn't come even close to winning. Peter Henley rode her, and she finished well down the field. But I think, as a result, Mike was paying particular attention to the race, and he had to have noticed the fact that I finished second on The Real Article. One of his riders riding something for someone else when he had a horse in the race.

The Real Article was actually brilliant for me. I rode him the following January in a bumper at Naas. He hung to his left again that day, which wasn't as big a problem as it had been at Clonmel given that Naas is left-handed, and we finished second again, to a horse of John Fowler's called Prodigal Prince, ridden by Tony Martin, who was having his first run on the racecourse. Then he won for me at Punchestown later that month, beating another horse of John Fowler's, Linden's Lotto, into second place. That was The Real Article's last run in a bumper, which was a shame. As bumpers are restricted to amateur riders and novice hurdles are not, Gerry was free to get a professional to ride him once he went jumping hurdles. That was fair enough. I had very little experience of riding over hurdles at the time, and he had done his bit for me anyway. He had got me noticed at Hourigan's, and that was a huge step forward.

In March 1994, Mike said I could ride one for him, For Kevin, in a winner-of-one race in a point-to-point at Corrin. Enda Bolger had ridden him to win his maiden, but for some reason Enda decided that he wasn't going to ride him at Corrin, so Mike told me that I could ride him. My first ride for Hourigan. I'm not sure if it was directly as a result of my exploits on The Real Article, but they had to have been an influential factor. I wasn't just one of the lads who rode out and mucked out and acted the maggot any more. He had seen me race-riding for somebody else, and he had obviously thought I was good enough to be given a chance for him in a point-to-point.

For Kevin won. Amazing. My first ride for Michael Hourigan was a winner. Robbie Byrnes was riding a couple for Mike at that meeting as well, but he had a fall early on and was concussed. In fact, it was rare that Robbie had a fall and didn't get concussed. So he was stood down for the rest of the day, and Mike said that I could ride the next one, Screen Printer, in the second division of the mares' maiden. This was absolutely unbelievable. I was at the meeting to lead up a couple and to ride one. I had won on that horse, I was floating around on the feeling of satisfaction that comes with achievement and progress, and here I was suddenly getting another ride. Screen Printer hadn't much form though. She would run 24 times on the track after her point-to-point days, and the best she would manage would be third place. But this mares' maiden really wasn't a good race and we managed to win that as well. I went to the meeting only having ever ridden one point-to-point winner, and I came home having ridden three. This was dreamland.

All of a sudden, things began to snowball. In the spring of 1994, here I was with a couple of point-to-point winners, a bumper winner, and more rides than I could possibly have expected. Robbie was off for a while after his fall. When you are concussed you are stood down for a mandatory 21 days, so I picked up a lot of his rides while he was away. He wasn't long back until he had another fall and was concussed again. Another 21 days. So that was 42 days of potential rides for me in the space of a short period of time, just when I needed opportunities in order to make a name for myself. I felt sorry for Robbie for sure, but I had to try to make the best of it myself.

Jonjo Walsh was great to me around that time as well. As well as the Hourigan horses, his mare, Mrs Pegasus, played a huge part in establishing my name as a point-to-point rider. I won a mares' maiden on her at Killeady in April 1994, I won an open race on her at Farnanes two weeks later, and I won another open on her at Dromahane three weeks after that. It was fantastic for me to be riding winners for an outside yard and I was really grateful to Jonjo for putting me up. I also finished second on Mrs Pegasus in a hunter chase at Kilbeggan in May that year, and I won a novice chase and a handicap chase on her on the track later that summer. I was riding a bit for Liam Burke as well, and for Jimmy Mangan. They were very good to me too. Jimmy trained a mare called What Thing for the O'Donoghues from Watergrass Hill, who were good friends of my Dad's. She gave me a few great spins in the top hunter chases at Fairyhouse and Punchestown against the best hunter chasers in the country, including Elegant Lord and Loving Around.

So, in the spring and summer of 1994 it began to look like I was second amateur in the yard. Mike never said as much to me, it just began to happen that I was riding everything that Enda Bolger wasn't. David Casey, Shane Broderick and John Cullen were professional, so I wasn't competing with them for rides. But I suppose I kind of skipped the queue. Some of the amateur lads who were there before me were actually after me in the pecking order at that time. But it never really felt like that. Everyone was competing for rides, and when you got one you were delighted. The appreciation came with the scarcity.

I was riding a lot of them on the track. Enda was winding down at the time and I had a seven-pound claim, which was proving to be extremely valuable, so I got to ride in bumpers and in the amateur riders' hurdle races on the track. Then other trainers started ringing looking for me to ride for them in bumpers. When you are riding well and riding winners, you are in demand. Of course the reverse is also the case. It's a fickle business. And timing is so important. That season was Enda's last, really, riding for Hourigan. He was cutting down in order that he could concentrate on his own operation, so I began riding all the point-to-pointers and all the bumper horses on the track, insofar as I could. Things were going really well. I rode fourteen winners on the point-to-point circuit that season and was joint champion novice rider with Kevin O'Sullivan.

One of the outside rides I got was on a mare called May Gale for Pat Rooney. I rode her first in a Flat race restricted to qualified riders at Leopardstown in June 1994. I got beaten a short head on her at Bellewstown after that, but then we went to the Galway Festival with her and won a maiden hurdle on the Monday evening. As it happened it was the first race of the festival, and it was live on national television, so it was a really big deal for me. Ted Walsh really gave me a lot of credit for the ride I gave her on RTE television afterwards. Ted has always been very good to me on television. After that, the phone started ringing even more. More outside trainers wanted to use me, and I was on my way.

But it wasn't all a bed of roses. The work still had to be done at Hourigan's, the mucking out and the grooming and the general caring for horses. It didn't matter how many winners you had ridden for outside trainers, or how many times the phone rang looking for you to ride at the weekend, you still had to do your horses. Peter Henley was telling me just recently that when he arrived at Hourigan's he was shown a line of about eight boxes, all of them with a horse's head sticking out over the top, and was told that they were his horses to do. Which ones? The top four or the bottom four? Actually, Peter, the top four and the bottom four. So you went from having four or maybe five horses to do on the Curragh to having eight or nine of your own to do down at Hourigan's. And they were just your own. That didn't include spares that you had to do when someone was away. In reality you'd have nine or ten. It wasn't easy. That's why everything was flat out at Hourigan's. No time for thinking, only time for doing.

Brian Moran took on the head lad role when Ros Easom left. Brian was great as head lad, but the poor man nearly lost his arm and had to give it up. I think he was just leading a horse into a box. He went under the bar at the front of the box, and he must have had the rope wrapped around his hand or something. The horse just shot back and wrenched his arm. It tore all the ligaments in it and nearly pulled it out of its socket.

Mike's daughter Kay filled in as head lass for a little while. I was actually going out with Kay at the time. In fact, I started going out with her over Christmas 1993, not long after I'd arrived at Hourigan's. Kay was my first real girlfriend. We didn't want people to know in the beginning, especially not Mike or Anne. Mike was very protective of Kay, as, I suppose, most fathers would be of their daughters. It is reasonable to assume that in an ideal world you wouldn't want your daughter to start going out with your latest recruit. So we kept it quiet in the beginning. We'd go into Adare, which was only a couple of miles away, or up to the Woodlands Hotel, which was literally just up the road. But Mike and Anne were friendly with the owner of the Woodlands, so we'd have to skulk around there a bit.

I remember one night we had to join a wedding party in the ballroom because Mike and Anne were up at the bar. We thought that nobody knew, but of course they knew. Anne certainly knew. Just a couple of months after we started going out, Anne caught us in the tack room together. Disaster. I remember her exact words to this day: 'Do you think I'm a fucking eejit?' And we were codding ourselves that Mike didn't know. I don't think he liked it, but he tolerated it. So we knew that Mike and Anne knew, and they knew that we knew they knew, but we didn't flaunt it and we certainly didn't talk about it. I couldn't imagine having a what-are-your-intentions-towards-my-daughter conversation with Mike.

There was drinking all right at Hourigan's, but it was more controlled and less intense than it had been on the Curragh. You wouldn't go out late on a Saturday night because you'd be riding on the Sunday – Sunday was the big day – and you wouldn't go out too late on a Friday or a Sunday because you'd have to be up early for work the following day. There was more thought put into the day after at Hourigan's. There was more professionalism, less reckless abandon. Work – the scourge of the drinking classes.

Kay and I also used to go over to Kilfinnan with a group of lads. Kay would have to sneak out of a window, as she wasn't allowed out. She was doing her Leaving Cert that year after all. Timmy O'Sullivan was one of the leading claiming riders at the time. I would share a house in England later on with him and Gerry Hogan. Timmy's parents, Timmy and Kathleen, had a bar in Kilfinnan, the Green Bar, although how anybody ever got to it I'll never know. There were no signposts that said Kilfinnan, no directions. You never knew you were on your way there until you arrived. I'd struggle to find my way there today. But there was a good group of lads there: Shane Broderick, Barry Fenton, Ciaran O'Brien and

Gerry O'Neill, who was working down the road at Austin Leahy's. For years afterwards, when we'd come home from England, we'd all go to the Green Bar. Jim Culloty, Gerry Hogan, Peter Henley. Kathleen was like a mother to us all.

Kay was great. She would be looking after me when we were out, reminding me that I had to be up early in the morning, or that I had two rides in the point-to-point the following day. She probably went through a lot with me. I wouldn't always listen to her, and that would cause a bit of aggro. Of course, in the vast majority of cases she was in the right and I was in the wrong. She acted as my agent for a while as well, insofar as an amateur rider can have an agent (who, obviously, doesn't get paid). Back then trainers could enter a horse in a couple of different races at the same point-to-point, which made things very difficult for riders. You wouldn't know in what races you'd be riding or in what races you'd be free to look for an outside ride. So Kay used to try to find out from Mike in which races he was intending to run the horses. Then we'd go up to the Woodlands on a Saturday evening with a handful of twenty-pence pieces and start phoning the trainers who had entries in the races in which I wouldn't have a ride for Mike.

I'm not sure if there was a feeling among the rest of the lads that Mike was only putting me up because I was going out with his daughter. I don't think there was, or if there was I didn't feel it. I didn't get anything easily. If anything, I had to work harder to get there because I was going out with Kay. I remember coming home from Gowran Park one evening after a filly had fallen with me and broken her leg, and Mike telling people that I had killed the filly. I had killed her! It was as if I had jumped down off her back and given her a kick!

Kay came over to England for a little while when I went there first. It was the first summer I was there, riding for Kim Bailey. Kay went home after the summer, but she was soon back out again. She had met Paul and Bridget Nicholls when they were over in Ireland buying horses, and they told her that there was a job for her with them if she ever wanted one, so she took them up on it. I guess she came over to be with me, but I was too busy drinking and messing and not cooperating with her efforts to look after me. Wasn't I well able to look after myself? She put up with a lot with me, there's no question, and she stuck it out for a long time. Much longer than any reasonable person would have expected her to. After six months with Nicholls, she went home to manage the yard at Lisaleen for Mike. She is still there today, doing a fantastic job.

Kay wasn't really old enough to run the yard when Brian Moran left – she was only eighteen at the time – so Mike recruited David Wachman as head lad. David was a young lad who was coming over from a yard in England. It turned out that it was Jenny Pitman's yard, which was a tough place to work, by all accounts. They joked at the time that the Alsatians at Pitman's used to walk around in pairs for protection.

My relationship with David at that time was less than harmonious.

He had already sacked David Casey well before the morning I came back to the yard on a horse with the quarter-sheet back. 'Pull up that quarter-sheet,' Wachman said to me as I was coming back in. I didn't think that I should, because the horse had just come back in after doing a little bit of work. I thought I should leave it off him, and I told Wachman as much.

'Look,' he said, 'pull up that quarter-sheet now.'

'But I think he's better off with it down.'

'Listen here,' he said to me. 'Either you pull up that quarter-sheet now, or you get out that gate.'

'Fine. I'm out of here.'

I got off the horse and walked towards the gate. Wachman didn't call me back. I didn't expect him to. Before I got to the gate, though, I knew that I had made a mistake. I hadn't really thought this through too well. No job, no accommodation. What was I going to do?

I walked out of the yard and down towards the house. The sense of regret got stronger. I was after messing up again, and things had been going so well. Why didn't I pull up the fecking quarter-sheet? It was only a quarter-sheet on a horse that probably wouldn't be able to run out of your way anyway. Wachman was the boss, there to be obeyed.

Shane Broderick came down to the house after he was finished in the yard that morning, and he said I should go up and talk to Mike later on. That made sense. Mike would understand. So I went up to Mike that evening and told him what had happened. Of course Wachman had already told him. Mike was fine about it, but he said, 'Look, if I take you back, the lads will have no respect for David, and that won't work. I have no problem with you coming back, but David will have to take you back, not me.'

David wouldn't.

I suppose it was fair enough. I probably had a bit of an attitude problem at the time, and I wasn't the greatest worker in the yard. I probably wouldn't have taken myself back if I had been in Wachman's shoes, I can see that now. But at the time I was right and everyone else was wrong. It was a good kick up the arse for me, and it didn't do me a great deal of harm in the long run.

I packed up my plastic bags and went back home. It was tough moving home with my tail between my legs, but where else was I going to go? I had no job and I didn't have enough money to pay rent. My Mam was delighted to have me back, even if I was a bit grumpy.

But unlike the times when I got sacked from Weld's and Gillespie's, I wasn't back to square one this time. Thankfully, the outside point-to-point rides didn't dry up. I suppose it didn't matter to outside trainers that I wasn't the best worker in the world, or that I had been sacked from Hourigan's for telling his head lad where to go. They only had to deal with me in the parade ring before a race and in the unsaddling area afterwards, and if I could ride, they were going to use me. I was lucky that I had managed to get my foot on the first rung of the ladder before I lost my job at Hourigan's.

I would have gone anywhere for a ride at that time, and I frequently did. I used to go racing with Warren Ewing, he used to drive. I'd be up north one day for one ride and down south the next day for another. I had a couple of winners as well, so things actually weren't working out too badly. I loved riding in point-to-points. There was a great group of lads riding with me at the time, and there was great camaraderie among them. Warren Ewing, Kevin O'Sullivan, Kenny Whelan. John Thomas McNamara was just starting off, and then there were the older lads like Timmy O'Callaghan and Nick Dee who were still riding when I was getting going. But while there was camaraderie off the track, there was no let-up on it. It was survival of the fittest on the track, and I had a couple of run-ins with lads along the way. There was only a round bale keeping you on the track and you'd have lads trying to nudge you out the far side of it. There were no cameras, no stewards' enquiries. If you were pushed out the far side of a bale, it just went down as a 'ran out' and you were out of the race, so you had to have your wits about you. You had to be able to look after yourself.

Down in Patrickswell, Hourigan didn't really have anyone to ride in point-to-points for him. Another huge stroke of luck for me. My career seems to be littered with them. He had Shane Broderick and Kevin O'Brien as professionals, but he didn't really have any amateurs, which was remarkable given how well stocked he had been with them just twelve months earlier. So he asked Kevin one day what I was doing with myself. Kevin told him that he didn't think I was doing much. So he put it to Kevin, if he could go and meet me and tell me that there were a load of pointers down in Hourigan's with nobody to ride them, maybe I'd come down with him a couple of days a week to ride out and I might get to ride them. It couldn't be seen to come from Hourigan, mind. He couldn't be seen to be asking me back.

So Kevin did. He did his job well. I started going down to Hourigan's two days a week with him. My Dad would drop me at Kevin's place in Kildare at five o'clock in the morning and we'd head down. So Mike started to use me again to ride his pointers and his bumper horses. It was just like it had been before, except that I wasn't living down there and I wasn't getting a wage, though he was giving me a few quid for riding out and for going down.

Things went really well for me that 1994/95 season. I rode 30 winners, finished second behind Tony Martin in the riders' championship and shared the novices 'riders' championship. I couldn't have wished for better. Two years earlier I would have been happy to ride three winners, or even get three rides. But it was to be my last season riding as an amateur. It was actually to be my last full season riding in Ireland. I was on my way.

CHAPTER SEVEN

ENGLAND CALLING

Ever since the days when I was riding Bluebell around the fields at home on Newberry Stud, I always thought I would ride as a professional one day, and when I thought of riding as a professional it was always England I thought of. Most of the racing I saw on television was from England. I wanted to be Jonjo O'Neill, and he rode in England. You couldn't be Jonjo O'Neill and ride in Ireland. When I began riding on the point-to-point circuit in Ireland, however, of course England wasn't on my mind. All I wanted was rides, just to get going, and then to ride winners and get more rides. But when I started seriously thinking of turning professional, I started to think of England again.

The number of rides I was getting on the track in hurdles and chases was increasing. Of course I was riding in bumpers as well, but the more I rode in hurdles and chases against professionals, the more I thought about turning professional. I was getting neater and tidier as a rider as well, and I was getting lots of experience. And there was money to be made when you turned professional. You could make a few quid as an amateur all right, but you wouldn't have made too much. You might get something from an owner if you won a race, but there wasn't really a living to be made from it.

In March 1995 I got a call from Tom Mahony. Tom was a good friend of Adrian Maguire's who used to call me from time to time to see if I was available to ride this horse or that horse in a point-to-point. Tom was also the person who got Adrian his first job in England, with Toby Balding. That was Adrian's break into England. Before that he had been riding in point-to-points, but it wasn't until after he joined Toby as his conditional rider that he really started to get noticed. It was Toby who provided Adrian with the stage and the ammunition to showcase his talents in England, which brought him to the attention of the likes of Martin Pipe. It was for Pipe that Adrian rode Omerta to win the Irish National and the Kim Muir in 1991. Adrian repaid Toby by winning the Gold Cup for him on Cool Ground in 1992 by a short head from The Fellow. There weren't too many jockeys riding at the time who would have won that Gold Cup on Cool Ground.

Back then there were people who used to keep an eye out around Ireland for young jockeys who might suit British trainers – scouts, if you like – and Tom Mahony was one. It doesn't happen so much these days, as the prize money and lifestyle in Ireland is so good that fewer young jockeys are looking to go to England. But back then, when there weren't many opportunities in Ireland for a young rider looking to make his way, there were plenty of young lads willing and eager to try their luck across the water. Tom asked me if I would ride a mare of his at Ballynoe the following week. He was trying to sell the mare to Toby Balding, and he was coming over to see her run. Tom wanted her to win, and he thought I would suit her. It would also be no harm for me if Toby were to see me ride. Balding was known as a trainer who used his conditional riders and gave them lots of opportunities. Look how well Adrian Maguire had done, and Tony McCoy was about to win the conditional jockeys' title that season with Balding. There was no reason why I wouldn't be able to do just as well if he liked me.

The mare, Goldenswift, trained by Pat O'Rourke, won easily with me at Ballynoe. Toby bought the mare and invited me over for an interview, so I went off to Balding's yard. It was my first time leaving Ireland, with the exception of a school trip to the Isle of Man when I was twelve. It was my first time on a plane, too. Exciting stuff. I thought the interview went OK. I doubt I wowed him with my charisma or my personality, but I didn't think I'd done or said anything that would militate against me. He wanted someone who could ride, not someone who could charm his way into Fort Knox, and he'd obviously thought I could ride if he wanted me over for an interview.

In Ireland, when you started out riding in those days you were allowed to claim seven pounds, which means that every horse you rode was allowed to carry seven pounds less than its allotted weight because an inexperienced rider was on board. After you rode ten winners your claim was reduced to five, and then to three after you rode twenty. It's a good system. It means that owners and trainers have an incentive to put you up, and a claimer who can ride well has a great chance of getting plenty of rides. And I was flying through my claim, which was great in one way, as it meant that I was riding winners, but it was a bit scary as well. Your claim is the one advantage that you, as an inexperienced rider, have over the seasoned professionals, and mine was already down to three pounds in Ireland as I had ridden 23 winners on the track at the time. But in England it wasn't reduced to three until you had ridden 25, so I could still claim five pounds in England, until I rode two more winners.

I thought it might be the case that I wouldn't be claiming enough for Toby. When Maguire and McCoy joined him they had their full claims more or less intact. So I was delighted when he offered me the job. However, around the same time Tom Dalton, for whom my Dad was looking after some horses, called me and asked me if I would be interested in riding out at Kim Bailey's during the Cheltenham Festival that year. I would just be riding out and helping out, but there might be an opportunity there as Bailey didn't have a conditional rider. He was a friend of Norman Williamson's, who was stable jockey at Bailey's at the time. Norman had heard a little about me a while before. He says that people were telling him that I was the second coming. Good point-to-point judges like Pat Healy were telling him I was very similar to Adrian Maguire. My Dad had introduced himself to Norman at a point-to-point once and Norman remembered that he seemed to be very proud of me, although he would never let me think that. Norman was over and back between Ireland and the UK a little bit in those days. He would mainly go over to Ireland to ride on Sundays, and I had met him a couple of times at the races. He had heard that I might be looking to move to England and he knew that Kim Bailey was looking for a conditional rider.

Of course I jumped at the chance to ride out for Kim Bailey. Bailey was one of the top National Hunt trainers in the UK. As well as being strong numerically, he was also high on quality. That year he had live chances in both the Champion Hurdle and the Gold Cup, with Alderbrook and Master Oats respectively. These days it would be like being asked to go and ride out at Paul Nicholls' yard during the Cheltenham Festival, or Nicky Henderson's, or Martin Pipe's. It was a no-brainer.

Then, another opportunity. It's quite uncanny. You go about for years, looking for rides, looking for an opportunity, just one break, and then when you get one the floodgates open and they all come tumbling through. At the beginning of my week with Bailey, Charlie Egerton asked me if I would go up to his place to school Talbot for him. Afterwards, he asked me if I would ride him in the Kim Muir at the Cheltenham Festival. This was dream stuff. A ride at the Cheltenham Festival at the age of twenty!

And it nearly got even better. Talbot was fantastic. We took it up at the third last and went clear going to the second last. Maybe I asked him to go on too early, as it was my first ride at Cheltenham and I didn't fully appreciate the reserves of energy you need to get from the back of the last fence up the hill to the line. But Talbot was proven over three miles so there was no danger of him not staying. It wasn't to be, however. A fleeting image of what it would be like to come back into Cheltenham's winner's enclosure was just that, fleeting, as Flyer's Nap and Peter Henley caught us before we jumped the last. Talbot kept on gamely to finish second and provide me with one of the greatest thrills of my fledgling career.

I rode out at Bailey's for three days, Tuesday, Wednesday and Thursday, the three days of the Cheltenham Festival. It was a bit strange, and in hindsight (twenty-twenty) it probably wasn't the best time for me to be riding at Bailey's. Everyone was so busy with Cheltenham that there was nobody there to really tell me what to do, or to see if I was any good.

Alderbrook won the Champion Hurdle on the Tuesday and Master Oats won the Gold Cup on the Thursday. Norman rode both of them. It was quite incredible, the first time that the same trainer/jockey combination had won the two big races at the Cheltenham Festival in years, and I was riding out at the yard when it happened.

When I was leaving at the end of the week, Bailey told me he was looking for a conditional rider, and asked me if I wanted a job. I told him I did. I didn't know if he expected me to stay or to go home to get myself together and come back. That was the sum total of our conversation.

'I'm looking for a conditional. Do you want a job?'

'Yes.'

And then I was off.

It wasn't a difficult decision to make between Bailey and Toby Balding. Toby was great for young riders, obviously. He had given Maguire and McCoy the opportunity their talent deserved. You still have to go and fully exploit the opportunity, of course, but getting it is half the battle for a young rider. But Kim Bailey was just after winning the Gold Cup and the Champion Hurdle, and he had over a hundred horses in training. There was no way I could turn his offer down. So I thanked Toby but told him I wasn't taking the job. No problem. Barry Fenton joined Toby soon afterwards.

I went home and started riding on the point-to-point circuit again. I wondered about Bailey for a little while, about whether I should call him and ask him if he was serious, and if so when I should go over. But then I started riding a couple of winners and I started to lose focus on England. I wasn't too good at long-term planning. I rarely looked beyond the weekend. Everything was geared towards the weekend: where the point-to-point meetings were, what runners Hourigan had, what other rides I could get, what trainers I should contact, where I would go drinking afterwards, and with whom.

Then, one evening, Norman Williamson called me. 'Are you coming over or what?' I was no longer totally sure that it was what I wanted, but the point-to-point season was coming to an end in Ireland anyway, and the timing felt right. As I said, I finished that season with 30 winners, second to Tony Martin in the riders' championship, who had 40, but I was leading rider in Munster and I was leading rider in Connacht. All in all, it was a fairly satisfactory season, and a major step up on the season that had gone before. So it wasn't a given that I would go to Bailey's. While I could see that it was a fantastic opportunity to ride for a top yard, and while I always thought that I would need to move to England if I was to make my mark as a rider, things were good in Ireland for me, and I knew that I would be giving up a lot if I went. Mike Hourigan wanted me to stay and turn professional with him. I think he thought that I was going to be with him for a long time, so when I did decide to leave for England it was a bit sad really. But I knew it was the right thing to do. I didn't actually tell Mike that I was definitely leaving. I should have, but I didn't. I wasn't good at thinking things through or doing the right thing like that. I just packed a bag one summer's evening shortly after the point-to-point season had ended, and headed off to Lambourn.

It was exciting and scary at the same time. Any venture into the unknown is scary, but I really was a greenhorn heading to a different land. And England was very different to Ireland. Everything was bigger. Bigger and faster. I don't care that much for London today, but back then I didn't like it at all. It was far too big; there was too much going on. I wouldn't have spent that much time in Dublin when I was growing up, and I thought that was massive. London was just in a different league. I was still a young lad from rural Ireland. I had never even been on a motorway before, now here I was zooming up the M4 from Heathrow to Lambourn, looking out the window at these fields. I couldn't believe the size of them. A hundred or two hundred acres. There are farms that aren't as big as that in Ireland.

There was a different atmosphere in England, too, a different smell in the air. Places do have different smells. There was always a very distinctive smell down at Uncle Mick's place in Shanballymore, and there was a different smell on the Curragh, and a different smell again at Hourigan's. I don't know what it was about England. It was warmer, and the air was heavier, more humid. It wasn't bad or good, it was just distinctive. And it wasn't Ireland.

I didn't like England in the beginning. Races were run more quickly, cars went faster, the pace of life was quicker and everything was more organised. Ireland was so laid back by comparison, and it took a lot of getting used to. I was lonely and homesick at first, and I didn't know anybody at all. I was living with Norman, and he was very good to me, as was Alan Normile, one of Bailey's top lads, who was Irish as well. I suppose the Irish kind of stuck together. Seanie Curran was living close by in Eastbury. I had met him a little while beforehand at the races in Limerick, and I had told him I was coming over. He said he'd keep an eye out for me. He did, and we became good mates quite quickly.

But it took me a while to settle down in England. I remember the first night out there that I really enjoyed, in this pub over in Kingston Lisle, the Blowing Stone. There was this Irish lad there, a fellow called Gerry Carwood, who played the guitar, the mouth organ and the bodhrán all at the same time. None of us would really have been musicians or anything, we weren't even necessarily into music, but this lad was brilliant. He didn't have any arrangement with the owner, he would just show up on a Sunday night and start playing. We used to go there every Sunday to see him, and the place would be hopping. They must have made a fortune out of him. But after a little while the owners decided that it was getting out of hand, that they wanted to run a quiet country pub, not this raucous bar it was becoming on a Sunday night, so they wouldn't allow him to play any more, and people stopped going there. It was a pity. At least they got their quiet country pub back.

Anyway, that night in the pub was good, and I remember thinking, 'Ah, this might not be so bad.' There were some really good people about, mainly Irish people, and it actually felt like it wasn't that far from home. There were a lot of Irish jockeys living around the area: Jim Culloty, Glenn Tormey, Johnny Kavanagh, Jason Titley, Seanie, Richard Dunwoody. Adrian Maguire wasn't too far away. Also, if I was ever feeling a bit funny or a bit lonely, I'd think, 'I'm only half an hour away from home on a plane. It's not as if I can't go back.' It was a strange and comforting feeling. I didn't want to go home, that would be like giving up, and deep down I knew that I wouldn't, but it was strangely reassuring to know that I could give it up and go home if I wanted to.

I did go home that summer, for the Galway Festival. I rode a mare for Paddy Mullins, Gaily Running, in the GPT Handicap, one of the biggest races on the calendar for qualified riders. She must have been Paddy's second string in the race as his son Tom, who now trains Asian Maze, rode his other horse, Boro Eight. Gaily Running and I got beaten a head by Noel Meade's horse, Heist, who had started favourite for the Cheltenham Bumper two years earlier. I tried hard to win the race, so much so that I got done for misuse of the whip. It was to be a common feature of my riding for a good few years to come.

I turned professional after that Galway Festival and went back to Bailey's. That was a bit daunting as well. Now I had to be paid for riding, so the only thing that differentiated me from the top jockeys like Dunwoody, Maguire and Williamson was my five-pound claim, which would soon be three pounds. But it made sense to turn professional then. If I was going to make it as a rider I was going to have to turn professional at some point, and that was the point at which to do it.

At least I was riding for a top yard. If I had been riding for a small yard, I could easily have squandered my claim by riding bad winners at low-profile meetings, and never got noticed. But because I was riding for Kim Bailey, I was getting noticed. Punters used to pick up the paper in the morning and look to see what Bailey was running that day. And who's this new fellow he has riding for him? T. J. Murphy? He must be OK if he's riding for Kim Bailey.

And Bailey did give me plenty of rides. I never got to ride any of the top horses like Master Oats or Alderbrook, but I did get to ride some good ones. I rode Mr Jamboree and Drumstick, and I rode Bertone in the big novice chase at Sandown's April meeting. He was owned by a lovely old American lady, Mrs Duffey, who also owned Mr Frisk, winner of the 1990 Grand National. All her horses used to have to run during the summer, because that was when she was around, so they used to try to buy good fast-ground horses for her.

The training at Bailey's was totally different to anything I was used to. There was no circle, no steady work done as there had been at Hourigan's or on the Curragh. We just used the hill. Up and down the hill. It took me a while to figure out how the horses were getting fit simply by going up and down the hill, nice and easy, or how you'd know that they were getting fit. Eddie Hales was Bailey's head lad at the time. He had some very good ideas about how to train horses, and I learnt a lot. It's not the hill that does the training, it's how you use the hill. It's not the gallop, the gallop doesn't do the work, it's how you use it.

The difficulty with the big yards these days is that all the horses are trained the same way. Two-milers, two-and-a-half-milers, it doesn't seem to matter. If you have a hundred horses, it's difficult to afford each of them individual attention. Just because they are all in the same yard doesn't mean they all enjoy being trained the same way. You often see horses improving after being moved to a different yard, simply because the different training regime suits them better. But it's a numbers game these days. The big yards are at a huge advantage because they have the numbers. Success is not measured in relative terms, but in absolute terms. For example, you ask anyone who had the more successful season in 2005/06, Jonjo O'Neill or Nicky Richards, and they will tell you, Jonjo O'Neill. Of course he did. He had 105 winners as opposed to Nicky Richards' 59. Almost twice as many. That's true in absolute terms, but in relative terms Richards was far more successful: his total of 59 winners was achieved from 277 runners while Jonjo had his 109 winners from 711 runners, a strike rate of 21 per cent against 15 per cent. Charlie Egerton had 21 winners from 85 runners, a strike rate of 25 per cent, but try telling anyone that he had a more successful season than Martin Pipe (13 per cent).

So in a world in which we take only the top line as a measurement of performance and don't delve too deeply into the details, it is in a trainer's interest to have big numbers, lots of horses. But the more horses you have, the more difficult it is to train them as individuals. That is why a yard like the Bowe family's down in Gathabawn in Co. Tipperary can have so much success. They generally have no more than four or five horses in training down there, and they have had two champions in Solerina and Limestone Lad and a host of other top performers like Florida Coast and Sweet Kiln. They say there must be something in the water down at Gathabawn for so many good horses to come from such a small pool, but, while you need to have a little bit of luck on your side as well, I suspect it is more to do with training methodology.

There is no question that different horses respond in different ways to different methods and intensities of training, but in a big yard you don't have the time to spend getting to know what works for each one. And even if you did have the time for that, you wouldn't then have the time actually to train them differently, as individuals. By and large, in a big yard with a lot of horses, the horses either respond to the method of training that is largely employed in that yard, with only a little room for manoeuvre, or else they do not succeed. Horses can slip through the net, talented horses that are not suited to a particular training regime and which don't get the chance to fulfil their potential because their training programme is not tailored towards them, and many have. But it is hard for the small trainer to survive, simply because he doesn't have the name or the numbers, even though he might be a better trainer than some of the big ones.

As I said, I learnt a lot from Eddie Hales about training, lots of little things that I will look to employ myself if I do go down that road. And sometimes I think I will, eventually. I like the idea of training a horse in such a way that he will get to realise his true potential. There are few things worse than unfulfilled potential. Then again, there is so much more to being a racehorse trainer than the actual training. Owners have to be acquired and looked after, staff have to be managed, a business has to be run. So many headaches. It's a tough call, but it might be worth it.

Despite listening closely to Eddie, I wasn't one for seeking much tuition in those days, but Norman Williamson swore by Yogi Breisner, and he introduced me. Yogi – his real name is Goran but he is known universally as Yogi since one of his students continually mispronounced his name – has a depth of experience in the eventing world. What Yogi doesn't know about horses or riding is either untrue or not worth knowing. Many of the top racehorse trainers bring horses to him who have problems with their jumping, and he invariably sorts them out. Norman took lessons with him regularly. Jamie Osborne used to go to Yogi as well, and I loved the way both Norman and Jamie rode. Osborne was a real Yogi Breisner jockey. If ever there was such a thing, Jamie was it. So maybe it was partly to be with Norman, partly to see if I could learn something, and partly to try to impress upon Bailey that I was making an effort. Whatever the reason behind it, I began to go down to Yogi's with Norman on a regular basis.

I was bowled over watching Yogi schooling a horse, the way he would present a fence differently for each horse, depending on what the horse needed. If a horse needed to be taught to stand off more, he'd have the take-off board a little bit away and he'd keep bringing it back and back gradually so that the horse was actually reaching in the end, without knowing it. The horse would end up with scope without even knowing it. Or if the horse was standing off too far, he'd position the poles at set distances so that the horse would have to skip over them. Then, by the time he got over the last pole and reached the fence, he'd be in tight and he'd have to jump out over it. And he'd repeat it, as many times as necessary for the horse to be able to go in and pop the fence without the poles. All that stuff really fascinated me.

He was great for riders as well. He taught me an awful lot. I was all the time building on what I had learned at Hourigan's. Like that you can't judge the height of a fence for a horse. The horse does that himself. It makes no difference how big or small you think the fence is, that's up to the horse to decide. It's nothing to do with you, so there's no point in launching him, trying to get him to jump high. All you have to do is keep him balanced and help him. You can't make him do it, you just have to help him. Keep your hands still and you should feel the horse shortening underneath you instead of you trying to make the horse shorten. I struggled with that one, though. 'If a horse is running away with you going into a fence, you can't just sit still,' I thought. Yogi said, 'Just raise your hands a little bit and raise yourself from the saddle a little bit before the fence. Then, the last couple of strides, just let the reins go.' It was amazing. If I was ever going down to the last fence with the race in the bag, I always used to shorten the horse up, bring him back on his hocks. Just all the time shortening. I thought that was the best way, the safest way. That was all I had ever done. And out in the country it was the same: I'd either pull the horse in the mouth to get him to shorten or hoof him into the fence to get him to lengthen. Yogi basically changed the whole way I rode over a fence. He changed the way I thought about jumping. I still kept the same style, but I became quieter over a fence.

Yogi said that I had a lot of raw talent, that I had a great position and movement over a fence, but that I was in too much of a hurry. I was too keen to do things instead of letting things happen. Of course he was right. It epitomised my life at the time. Gradually I began to learn to let the horse jump the fence instead of trying to jump it for him, though it was very difficult to do in the beginning. I suppose it's always difficult to break the habit of a lifetime, but I figured it was worth a try. I was riding this horse who was really keen. It's very difficult to do nothing when you are running into a fence and you feel as if you're out of control. But I did this time. Be brave. Try this once. What's the worst that can happen? You end up on your arse – OK, so don't try it again. He was running freely and I said to myself, 'Right, hold him, hold him,' and then I just let him go at the second last stride before the obstacle. You could feel him changing his stride. He flew the fence, and I thought, 'Wow, that was amazing.' He did it again and again. After that, I believed everything Yogi told me.

Yogi was all about balance, not sitting too far forward or too far back, always keeping your horse balanced and letting the horse do the jumping rather than you. A horse can jump fine when he's on a loose rein; it's the jockey that messes him up. Yogi was a great man to get your confidence up. He was just so easy to learn from, so easy to listen to. He never lost his head or bawled you out of it, which was what I was used to. He just told you what to do in plain terms. Simplified it for you, and told you why. Everything he said made perfect sense and almost everything he suggested worked for me. I improved immeasurably as a rider after lessons with him.

I lived with Norman Williamson when I first went to England. Everything was in Lambourn, right there, self-contained – my job, my social scene, my career. You didn't have to leave the confines of Lambourn for anything, and few did. It was like the goldfish bowl that is the Curragh multiplied by about a hundred. Everybody knew everybody else, and if you didn't know everybody, you knew about everybody and talked about them. You'd end up going down to the pub, the Malt Shovel, every evening when you weren't racing or working. There was nothing wrong with going down to the pub, but it was all you did, simply because there was nothing else to do. And everybody did it. You either went down to the pub or sat at home on your own, and I wasn't really one for sitting at home on my own.

I was getting on to the treadmill again: work to pub to racing to pub to bed. And it was worse than on the Curragh. All the Irish used to stick together, as is the case the world over, and there was a lot of pressure on you to go out and do the social thing. We all exerted pressure on each other. You stick closer together when you are away from home. Friday night was a big night. They had happy hour in the pub on Friday night which lasted from five o'clock until nine. I guess that's an Irish happy hour for you. A fiver for a steak and drink was half price for the evening, so we'd all be locked by nine o'clock. That didn't help. Don't get me wrong, they were great times and we had some great nights, but it wasn't good for the long term, and there comes a time when you have to grow up a little. I'm not sure we really realised when that time came.

I was living right beside the pub, and I used to go down to Seanie Curran's house on a Friday night and drag him out. 'It's happy hour,' I would tell him. 'You have to come out for happy hour.' Kay hated happy hour when she was over. 'Happy fucking hour' she used to call it. She was riding out for Paul Nicholls and she used to come up to Lambourn to see me at weekends, but it was no fun for her. I would be out having the craic with the lads, getting progressively more drunk, while she would sit there feeling that she had to stay sober so that she could make sure I wouldn't come to any harm, or do any damage to myself. Of course I used to give her a fierce hard time, and I'm sure I came across as stupid and silly, as a drunk person invariably does to a sober person. Like I said before, Kay was fantastic to put up with me for as long as she did, but it was never going to work. I just wasn't in the right place mentally.

I was probably a little wilder than most. Jockeys are generally a fairly wild bunch anyway, hence the saying 'You don't have to be mad in the head in order to be a jockey, but it helps'. But I probably pushed the boat out a little further than most. When I partied, I didn't know when to stop. Anything Seanie did, I just had to go one step further. But Seanie knew when it was time to go home, whereas I didn't. I would often give him a head butt. Just a little one, a playful one, if there is such a thing, and that was the sign for Seanie. That was time up, time to go home. He'd grab me and throw me into a taxi. The head butt was a sign to him that I had had enough.

Once, a whole gang of us went on holiday to Lanzarote. There were about ten of us – Robert Widger, Liam Cummins, Barry Fenton, Richie Forristal, Seanie and me, among others. I went down to the beach one day and someone stole my flip-flops. I came back at the end of the day barefoot, feet killing me, burnt to a cinder, and we went for a couple of beers in this bar that was on the second floor. There was a palm tree outside the balcony and Robert Widger decided that he would climb down it. I decided that I would do better – the usual – and slid down it, promptly grazing the whole front of my body. That night I was complaining so much about my feet, my sunburn and my grazes that Seanie said I'd be better off sleeping outside. So I slept on the balcony, and got eaten alive by mosquitoes. I was in pain for days afterwards.

My drinking wasn't helping my career either, or my relationship with Kim Bailey. I found it very difficult to get up after a night out. Poor timekeeping was a common thread that ran right through my early career, and it was all down to drink. I just wouldn't hear the alarm after a night out, or I'd hear it and turn it off, or hit the snooze button and just ignore it.

There was this small Irish trainer who was based down near Plumpton, Paddy Butler, whose son Robert rides now and, for whom I used to go down and school a couple sometimes. There were a few occasions when I'd wake up on Seanie's sofa late for work, so I'd ring Paddy and tell him that if anyone asked, I was down at his place schooling that morning. So I'd just go into Bailey's the following morning, say nothing, and wait for the bollicking.

'Where were you yesterday?'

'I was down at Paddy Butler's.' Nonchalant.

'And what were you doing down in Paddy Butler's when you were needed here?'

'Did I not tell you I was going down? Ah, sorry about that.'

So Bailey would ring Paddy.

'Was Murphy down with you yesterday?'

'Ah, Timmy, yeah, yeah, he was down here schooling a couple for me. Why?'

None of this helped me to get along with Bailey, but it was an uphill struggle from the start anyway. It didn't matter that I had ridden 45 point-to-point winners in Ireland, to him I was starting off all over again. Even if I had ridden 450, it wouldn't have mattered. I had to prove myself again.

I used to go out of my way to be cooperative, to communicate with him. I wasn't the best communicator in the world, that was for sure, but I used to make an effort with Bailey in the beginning. I really did.

My Dad met Bailey at Doncaster Sales that first year I was in England and went up to him to ask how I was getting on. That would be a fair deal for my father. He wouldn't usually go up to people like that to check on me. If it was to check about a horse, absolutely, but his son? Fairly rare. 'Oh, he's doing OK,' said Bailey, 'but he just doesn't communicate enough with me.' What? I couldn't believe it when Dad told me. Me not communicate with him? It was by far the greatest effort I had ever put into communication with a trainer at any stage of my career up to that point.

We had an open day that year, and I remember that Princess Anne came along to it. Whatever way it happened, I ended up showing her around the yard. As we were walking round, and I was explaining to her the intricacies of washing a horse, or some such gem of information on equine care, Bailey came up to introduce himself and ask if he could show her around. 'No, I'm quite all right with this young man, but thank you,' she said. I was stunned. Stunned and delighted. I carried on with Princess Anne. I'm sure Kim couldn't believe it. This young upstart from Ireland who drank too often and too much and was regularly late for work, and who probably didn't even really know who Princess Anne was, showing her around? A member of the royal family in his yard, and Timmy Murphy was showing her around? I have to admit, I got a good kick out of that one.

But Princess Anne apart, I wasn't really going anywhere that quickly. Norman left in October 1995, but that still didn't mean many more opportunities for me. Andrew Thornton was there, and Conor O'Dwyer started to come over from Ireland at weekends to ride Bailey's horses at the high-profile meetings. It didn't bother me too much. I was happy enough with my lot, but when I thought about it I felt like I was kind of stuck in slow motion. Things had happened quickly for me in Ireland in the end. It might have taken me a little while to get going, but once I did, things happened quickly. To ride 30 point-to-point winners there was a fair achievement in only my second full season.

I suppose it was just that when I came over to England, I had to start all over again. Very few people knew me or knew of me, and I had to make a bit of a name for myself all again. I knew I would have to do that, but it was taking a while, and that was while riding for one of the most powerful yards in the country. It would have been impossible if I had been with a small yard. But England is so big, so much bigger than Ireland. It just took longer to build up your contacts.

I had set a target for myself of 50 winners for my first season in England. That was a little bit naive of me, given that I had no parameters within which to set targets and nothing on which to base them. It would be like deciding that you were going to try to dig five holes in an hour without having a clue how long it should take you to dig one hole. Why 50? Why not 80, or 20? I had ridden 30 winners during my last season in Ireland, so 50 sounded good, I suppose. No regard for what would have to happen in order for me to achieve it. Things did in fact go quite well for me on the track in that 1995/96 season. I got a good few rides and rode 26 winners. Not fantastic, but not bad, and I was getting a little bit of recognition. But those 26 winners fell some way short of my target, and I got a bit frustrated when I realised I wasn't going to hit it. But that taught me a lesson. There is no point getting older if you are not going to get any wiser, and the most important subject you will ever learn about is yourself. I never set myself a target again after that.

In Ireland, I was at my happiest when I wasn't putting pressure on myself, when I wasn't walking my box wanting things to happen. At Weld's and at Gillespie's I would get frustrated because I wasn't getting rides, simply because I expected to get rides. That was when I was at my most disillusioned. But when I went to Hourigan's I didn't expect rides. I just went to ride work and to school, and then it happened. The rides came, and it happened easily. I didn't force it, I didn't have to, or feel that I needed to because my expectations were so low. It's like a horse that is difficult to settle. The more you pull on his reins, the more you try to physically restrain him, the more he will fight against you. But if you just let him be, if you relax on him, he will settle into his rhythm and carry you with him. Some people respond to targets, but they demotivate others. And what's the point in setting a target anyway? Just because you set a target for yourself of, say, a hundred winners, it doesn't mean you will ride a hundred winners. It doesn't mean you are going to ride any differently. And what do you do when you reach a hundred? Do you stop, target reached, objective achieved? Or do you keep going and try to ride as many winners as you can? If you do, what was the point in setting the target in the first place? If someone asks me how many winners I want to ride these days, I tell them, 'As many as I can.'

Alas, my time ran out with Kim Bailey before it could really get going. Looking back on it now, it really was a case of when rather than if. You can't continue in somebody's employ indefinitely if you have a relationship with him like I had with Kim, and there was no sign of any improvement in it.

The inevitable end came one morning in October 1996. I had been out late the night before, but I'd managed to get up OK and I drove to Bailey's for 6.30. I fed my horses, the same as all the other lads, and had mucked out by 6.45. Then it was a cup of tea for fifteen minutes before tacking up and riding out. This particular morning, however, I was knackered, so I figured I'd try to catch a nap before first lot instead of joining them for a cup of tea. Unfortunately, it turned into more than just a nap. I was sound asleep in the car when the lads were going out for first lot. I was awakened up by this rat-tat-tat on my window. It was Bailey himself. That's it, he said, final straw. You're out.

CHAPTER EIGHT

WILDERNESS

I had been planning to stay at Bailey's for a while, insofar as I managed to plan anything in those days. Why wouldn't I? It was one of the top yards in the country, I was riding some winners – good horses that were fit and could jump – and I felt I was getting noticed. OK, so things weren't happening as quickly as I would have liked, but I was comfortable that I was in the right place. Progress was steady, and you never do know when you're going to get your next break. Also, the craic was good. I certainly had no intentions of leaving. But there I was at the end of 1996, jobless again, only this time I was in England. Though of course there isn't a great deal of difference between being jobless in England and being jobless in Ireland. They both amount to the same thing, essentially. Same predicament.

Funny thing, I didn't consider going back to Ireland. I wasn't really in touch with Michael Hourigan at the time. It wasn't that we had fallen out, I just hadn't spoken to him since I upped and left for Bailey's. I didn't consider that Ireland was an option anyway. I would have viewed it as a step backwards. Back in 1996, the prize money in Ireland wasn't anything like it is now, and the industry wasn't nearly as buoyant. The way I looked at it, I had ridden 26 winners in my first season in England, and that was from a standing start, without any real contacts to begin with other than the yard for which I was riding. To ride 26 winners in a season at that time in Ireland you would have to have been among the top ten jockeys in the country. So I figured if I could ride 26 winners in my first season in England, there was no reason why I could not do better in my second and third. I had made some contacts, I was getting used to the lifestyle, I was beginning to get a feel for racing in England, and I was reluctant to leave.

I had quite a few contacts around Plumpton – Paddy Butler and a couple of other small trainers around there – so when I'd be going to Plumpton I'd ring one or two of them in advance and ask if I could come down and ride out for them that morning. There was Tony Carroll close to Stratford, and various others dotted around the country. Jeff King was very good to me at this time. I had ridden a couple of horses for him while I was at Bailey's. Spares, really, here and there. Dunwoody used to ride most of the good ones. I just rang Jeff a couple of days after losing my job and told him, 'Jeff, I'm after losing my job. Can I come in and ride out for you?' Basically, it was all graft, but I didn't mind. I quite enjoyed it actually. If I was racing close to one of my contacts, or if I just had a blank day, I'd ring them and ask them if it was OK for me to come down and ride out the following day, or I'd ride out for Jeff. It was my way of letting those trainers know that I was available to ride for them if they needed me. You were rarely paid for riding out. In fact, it was a bad sign if the trainer paid you as it meant that he probably wasn't going to give you a ride. If they didn't pay you, that was good. It was like they were saying, 'Thanks for coming down, I'll keep you in mind.' I rode out for Henrietta Knight a couple of times in those days too, but that didn't last. My poor timekeeping did for me there as well. I was late a couple of times, and things fizzled out. The only surprise was that it took a couple of times. When you go to Hen's you can't be late. Everyone has a five-minute slot within which to pull out. If you are not there to pull out on time, you upset the whole show. It's a bit like air traffic control there. But Hen was great. I had a few winners for her, I had a few winners for Jeff, and I had a few winners for Peter Bowen, so at least I was able to keep ticking over.

It was a tough year, though. It really was a case of living from day to day, and riding out for as many small trainers as I could so that I would be on their list when they were looking for a rider. But I had no set stable, and there was very little consistency. I could have no rides for a couple of days and then be wanted by two different trainers at two different meetings, which meant I had to decide where I would go. It was like being sacked from a job with Microsoft and going out on your own as a freelance computer programmer.

Chris Broad was very good to me at the time as well. He had been a trainer cum farmer who became a trainer cum jockey's agent in 1996 when he figured that he was losing money training racehorses. He won the Cleeve Hurdle in 1995 with Mudahim, which went on to win the *Racing Post* Chase for Jenny Pitman in 1997. He trained a couple of horses for Tom Dalton, my Dad's friend who had made the initial introduction for me to Norman Williamson and Kim Bailey, and it was through Tom that I got to know Chris.

Chris began as my agent. He needed jockeys and I needed an agent, so it suited both of us. At the time he had Carl Llewellyn, Warren Marston and me on his books. Jim Culloty joined him later. I suppose our relationship would have been a little fiery in the beginning. Actually, still is! He will tell you that I'm a fiery character and that I often need kid-glove treatment, and that sometimes he is not in kid-glove mode, and I have been known to hang up on him on occasion. Actually, he is a fiery enough character himself. We are quite similar in character, which is why we can often clash. But it was always great to have Chris in my corner. When I was drinking, I often found it difficult to focus on the job. I would often ring Chris in the morning and ask him where I was riding that day. Of course we'd have discussed it and he'd have told me the day before, but I'd have forgotten. He was like an extra pair of eyes and ears when I needed them. The fact that we are still together as jockey and agent after ten years is testament to the depth of our relationship. Some jockeys change agents as often as they change underpants, but I have never seen the need to move away from Chris. As well as being my agent, he has become a close friend over the years. He was one of the people who was there for me when I was going through some bad times.

I was living with Gerry Hogan at the start of the 1996/97 season, but halfway through it I decided I would buy a house of my own. It wasn't easy to get a mortgage – occupation: freelance National Hunt jockey – but the bank manager at the AIB in Birmingham, Mike Donovan, was great, as was Frances Purcell. In fact, a lot of Irish jockeys are with the AIB in Birmingham, and I am still with them today. Mike was happy that I would be able to make the repayments, and I bought my first house in Faringdon.

I was lucky that, while I was a bit off the wall in many ways, I did have my head screwed on when it came to certain things. Money management was one. As I said before, even when I was carousing on the Curragh I always made sure I paid for my digs every week before I went out to spend whatever I had left. It was something my Mam drilled into me and Brian from an early age, and it has always stayed with me. I figured that I was spending too much money on rent, so why not put the same money into a mortgage and at least have something to show for it?

I was also quite good at putting my head down and grafting when I needed to, and I could see that I needed to at the start of that season. With no fixed employer, I needed to make as many contacts as I could, and I could see that the only way to do that was to go and ride out for as many small trainers as I could. Any time I rode for a new trainer I would always let him or her know that I would be delighted to go down to school horses for them if they wanted. All the big yards had their own jocks, so the only potential openings were with the small guys. Race-riding paid the bills, so you needed to be getting mounts at the very least, and you never knew when a small trainer was going to unearth a big winner.

That December I was asked to ride Terao for Martin Pipe and Brian Kilpatrick in a handicap chase at Lingfield. I rode him again in a handicap chase at Chepstow the following February, and we finished last of the nine finishers behind Bells Life. So I didn't get too excited when I was asked to ride him in the Mildmay of Flete at the Cheltenham Festival in March 1997. McCoy was in his first season as Pipe's stable jockey. He was riding a French import of Pipe's in the race, As Du Trefle, owned by David Johnson. He had been a prolific hurdler and had won an egg and spoon race at Southwell on his previous run. He was a nine-year-old and still a novice over fences, but that didn't seem to matter. They put him in as favourite for the Mildmay of Flete, and sent Terao off an unconsidered 20–1 shot.

Of course I didn't expect Terao to win. He was an eleven-year-old, handicapped to the hilt, probably not improving, and had been pulled up in the same race the previous season. McCoy had chosen to ride As Du Trefle, and he should have known their relative abilities. There was no pressure on me, so I just set out to enjoy riding at the Cheltenham Festival.

McCoy led in the early stages. Terao liked to be ridden handily, so I just tracked McCoy and concentrated on getting him jumping. At the sixth last at the top of the hill, Terao was travelling so well that I let him go on, but by the time we got to the fourth last he felt like a spent force, and McCoy went on again. However, coming down the hill I felt that Terao was getting his second wind. He flew the second last and started to run on again. We took it up just before the last, winged it, and scorched up the hill to win by just over a length from J. P. McManus's horse All the Aces, and Charlie Swan.

I couldn't believe it. It could have been Kilmuckridge all over again, except this time there was no potentially dodgy photo finish and no Dyser to throw everybody out of our way on the walk back to the winner's enclosure. If it was a long walk, I didn't feel it. I was trying to savour the moment. OK, so it was the Mildmay of Flete, it wasn't one of the championship races, but it was the Cheltenham Festival, and it didn't get much bigger than that. The walk back down past the stands was magic. Even though he was a 20–1 shot and not many people would have backed him, the crowds still gave us a great reception the whole way back into the winner's enclosure. Perhaps the majority of people cheering were bookmakers. Pipe was delighted too, and Brian Kilpatrick was over the moon. Even McCoy was fairly magnanimous! It was just about the only thing he didn't win that week. He had won the Champion Hurdle the previous day on Pipe's Make a Stand, and he would win the Gold Cup the following day on Mr Mulligan, trained by Noel Chance.

That was unquestionably the highlight of my season. In fact, I was asked by the press shortly afterwards what the best moment of my career to date was, and I said that it was winning the Mildmay of Flete Chase on Terao. And I wasn't lying. It was certainly the most high profile, and it was definitely one of the best. Was it better than winning my first point-to-point at Kilmuckridge? Probably not. Was it as good? Probably, but they were both different. They were both hugely unexpected. On both occasions the realisation dawned on me slowly, gradually. My first winner and my first Cheltenham Festival winner. They were both fantastic. But I thought it better to go with the Cheltenham one for the press. Try explaining where Kilmuckridge is to a member of the British Press Association.

So, all things considered, that 1996/97 season didn't go too badly for me. If you had told me on the day I lost my job with Kim Bailey that I would ride more winners that season than I had the previous season, and that I would ride a winner at the Cheltenham Festival, I doubt I would have believed you. But I did. I ended up with 28 winners, two more than the previous season, spread among about twenty different trainers. As well as that I had managed to get myself a mortgage and buy a house. And all the while I was generating more contacts and becoming better known.

I didn't know it at the time, but my career was about to take another huge leap forward. Another ladder in the game of snakes and ladders that is the lot of the National Hunt jockey. The trick is to maximise your chances of landing on the ladders, and avoid the snakes. Not always possible.

CHAPTER NINE

TOP JOB

C hris Broad rang me early one morning in August 1997. Good news: he had just had a call from Paul Nicholls to enquire if I would ride one for him at Newton Abbot the following Monday.

Now, a ride on a Monday at Newton Abbot wasn't really anything to get hugely excited about. But when that ride was for Paul Nicholls, it was something to think about.

Of course, the Paul Nicholls of 1997 wasn't the Paul Nicholls, champion trainer, of 2006, but he was a young trainer on the up. As a jockey he had ridden Broadheath to win the Hennessy in 1986 and Playschool to win it in 1987, both for trainer David Barons. He had also ridden Playschool to victory in the Welsh National in 1987 and the Vincent O'Brien Gold Cup in 1988, beating Forgive 'N Forget. But Nicholls always struggled with his weight as a rider. The knell of his riding career was sounded when he broke his leg in a fall in 1989 and was hospitalised for a month. He was never going to be able to get back down to riding weight after that, so he took out a trainer's licence. Actually, he was always more interested in training than in riding; he just used riding as a means to get into the industry in order that he could train. And fair play to him for doing it. It can't have been easy, given that his family had no involvement whatsoever in racing. His father, Brian, was in the police force, as was his father before him. It was easy for me and my likes by comparison, being born on Newberry Stud, having horses around all the time and a father who was well respected and connected in the industry. Would I have managed to make my way in racing if my father had been a garda, a builder or a plumber? I seriously doubt it.

Nicholls had taken on the role as Paul Barber's trainer only a couple of years earlier. Paul Barber is a dairy farmer whose two ambitions in life were to milk a 1,000 cows and own a Gold Cup winner. He wanted to have one trainer who would train his horses on his farm in Ditcheat in deepest Somerset. Jim Old had had a go at it first, but that didn't work out, so Barber had recruited Nicholls, an ambitious, enthusiastic young ex-jockey who looked like he could train racehorses.

The horse Nicholls wanted me to ride in a three-and-a-quarter-mile novice chase was a mare called Mutual Agreement. She had run twelve times and never won, although she had run only once for Nicholls. That had been in a novices' chase at Hereford almost a year earlier to the day, when she was ridden by McCoy and looked like a winner going to the last only to fall. It had been quite a heavy fall, and she hadn't run since, so they were travelling more in hope than anything else.

Newton Abbot is right down in the south-west of England. Go any further west and you are into the tip of Cornwall; any further south and you are on your way to France. But there was never any question of not travelling. I would have gone anywhere for a good ride, and this was my first for Paul Nicholls. The fields were small on the day, and Chris didn't manage to book any other rides for me, but I didn't mind travelling at all, even if it was only for one ride. I remember driving to Perth one day with Glenn Tormey – a fourteen-hour round trip for one ride each.

Turned out this one was worth it. Nicholls didn't give me very strict instructions before the race. He just told me that, in spite of the fact that she hadn't run in a year, she was fit and could jump, so not to get too far behind. He always prided himself on having his horses very fit. It was only a five-horse race, so I settled her towards the rear but not too far from the lead. McCoy, on the odds-on favourite General Mouktar, went to take it up at the second last, but I was travelling well in behind, and I passed him between the last two before going on to win well.

I rode a couple more for Nicholls in the next few weeks, but I was still essentially a freelance, riding for whoever would have me, and mainly for Jeff King. Later that autumn Nicholls asked me if I would go and ride as first rider for him. It came as a bit of a shock. Like I say, Nicholls wasn't champion trainer or anything at the time, but it was still a pretty big yard with some very decent horses. I asked Chris what he thought, but there really was nothing to think about. Then I had to tell Jeff. That wasn't easy, because Jeff had been so good to me, but he was great. 'Ah, fuck him, fuck him,' said Jeff in his own inimitable way. 'That's a fucking great job, sure you have to go and take that. Fuck him.'

Joe Tizzard was Nicholls' conditional rider at the time. Joe had been with Nicholls since he was sixteen, but Nicholls thought he was just a little too young and inexperienced to take on the role as stable jockey in such a burgeoning operation. I wasn't much more experienced, just sufficiently. Apparently, Nicholls liked the way I rode. He had seen me riding a couple for Jeff and he just liked my style. He had been using different jockeys up to that point. He had used McCoy a lot while he was still with Toby Balding. In fact he had had second call on McCoy after Balding for more than half a season, but then McCoy joined Pipe and he couldn't use him any more, so he wanted someone who wasn't attached to any other yard and who could ride a bit. That was me. Right time, right place.

I didn't have a great reputation at the time. When I lost my job with Bailey, it was all over the *Racing Post*. Bad timekeeping, they said, and they weren't wrong. Nicholls was aware of this, and he had heard that I wasn't the greatest around the yard in the mornings, but, fair play to him, he just ignored what he was hearing and figured he'd find out for himself.

My role at Nicholls' was different to my role at Bailey's. Indeed it was different to any other role I had had up to then. Nicholls didn't want me to ride out every morning, which suited me great. I would go down maybe one morning every two weeks or so, just to sit on one or two that he wanted me to sit on, or to do a bit of schooling, but I didn't have to be there pulling out at 7.30 every morning. He wasn't looking for someone who would be there every morning, he was looking for someone who was good in the afternoons. Also, he had been advised by a couple of people not to try to have me there seven mornings a week. 'He won't be there,' they told him, 'and you'll end up falling out within a week, which would be a shame, because he's a good rider and could be exactly what you need.'

And it makes sense. Jump jockeys are athletes. It doesn't seem right that top athletes should have to be there every morning, grafting, mucking out and riding out, before going and travelling to the races and being expected to perform at the highest level. There was a time, not too long ago, when you had to do it all as stable jockey, but that is becoming less and less prevalent these days. You wouldn't see Wayne Rooney washing and polishing a couple of pairs of football boots or playing three five-a-side matches in the morning before going off to play at Old Trafford in the afternoon. Nicholls wanted his stable jockey to be at his best in the afternoon, and whatever needed to be done in order to ensure that that was the case, he was willing to do it. He figured it was important that I come down to the yard every now and again just so that I would get to meet the lads and be a part of the team, but even now, Paul hardly ever sees Ruby Walsh except at the races, and maybe at the odd awards ceremony or wedding.

As I said, there were some very decent horses at Nicholls' at the time. Court Melody followed me over from Hourigan's, but I had never ridden him there. The first time I rode him in a race was for Nicholls in the Becher Chase over the big fences at Aintree in November 1997 when he gave me a great spin and finished second to Samlee. Lake Kariba won two for me in the early part of the season and was looking like one of the best two-mile novice chasers around. Call Equiname won the Mitsubishi Shogun Chase at Cheltenham's November meeting and looked like he just might be able to make the leap required to be competitive at the highest level if his glass legs would stand up to the strain. Strong Chairman looked like a decent staying novice chaser, and See More Business was just coming of age. Dorans Pride had beaten him twice the previous season in Ireland when they were both novices, but on his debut for me in November 1997 he finished third to Suny Bay in the Edward Hanmer at Haydock, giving him weight, and then went and won the Rehearsal Chase at Chepstow, giving weight to Indian Tracker and Banjo. We didn't know it at the time, but Indian Tracker wouldn't have to wait too long to exact his revenge in the most bizarre way possible.

This was the big time for me. It was like being promoted from League Two to the Premiership in one go. I had gone from scraping around Plumpton, Taunton, Stratford and Ludlow, riding whatever I could, to riding good horses at Cheltenham, Newbury, Sandown and Chepstow. And it was enjoyable. Of course it was. If as a jockey you don't enjoy riding good horses in good races then you are in the wrong profession. Also, for the first time in my career there was plenty of money coming in. I wasn't on the breadline or anything before I joined Nicholls, but suddenly I began to notice the coffers swelling, and I had never noticed that before.

There were many good things about riding for Nicholls. For starters, I got on quite well with him, which was a big change for me from Bailey's. He would listen to me when I had something to say, and he seemed to value my opinion. It helped that he had been a jockey not too long before he started training. Of course, what a jockey says about a horse isn't gospel, but it is an important element in determining what is right for the horse and under what conditions he is most likely to achieve his potential. I think Paul and I were on the same wavelength a lot of the time. He had an excellent understanding of horses. I'd often come in after a race thinking something about a horse, and Paul would invariably be thinking the same. Like, when I'd come in to unsaddle, I might be thinking that this one wanted further, but before I could say it to him he'd say to me, 'He wants further, doesn't he?'

The best thing about riding for Paul, however, was the fact that his horses were always fit and well, and they could jump. These aspects are interlinked. It wasn't that he schooled them any more intensively than other trainers, it's just that when horses are fit they simply jump better. They are like humans in that sense. You might be able to jump over a barrel no problem, but try jumping over the same barrel after you have run five miles and you might not find it so easy. Take the 3,000m steeplechase race in athletics: you generally don't see lads falling in the early part of the race unless they are unsighted at a barrier, but on the last couple of laps, after they have run their legs off for 2,200 metres, you can see some horrible and painful falls.

Riding instructions rarely deviated from 'jump off, make sure you're handy and kick on turning in'. Sometimes that was difficult. If you are handy and the leaders die away in front of you, suddenly you are there too soon and there's not a huge amount you can do about it. Paul's horses were fit, fitter than most, especially in the early part of the season, so there was no point in lobbing along in behind where you might find trouble, or from where you just might not be able to make up the ground. Considering my experience at the time, it was a good way to be riding. But I did find it a little bit difficult to be tied to instructions. Sometimes you can't foresee what is going to happen in a race. Maybe they go off too quickly, or too slowly, or the horse you were planning on tracking doesn't lead, or doesn't perform, or isn't jumping well, or they go quickly initially and then slow down, or the ground rides softer than you thought it would when you walked it. There are myriad of things for which you can't legislate. It is decision-making as much as riding ability that differentiates a good jockey from a moderate one, and if that decision-making power is taken away from you by strict riding instructions, you lose the power to utilise one of your attributes as a jockey.

There was also a certain amount of pressure. I think Paul felt that he was under pressure from his owners. He was still just a young trainer on the up. While he was well respected and wasn't far beneath the top echelons of the training ranks, he still wasn't a Martin Pipe or a Nicky Henderson or a David Nicholson. The pressure he undoubtedly felt was communicated to me – not in any overt way, but you could sense it nonetheless. 'This'll win.' I found that difficult. There is always more pressure on you in any walk of life when you are expected to deliver, like if you are riding an odds-on shot, or standing over a two-foot putt, or taking a penalty kick. There is never any pressure on the goalkeeper. 'This'll win. Just ride him handy and don't get there too soon.'

I also put pressure on myself. I sensed that there was a feeling around that I didn't deserve such a big job. It wasn't very obvious, and maybe it was my imagination, but I sensed it was there all right, in little pockets of the weigh room. What did he do to deserve a job like that? If I stayed in bed all morning would I get a job like that too? So that added to the pressure. I always felt I had to prove something: to Nicholls, that he wasn't wrong to appoint me; to his owners, that I was as good as Nicholls had obviously told them I was; to the begrudgers in the weigh room, the ones riddled with jealousy who couldn't ride a clothes horse; to the punters and the public; and to myself. Mostly to myself. It was a bit like being in a pressure cooker. It was full on, mentally and physically, maximum concentration required in order to get it right, or at least to not get it wrong.

Which meant that when the valve was released at the weekends, the pressure was really let off. I wasn't drinking more, or rather I wasn't drinking more intensely. They didn't have Budweiser in Faringdon so it was pints of Foster's I drank. I was never one to come home on my own and open a bottle of wine. I would go out at the weekends and get home, locked, but that would be the end of it. But I would usually push the boat out a little further than most people ever would.

I went to an English Grand National dinner one evening at The Belfry. There were rooms there for all the jockeys to stay over, so we figured we'd give it a bit of a lash. Not for the first time, however, I gave it slightly too hard a lash. Adrian Maguire was one of the few who wasn't drinking. He saw that I was getting a little out of hand, so he took me with him and drove me home. I was going mad. I wanted to stay and have the craic. I'm sure it was a terrible journey home for Adrian with me going berserk the whole way home, but he did it for my sake, and there was no doubt it was the right thing to do. I am lucky in that I have had people to look out for me all my life. Well, almost all my life.

We'd go racing on a Saturday and plan from there. Depending on where racing was, that would determine where we would go out or what we would do. There was very little Sunday racing in the UK in those days, and I generally wouldn't be going over to Ireland where there was Sunday racing, so you'd be able to give it a good kick on Saturday night. Then you'd get up late on Sunday, usually dying, go for Sunday lunch, have a couple of pints over lunch, then go again from there until Sunday night. You'd be suffering on Monday morning, that was for sure, but it didn't stop you doing it again the following weekend.

I didn't think there was any problem with that. I didn't think I had a problem at all, but I had, as I realised later when I was able to look back on it all. Sometimes you can't see the wood for the trees. When you are in the middle of something bad, you are the last person to see it, simply because it's you in the middle of it. You can't look at it objectively. You can't see the big picture, the long term; you can only see what is happening on a day-to-day basis. It wasn't until I went to The Priory that I began to realise I had a problem. If you go out to get drunk, you have a problem. It might be only a small problem, but it is still a problem. If you didn't have a problem, why would you need to go out with the specific objective of getting drunk?

What I was doing was binge drinking. Because I wasn't drinking during the week, I didn't think I had an issue with alcohol. I wasn't dependent on the stuff. Actually, I was. The difficulty lies in where it leads to. They say that what starts as binge drinking can lead to more serious problems, like drinking during the week, during the day, losing your house and your family. You don't start like that, but you can end up like that. That's the bit that got me. If you had asked me then if I was an alcoholic, I would have laughed in your face. To me, an alcoholic was a fellow who drank 24 hours a day and was never sober. That wasn't me. No way. I only drank when I was out, and that was mainly at weekends. No way was I an alcoholic. I had it all under control. But people who are rarely sober didn't start off like that, and that's the bit that hit home with me. They didn't say, 'There's a nice park bench there, I think I'll live there, stay there seven days a week and just get locked all the time.' They started on the slippery slope somewhere, and I was on that slope. Nearly everyone I met when I started going to AA told me how lucky I was. I was incredulous. How am I lucky? I'm an alcoholic for Christ's sake. What they meant was I was lucky to find out while I was still young. The majority of the people with whom I spoke reckoned that they had wasted 50 years of their lives before they found out.

You drink on feelings. I drank because I found it difficult to communicate with people when I was sober. But when I drank, I drank so much that I wouldn't be able to string a coherent sentence together. So when I didn't drink I didn't have the courage to talk to people, and when I did I physically couldn't. People drink to get away from their problems, but the problem is still there in the morning, and then you're dying as well as having to deal with it. It just keeps building up, and the problem never gets solved. I thought it was normal. I couldn't see anything wrong with going out at the weekend and getting hammered. Everyone else was doing it. But everyone else wasn't doing it like I was doing it. Everyone else was able to get up for work the following morning. I wasn't. It just didn't suit me.

But I'm a firm believer in things happening for a reason. Who knows, if I had been able to get up in the mornings, and if I had always been in on time, I might still be at Dermot Weld's riding out and mucking out and not even getting to ride work. And I think, now that I'm not drinking, perhaps I'm able to appreciate life more than someone who never had a problem. I think I can appreciate the freedom of not having to drink. It was like a noose around my neck. Waking up in the morning thinking, 'Oh no, what did I do last night? What did I say to him or her?' And you're feeling awful as well, and you're going out and trying to do a job, feeling dreadful. That I don't miss.

Still, on the racetrack I was trying hard. Too hard, in the opinion of the stewards. I spent 52 days on the sidelines in my first season with Nicholls because of suspensions for misuse of the whip. That was quite an incredible number of days. The Jockey Club told me that if I didn't change my ways they would have difficulty giving me a licence to ride the following season. Frequency, force, style, you name it, if it had to do with the whip and you were going to get a suspension for it, I did it.

I had a strong will to win, but there was more to it than that. I had a temper. I still do, but I think I have it much more under control now. I used to get angry with horses when I felt they weren't trying for me, horses that weren't putting it all in, keeping a little back for themselves and not going as fast as they could when I asked them to quicken. If he was just a slow horse, it wasn't his fault, and I recognised that, but when I was riding one I felt had the ability but just wouldn't do it, that used to drive me mad. I got the majority of my suspensions, unusually, when I was riding horses that got beaten. I rarely got done for the whip on a winner. It was always something that wouldn't try for me. It wasn't until the last couple of years that I learnt to fully appreciate that often it doesn't matter how hard you hit them, they're not necessarily going to go any faster for you. The strange thing is that when I was hitting a horse, I don't think I ever really felt he would go quicker. I should have realised after a short while that very few of them did. But I was angry. I'd teach him a lesson. If he wasn't going to put it in for me, I'd make sure he knew about it. It was my frame of mind at the time, my aggressive frame of mind, and it permeated my entire life. It didn't matter if I was on a horse or in a pub.

Adrian Maguire tells the story of a beginners' chase at Newton Abbot in which we were both riding. He fell at the first. When we went round the second time, Adrian was standing at the fence and saw me, tailed off last, kicking and scrubbing my fellow along. When we came round again I was even further behind, but I was still going, pushing and shoving. 'Would you ever pull him up!' Adrian shouted after me as he made his way back to the enclosures. 'You'll kill the two of you!' When he met me in the weigh room afterwards, he asked me, 'Did you manage to finish the race on that thing?'

'I did,' I replied.

'You must be off your fecking head.'

I was suspenced on St Stephen's Day 1997. St Stephen's Day is not an ideal day to be suspended any year, given the quality and quantity of racing that goes on, but St Stephen's Day 1997 was a particularly poor day for me to be suspended. See More Business, the horse on which I had won the Rehearsal Chase at Chepstow, was being prepared by Paul for a tilt at the King George VI Chase, the highlight of the St Stephen's Day programme. And he had a chance. One Man, who had won the race for the previous two years, was going to be favourite, but he had proved in a couple of Gold Cups that he wasn't invincible. Suny Bay, who had beaten us in the Edward Hanmer that November, was also in the race. He had gone on and won the Hennessy in the interim and was going to be tough to beat, but I knew that our fellow was in great form. He was only seven and was still improving. Paul Nicholls and Paul Barber, part-owner of See More Business, were searching for a replacement for me for days. All the top jocks were gone. McCoy was riding Challenger Du Luc for Pipe, Dunwoody was, of course, riding One Man, Mick Fitzgerald was on Rough Quest, and Maguire was committed to Barton Bank for David Nicholson. Eventually they came up with Andy Thornton. A good horseman, and a good lad to boot.

I watched the race in the sitting room of my first house in Faringdon with Davy Kavanagh. David was also known as Davy Duck, because he looked very like Charlie Swan. A lot of the girls thought he did anyway! You often hear jockeys who are injured or suspended being interviewed before a big race in which they should be riding. They always say the same thing: hope the horse wins, great for the yard, great for the horse ... all a load of crap! If you dig deep into your heart, way down at the bottom of your gut, and if you are honest with yourself, the very last thing you want is for the horse to win. But there was an inevitability about this one. I watched as Andy settled See More Business towards the back. He wasn't jumping that well, but that was him: he never was a brilliant jumper, but he was adequate this day, wasn't losing much ground at his fences and never looked like falling.

See More Business took it up off Suny Bay on the approach to the third last, the first in the straight. One Man was gone, Barton Bank was long gone, and Suny Bay began to beat a retreat. Challenger Du Luc and McCoy loomed large at the last. If you didn't know Challenger Du Luc, you would have said he was a 10–1 on shot at that stage. But you did, and you knew that if there was one horse you wanted cruising up to your withers on the run-in in a King George, it was Challenger Du Luc. I could hardly bear to watch as McCoy began to stoke up his unwilling partner, but the more he stoked the more unwilling his partner was getting. Thornton just kept driving and kicking with his long legs almost wrapped around his horse's belly, and See More just kept responding, as game as you like. At the line, See More and Andy had two lengths to spare over Challenger Du Luc and McCoy.

I buried my head in my hands. To say that I had mixed emotions would really be to tell a lie. I was gutted. Sick as a pig. I should have been there. Right there, on See More's back, right where Andy Thornton was now. Well, he may well grin a grin as wide as his head. It should have been my King George. You don't get the chance to win a King George too often in your career. This one was mine, and it had passed me by. As I sat in my sitting room and watched Derek Thompson interviewing King George-winning jockey Andy Thornton, it was difficult.

When the dust settled, though, I was delighted for Paul Nicholls and Paul Barber, and for the yard. It is these big race wins that make going into work on a Monday morning that much easier for everyone. And I was delighted for Andy. I really was. Andy is a great guy and a really good jockey, and if anyone had to take my place on a King George winner because I beat some useless thing too much in an egg and spoon race that would hardly have merited a mention in the *Racing Post*, it might as well have been Andy. In fact, I didn't know this until much later, but when I was away at Her Majesty's Pleasure Andy wouldn't allow anybody to use my peg in the weigh room. That is the type of guy Andy Thornton is.

Andy seems to be at the receiving end of a lot of the practical jokes in the weigh room – and there are many lads who fancy themselves as practical jokers in there. I guess Andy gets it because he takes it so well. We have been known to put squished-up bananas into his light boots. We have also put black boot polish on the chin-strap of his helmet so that when he took it off after sweating he had a big black mark on his chin. All very childish, I know, but it was always good for a laugh, and everybody in the weigh room would be in on it except Andy. Two years ago, when I was just getting going again as a rider after my spell in prison, I would be at a race meeting for just one or two rides, and consequently would spend a lot of time sitting around the weigh room. I decided one day that I would put my sewing skills to good use, so I sewed the sleeves of Andy's shirt together. It happened that he had a ride in nearly every race that day, so I had more time than I had thought. I decided that I would sew the legs of his trousers together as well. I'm not sure what Andy wore going home that evening.

I was back well in time to ride See More Business in the Pillar Property Chase at Cheltenham the following month. That was important. Some of the owners were beginning to get a little anxious that I was spending so much time on the sidelines, and it was crucial for me that I got back quickly and kept my nose clean. The Pillar Property Chase is one of the main trials for the Cheltenham Gold Cup. At three miles one and a half furlongs, the Pillar Property is run over almost the exact same course and distance as the Gold Cup, although the ground at Cheltenham in January is often a lot softer than the same ground in March. See More had been a high-class staying novice chaser who had now won the King George, so we were within our rights to think of him as a real Gold Cup contender. The Pillar Property would tell us a lot more.

It was a funny old race. I settled See More out the back. He didn't jump that fluently – the usual – and I had to get after him a little going up to the top of the hill. Then, just as I was beginning to think that we would win, he clouted the fourth last. Absolutely clobbered it. He did well to stay on his feet, and the fence did well to stay in the ground. I thought our chance had gone, but this horse had a serious engine. He got himself going again almost immediately and was in front by the second last. He stayed on really well up the hill to win by four lengths from Cyborgo and Tony McCoy (again), with Andy Thornton deputising for Mick Fitzgerald on Rough Quest back in third.

The six and a half weeks between the Pillar Property and the Gold Cup were filled with expectation. That's one of the many great things about this game. The expectation. The anticipation. The hopes and the dreams. Trainers tread on eggshells in the days before Cheltenham, or before any big race in which they have a live contender. Tread carefully, for you tread on my dreams. In the last week or so before the Gold Cup I was almost afraid to speak to Paul Nicholls in case he told me that something had gone wrong with the horse. He never did.

Most people will tell you that there is no such thing as a poor Gold Cup; or if you suggest to a trainer that this year's Gold Cup does not have great strength in depth, he will tell you to try training the winner of one. But it didn't look to me like a very strong Gold Cup field that year. Dorans Pride was favourite. In fact, in my book he was the only danger. He had disappointed in a handicap chase at Naas in January, but he'd bounced back fairly well with a win in an uncompetitive Hennessy at Leopardstown the previous month. He was, of course, trained by Michael Hourigan. It was ironic: had the ball bounced a little differently, I could have been riding him in that Gold Cup. I was very happy to be riding See More, however. In fact, I wouldn't have swapped him for anything.

I went through everything in my head before that race. I would ride him towards the outside because he liked his space and he wasn't such a fluent jumper, and it would be better for him to have a little bit of room at his fences. Cheltenham is a turning track, and you do give away a little bit of ground when you go wide, but with some horses it is worth it, and I figured that it was with See More. What we would give away by going wide we would gain by jumping more fluently and by keeping away from the congestion on the rails. I was prepared for everything. I was prepared to win, prepared to get beaten, prepared to fall, prepared to find out that he just wasn't good enough. At least I thought I was prepared for everything.

We were travelling well on the outside going to the seventh fence, the one just after you've turned left-handed at the top of the hill. I was happy with how the race was going. See More was jumping well for him, and seemed happy to be going the pace they were going. It all happened in an instant, yet at the same time it seemed as if we suddenly regressed into

130

slow motion. I could see McCoy pulling out on Cyborgo on my inside. At first I wasn't sure what was going on, but I was well away from him anyway. As he pulled the horse to his right, however, he began to carry Jonothan Lower on Indian Tracker with him. Indian Tracker was directly on my inside, and suddenly he began to carry me right. Jonothan tried to race around McCoy in order that he could jump the fence, but he was struggling to get there. I was just sitting on their outside, powerless, a passenger. It was as if I had been suspended in the air, as if I was on the William Hill blimp looking down on everything that was going on and thinking, 'Oh no.' It was almost like a dream, where you can see exactly what is happening and you know exactly what is going to happen but you are incapable of doing anything about it. The next thing I knew, the outside wing of the fence had passed me by on the inside and we were out of the race.

I'm not sure what I felt or what I did. I think I let out a long and loud scream as the realisation dawned. We were out of the race, out of the Gold Cup. All the talk, all the preparation, all the expectation, all for nothing. We were slowing to a trot now, then a walk. I screamed again. There wasn't a shout or anything. No warning. But what could McCoy have done? His poor horse had broken down before the fence, so of course he was going to do all he could to avoid jumping the fence. He didn't have time to shout a warning, and it probably wouldn't have done any good anyway. It all happened so quickly. But surely we could have had some notice. Surely some kind of warning. If it had just been him and me, I'm sure we would have been fine. We would have been able to avoid him. I would have been able to manoeuvre See More around him, or I would have done something to make sure he jumped the fence, the seventh fence. But because there was another horse between us, it made it more difficult. It made it impossible to avoid. I screamed again.

McCoy didn't say anything to me. He was too busy looking after the stricken Cyborgo. I cantered back to the enclosures, me and See More. We could have been coming back to a hero's welcome, but as it was we were coming back under cover, anonymous. No need to take any notice of us, we're not the story. Paul Barber was livid. Paul Nicholls was livid. He hadn't had a winner at the Cheltenham Festival before and he thought See More could have been it. He really did. A Gold Cup, up in smoke, right there.

There were all sorts of conspiracy theories afterwards. In the immediate aftermath we really did believe that we had been done. In fact it was a good thing that none of us said too much to the press directly after the race as we could have got ourselves into serious trouble. It just would have looked like sour grapes. Of course we were disappointed. Best to leave it at that. There was some circumstantial evidence around, though. We were amazed that Cyborgo even ran in the race. Some of the girls at Nicholls' used to hang around with some of the girls at Pipe's, and there was talk of Cyborgo not being right and unlikely to run in the Gold Cup at all. Talk among stable staff is rarely too far wide of the mark, so we were surprised when Cyborgo showed up. But to think that they used Cyborgo to take us out? And to take out Indian Tracker, his stablemate, as well? Why? To increase the chances of their other runner, Challenger Du Luc? Hardly. And how would you do it? How could you plan it? Make sure that See More Business and Murphy are on your outside and then pull out without any warning? And even if you somehow convinced yourself that all that was possible, there is no way that McCoy would be complicit in something like that. No way. The conspiracy theory was unfounded.

Amazingly, Paul Barber had had a dream a couple of days before the Gold Cup that something like this would happen. And it wasn't made any easier to swallow by the fact that the race was won by Cool Dawn, an ex-hunter chaser whose previous win was in a handicap chase off a mark of 148, about two stone inferior to See More Business, trained by one of racing's gentlemen, Robert Alner, and ridden by the ubiquitous Andy Thornton. It capped a hell of a season for Andy. A King George and a Gold Cup on two different horses in the space of three months.

I beat myself up for weeks afterwards. I should have seen it coming. I should have seen the horses pulling out towards me. I should have pulled back, or kicked on, or run through Indian Tracker just to get to jump the fence. It's human nature that when something goes wrong you wonder what you could have done to avoid it. If you have a car accident, you think, 'If only I had left the house two minutes earlier, or two minutes later, or if I hadn't stopped at the shop.' Or if you get beaten a short head in a race, you think, 'If only I had kicked on sooner, or left it later, or asked him for a long one at the second last.' If something like this had happened in a selling hurdle at Fontwell you would have been annoyed; for it to happen in the Gold Cup when you were riding what many people thought was the most likely winner of the race, it really was quite incredible. If you read it in a book you would think it was too contrived, too far-fetched. Roy of the Rovers stuff.

Nobody blamed me for what happened. No reasonable person could have. Even so, it wasn't a positive, and it just added to the pressure on everybody. I'm sure Nicholls was coming under pressure from the owners about me, and he was relaying that pressure to me, because I felt it. There is nothing like success to alleviate pressure. A little success can paper over a lot of cracks. You put up with the little things that aren't right when you are winning, but as soon as things begin to go a little awry, relationships can come under strain.

I have no doubt that if I had won the 1998 Gold Cup on See More Business I wouldn't have lost my job with Nicholls at the end of the season. It wasn't because of what happened that I lost it, you understand, but a Gold Cup would have saved it. Of course, at the time I had no idea that I was going to lose it, but some of the owners weren't too happy with me. Nicholls wasn't as established then as he is now. I suppose it's difficult to blame him. It is the owners, after all, who pay the bills, and they have to have some input into the piper's tune.

Barber might come up to the yard on a schooling morning to watch his horses and see how they jumped, but he wouldn't come round that often. I wouldn't say I was his best buddy or anything. He owned the place. He was my boss's boss, so I suppose I had to make some kind of an effort. But I wasn't great at talking to owners. Nicholls wanted his stable jockey to wax lyrical about a horse with the owners when he came in to unsaddle after a race. He was unlucky, or he wants further, or he'll be better on better ground, or I should have asked him for a long one at the fourth last. Owners love that kind of thing. They love to have a straw to clutch even if everyone knows the horse is useless. But that wasn't my style. I generally like to call it as it is, and I found it difficult to do the owner thing directly after getting off something that just hadn't wanted to know. When I got beaten I would generally just dismount and say nothing, and Paul would have to talk to the owners.

I remember one day at Wincanton, finishing third on this horse that wouldn't have been out of place on Grafton Street with a cart tied to its back. More than that, whatever modicum of ability he possessed, he was intent on not using it. A flailing couldn't convince him to put it in during the race, so when I pulled him up and his lass came to lead us in, I just dismounted there and then. Get this thing out of my sight. I walked straight back to the weigh room without talking to Paul or the expectant owners. Paul was livid. He had every right to be. He came into the weigh room after he had obviously appeased the owners as well as he could and pulled me aside. 'Don't you ever do that again. When you finish a race, no matter where you finish, you come back into the unsaddling enclosure like everybody else and you talk to the owners.'

It didn't get any better as the season went on. I didn't get any better. In fact, if anything, I got progressively worse. I didn't talk that much, and I'm sure Paul found it increasingly difficult to communicate with me. And that made his job difficult. Of course I had a huge will to win, but sometimes the boundaries between my will to win and my temper would become blurred. And whatever chance there was of me talking to Paul, there was very little chance of me talking to the owners. Paul used to end up sticking up for me a lot with owners, making excuses for me, telling them that I wasn't the best of communicators but that I could ride. And which is the more important attribute?

But it was a finger-in-the-dam job. Perhaps if Paul had been as strong and established as he is now, he could have said, 'Look, Timmy is my stable jockey, so you can either accept that or take your horses somewhere else.' But he couldn't have done that then. And I wasn't helping him, or rather I wasn't helping him to help me, with my strops, my temper, my economy of speech and my bans. Joe Tizzard was in the wings, the stable's conditional rider. He was only eighteen at the time, but he was a decent rider and it looked like he would be able to step up to the mark quite soon and take over as stable jockey if they wanted him to. Just as importantly, he was a nice lad who would talk to the owners and smile and agree and give them all the straws they wanted. Not like me, then.

I rode for Nicholls at Aintree that year. I rode With Impunity to finish third behind a remarkable five-year-old gelding owned by David Johnson and trained by Martin Pipe called Cyfor Malta in the John Hughes Chase over the Grand National fences; I rode Lake Kariba to finish third behind the Arthur Moore-trained Jeffell in the Red Rum Chase; and I rode Court Melody in the Grand National, who took me as far as Becher's first time before hitting the deck. Over the months that followed, however, the pressure on Nicholls became too great to withstand. Some of the owners became quite dogmatic in their desire not to have me as stable jockey, and Paul relented in the end. John Keighley had taken out a retainer on Joe Tizzard. Paul figured it would be difficult to have me as stable jockey and have Joe riding all the horses for one of the main owners in the yard. In November he rang Chris Broad to tell him, and Chris told me, 'Too bad, you're out. The owners want Joe. Sorry.'

Another job lost. I suppose if you do something often enough the novelty wears off after a while. I was disappointed to lose this one though. Still, even when I lost it I thought I would be OK. I thought I had built up enough contacts in the UK to be able to get by. I wouldn't have the pick of the horses that had been at my disposal at Nicholls', but I knew I would be OK. It was all a bit frustrating, but I wasn't too despondent, because I knew I hadn't really done that much wrong from the point of view of riding. I rode 60 winners that season, even with 52 days off due to suspension, the majority of them for Nicholls. I had been riding quite well and, the Gold Cup notwithstanding, the number of races I lost that I should have won was negligible. At no stage during the season did Nicholls take me aside and say, 'Listen, Timmy, some of the owners think you are being too hard on their horses,' or, 'If you keep getting banned I'm going to find it difficult to keep you on as stable jockey.' His will to win was as strong as mine. He didn't care how he won and he knew that I was trying my heart out. Also, from his perspective it was me who was getting banned for trying so hard, not him. There was an inconvenience factor through not having his stable jockey available for 52 days during the season, but it wasn't as great an inconvenience as I was suffering.

Of course I had nobody to blame. It was all self-inflicted. The thought crossed my mind that I was only filling in a year until Joe came of age and that it had always been the plan to put Joe in for the 1998/99 season and get rid of me, but I don't think that was the case. I think I brought it all on myself through not making an effort to get on with some of Nicholls' bigger owners. Add in the bans, how hard I was on the horses, and the Gold Cup, and you had your case for dismissal right there.

There was no acrimony about the split. I just accepted it and got on with things. That's the way I was back then. I wasn't good at talking things out and I wasn't good at conflict. I preferred to sidestep issues rather than take them on, and I wasn't good at making my feelings known. So although I was disappointed at losing the job, I didn't really let it be known that I was. I still rode out at Nicholls' once a week or once a fortnight after that, and I still rode for Paul when Joe wasn't available. It was a strange one, going from being the stable's number one to being the stable's number two. I know how Oliver Kahn must have felt sitting on the German bench during the 2006 World Cup.

The end of my spell as stable jockey for Nicholls had a little bit of a sting in the tail. I had my final rides in my capacity as stable jockey for him that year at Sandown on the Saturday after the announcement was made. Nicholls was at another meeting, so he sent Tim Cox to look after things in his place. I had three rides for him on the day – the two-mile novice chase on Laredo, the two-and-a-half-mile handicap chase on Mr Strong Gale, and the three-mile chase on my old friend Court Melody. I won on all of them. Maybe this fellow isn't such a bad jockey after all. I also won the two-mile handicap hurdle on Chai-Yo for Jim Old, which meant that I completed the first ever four-timer of my career.

If you were looking for symbolism in a day's racing, you had it right there. The end of one era, the beginning of another. When See More Business ran in the Edward Hanmer Chase at Haydock the following week, Joe Tizzard rode him. When Laredo and Court Melody ran at Ascot two weeks later, Joe rode both. And when Chai-Yo ran in the handicap hurdle at Cheltenham the following week, I was on board. And I was on board almost everything else that Jim Old ran for the rest of the season. That was me, landing on my feet, off and running again.

CHAPTER TEN

OLD FRIENDS

I first met Jim Old in January 1996 when I was up schooling a couple of horses for Jeff King. Jeff and Jim are next-door neighbours, insofar as you can have a next-door neighbour in Wroughton in Wiltshire, and they shared an all-weather gallop during the winter when the ground was just too bad to gallop on grass. 'Jim, Timmy, do you two know each other?' Jeff asked. Jim shook his head and extended his hand. I shook my head and shook his hand. 'How's it going?'

Two months later I knew who Jim Old was, as I watched Graham Bradley push and kick Collier Bay home clear of odds-on favourite and defending champion Alderbrook in the Champion Hurdle at Cheltenham. Strange the way fate deals out the cards. Bradley was supposed to ride Alderbrook in that Champion Hurdle, but he didn't turn up on time at Kim Bailey's for a schooling session beforehand, with the result that he was jocked off and Richard Dunwoody got the ride. Bradley said that his alarm clock didn't go off that morning, and the images of him being led into the winner's enclosure after that Champion Hurdle looking at his imaginary watch are what most people remember. I'm not sure that Collier Bay or Jim Old got the credit they deserved for winning that Champion Hurdle as a result. All the talk was about Bradley and Alderbrook, and the strange turn of events that led to him getting the ride. But Collier Bay had a serious engine, and Jim had him spot on on the day.

It was another twist of fate that led to me getting to know Jim. Jim used to give Chris Broad a call when he was looking for a jockey. Carl Llewellyn was a good friend of Jim's, and he was with Broady, so it made sense for Jim to use him. The day that Chai-Yo was due to run in the handicap hurdle at Sandown, Jim didn't have a jockey for him, so he gave Broady a call. 'What about Murphy? He's all I've got.'

Everything went right for me on Chai-Yo. In fact, most things went right for me throughout the entire afternoon. It would be unusual to ride a four-timer and come back in and say that things didn't go right. But Chai-Yo really zinged. I dropped him in at the back and only really asked him to make any ground when we got into the home straight. He picked up lovely for me at the second last. I hardly had to ask him to quicken, he just went away and did it all himself. We won by eight lengths in the end from Papua, who had run in the Epsom Derby the previous season.

Jim was delighted afterwards. He really was. He thought a lot of this horse, and he figured that he had been just waiting for someone to ride him like I had just ridden him. And this was a fair performance, to carry top weight and win so easily in what looked like a competitive little handicap. I went off to ride Court Melody in the handicap chase – thanks very much for the ride – and Jim went up to the box where Wally Sturt and George Ward were. Wally and George are great mates. Wally owned Collier Bay and a whole host of other horses that Jim trained, and George Ward is George Ward of Doubleprint and Tripleprint fame. George had a horse going in the last, the bumper, that they thought would go well, so they were all in high spirits.

Apparently Wally and George were keen for Jim to sign me up as stable jockey. It made complete sense to them. They were impressed with the ride I had given Chai-Yo, I was without a job, and Jim needed a rider. There was no downside. Jim disagreed. Sure, I could ride, but my reputation had preceded me. My reputation preceded me to most destinations in those days, in fact. He had heard about me mainly through Carl Llewellyn and Mick Fitzgerald, that I liked to socialise intensely and sometimes my socialising time ate into my work time.

'Your problem is that you're not decisive enough,' said George to Jim. 'You need to be more decisive, and grab an opportunity when one presents itself.'

'I am decisive,' protested Jim. 'I'm deciding that I don't want him! There are several things that I can't stand in people, and if what I hear is correct, they are all wrapped up in that jockey.'

Jim didn't think any more of it. That was the end of it as far as he was concerned. They watched me ride Court Melody to victory and they watched me get Mr Strong Gale up on the line. Then Jim went off to saddle George's horse, Native King, in the last. What he didn't know was that George and Wally had sent down for me to come up to their box to watch the race.

Native King ran well to finish third. Although George and Wally fancied him well, and he was sent off favourite, they were pleased with his run. He had been working well at home, but this was his first run ever on a racecourse, and he had run with a lot of promise. Monsignor won the race, the Mark Pitman-trained horse who was also making his racecourse debut and who would go on to win the Cheltenham Bumper later that season. Richard Guest was reportedly so impressed with Monsignor at Sandown that, once he'd dismounted in the winner's enclosure, he told his owner Malcolm Denmark that if he was offered £100,000 not to accept it! Guestie's judgement would prove to be more than vindicated as Monsignor went on to win all six of his hurdle races the following season, including beating Best Mate in the Tolworth Hurdle and winning the SunAlliance Hurdle at Cheltenham.

George Ward's prize asset at the time was a horse called Dawn Leader, a top-class bumper horse who had been just beaten in the Top Novices' Hurdle at Aintree the previous April and who was about to embark on a chasing career. George was anxious to sign up a jockey who would be committed to riding him regularly. As well as Collier Bay, who had himself just begun his career as a chaser, Wally had a number of decent horses, including Sir Talbot, who had shown a lot of promise when trained by Richard Hannon on the Flat and who had looked good when winning a hurdle race for Wally the previous week.

By the time Jim got back up to the box after seeing Native King back in, Wally Sturt had offered me a job. I didn't accept the offer immediately.

I told him I would have to have a think about it, which was very mature of me. But what was I going to do? There I was, without a job. Sure, I had Jeff King, who was great, and a couple of other small trainers who would put me up, but they didn't have enough horses between them to allow me to ride as many horses as I wanted to ride, as many as I needed to ride. Wally Sturt had some decent horses. Jim Old had about 45 horses altogether, and there had to be a good chance that I would get to ride the horses there that weren't owned by Wally.

Within about a week of accepting the offer, I rode Juyush in the PricewaterhouseCoopers Hurdle at Ascot. Juyush had won four on the bounce as a novice but had been desperately disappointing the previous season when it looked like he might turn out to be very good. They had gelded him during the summer and this was his first run over hurdles since then. I had never sat on Juyush before Jim gave me the leg up in the parade ring at Ascot. He told me to ride him patiently and not to get there too soon. That wasn't difficult. Mick Fitzgerald on Bimsey set off at a rate of knots. He simply went far too fast, so I had no difficulty sitting well off him and biding my time. Even when he was twenty lengths clear coming out of Swinley Bottom with just four flights of hurdles to jump, I wasn't panicking. Juyush was just feeling his way into the race, and I let him get there in his own time. We took it up going to the last and we quickened away to win impressively from Mary Reveley's stalwart Turnpole, in second, with Castle Sweep, who had finished third in the Coral Cup the previous season, back in third.

There is nothing like a little bit of success to cement a new relationship. Wally was delighted with Juyush, and with the ride that I had given him. Jim was thrilled. Juyush was only six years old and was a real prospect. All the talk afterwards was whether he would go for the Champion Hurdle or the Stayers' at Cheltenham the following March. I was just delighted to have been able to win such a good prize for my new employers. It took the pressure off a bit.

Not that there was ever any real pressure riding for Wally or Jim. In spite of Jim's reservations about – nay, dogged opposition to – my appointment in the beginning, we struck up a really good relationship. Jim is a gentleman, and he was a real pleasure to work for, although it never felt like I was working for him. He was never the boss. We were in it together, as a team, which made sense as we both had the same objectives. It was a relationship of mutual respect. He is a top trainer of racehorses. He understands horses, he understands that they have different needs, and he trains them as individuals.

A lot was happening for me around that time. McCoy had been suspended for fourteen days for misuse of the whip. It was only a minor offence in a little race at Fontwell, but it triggered other bans that had been suspended under the totting-up system. McCoy was going through a torrid time with his use of the whip. He did mention that he might just give up riding and become a professional golfer, but we knew that his handicap of 28 was genuine, so it was unlikely he would ever make it as a golfer! He ended up working hard on changing his style, and he vowed that it would be a long time before he would be up before the Jockey Club's disciplinary committee in Portman Square again to answer questions about his use of the whip and how his style contravened the Jockey Club's guidelines.

The ban meant that McCoy could not ride in the Hennessy Gold Cup at Newbury that year. His boss Martin Pipe had two horses in the race, Cyfor Malta and Eudipe, both owned by David Johnson, and he asked me if I would ride for him. In the end, they decided to keep Cyfor Malta for the Tripleprint – he had just won the Murphy's – and run Eudipe in the Hennessy. He asked me to ride Eudipe.

I have to admit I was a little taken aback, but I was delighted at the same time. I didn't think I was a Pipe type of jockey. I wasn't a Scudamore or a McCoy; I wasn't an aggressive rider who would go like hell from early on and hope that the horse would be able to sustain the effort to the line. The Pipe philosophy seemed to be that the quickest way to get from one point to another was to go as fast as you can from the outset. Sprint the whole way. And there is a lot to be said for being handy in a race. It was a similar philosophy to the one Nicholls adopted. There is no doubt that it is effective in fully exploiting any fitness advantage you have over your rivals, but it didn't work for every horse. My thinking was that you had to ride every horse as you found it.

To tell the truth, I was flattered even to be considered by Pipe and David Johnson as a deputy for McCoy. Eudipe ran a cracker for me in that Hennessy. I rode him handy, as I had been instructed to do, and he stayed on up the straight well to finish second, but he had no answer to Teeton Mill's resolute gallop. That was hardly surprising, as Teeton Mill went on to win the King George at Kempton four weeks later, and we had been trying to give him eight pounds in the Hennessy. But I was happy with my debut in David Johnson's blue and green silks. I didn't know at the time that no more than six years later I would be putting those silks on my back more often than I would be putting my baseball cap on my head.

Life wasn't bad. I used to go up to Jim Old's to ride out once a week, or maybe three times every fortnight. I loved riding for Jim. I got a great kick out of riding winners for him because you knew that he appreciated it. He was like Jeff King in that respect. There must be something in the Wiltshire air. Jim and his wife Anne Marie put some amount of work into training, and whatever reward or result they get out of it they fully deserve. It's a big day when they have a winner. All the work that has gone in has paid off.

In February 1999 I won the Agfa Diamond Chase at Sandown for Jim on Clever Remark. I was pretty pleased with the ride I gave him. He was doing nothing for me in behind, so I decided to be aggressive with him at the end of the back straight and he just kept picking up over the last three fences and all the way to the line.

So I was ticking over fairly well. I was making a living and riding some nice horses, though I wasn't necessarily setting the world alight. By contrast, Paul Nicholls was. Call Equiname had won the Victor Chandler Chase and was a live contender for the Champion Chase at Cheltenham, Flagship Uberalles looked like one of the top two-mile novice chasers in the country, and, though See More Business had disappointed when favourite for the King George, he was still well on track for the Gold Cup.

I was still getting into trouble with the stewards. I was banned for ten days that February for holding my ground on Challenger Du Luc in the Mitsubishi Shogun Ascot Chase and not allowing Richard Dunwoody on Direct Route up my inside, which had a concertina effect and resulted in Carl Llewellyn and Chief's Song being hampered. All I did was hold my ground. Richard shouldn't have been going there. If anything, he was the one guilty of recklessness; I got ten days for not moving out of his way. I didn't appeal, however, as the ban ended just before Cheltenham, and there had to be a small danger that if I did appeal the ban would be extended and I would miss the festival. It wasn't worth the risk. You just don't know how these things are going to go. I had the feeling that the stewards had a special eye on me.

Actually, I didn't have any outstanding rides to look forward to at Cheltenham. I didn't have a ride at all on the first day. The closest I got in any of the first nineteen races was a fourth placing on Collier Bay in the SunAlliance Chase on the Wednesday, a distance behind Looks Like Trouble, in a race that was marred by the awful injury to Nick Dundee. That was before the last race on the last day, the Vincent O'Brien County Hurdle, in which I was riding Sir Talbot for Wally and Jim. He was nicely weighted, and before the week started I considered him to be my best chance of having a winner. But it is difficult to be confident or even hopeful when you have had seven rides, none of whom has even really got competitive.

That all changed with Sir Talbot. Jim had taken him out of the Imperial Cup at Sandown the Saturday before because he thought that the ground was too soft for him there, so he was fit, fresh and well for the County Hurdle, and he bounced off the ground. I had him handy for most of the way, moved him up at the third last, took it up over the second last and kicked for home from there. Two miles was actually a little too sharp for him, but this was two miles and a furlong at Cheltenham, where they go almost flat out the whole way, so you actually need a horse that stays much further than two miles to win a County Hurdle. Sir Talbot kept going all the way over the final flight and to the line, easily holding off a constant challenge from Norman Williamson on the favourite, Decoupage.

It was great to come back into the winner's enclosure at the Cheltenham Festival. It was the last race on the Thursday, the last day, and there might not have been as big a crowd to welcome us back in the fading light as there would have been if it had been the third race on the Tuesday, but it wasn't any less sweet as a result. If you had asked me at the start of the week if I would have settled for winning the County Hurdle on Sir Talbot as my bounty for the week, my answer would have been a resounding yes.

I couldn't help looking over my shoulder at Nicholls during the week. That's human nature, I suppose. If the owners hadn't wanted me out, I would have been riding the majority, if not all, of the Nicholls horses. The trainer who had never had a winner at the festival, and on whose See More Business I had got carried out the previous year, lost his Cheltenham virginity in style: Flagship Uberalles won the Arkle, Call Equiname won the Champion Chase, and See More Business, in his first-time blinkers, won the Gold Cup.

Interesting thing, I thought. Joe Tizzard rode Flagship Uberalles all right, but Mick Fitzgerald, Nicholls' brother-in-law at the time, rode the other two. Joe had ridden See More Business in his previous four races, but Mick rode him in the Gold Cup. Joe rode Double Thriller, who was actually a much shorter price than See More. But Joe had never ridden Call Equiname. He actually rode the Nicholls second string, Green Green Desert, in the Champion Chase. They put it down to experience – Joe was young and Mick had all the experience of riding around Cheltenham – but it was a sign that everything was not right. Mick continued to ride both See More Business and Call Equiname when he was available after that.

It's another difference in the Nicholls outlook versus the Old outlook. I'm not saying that one is better than the other, but when Jim Old has a regular rider, he sticks with him, gives him as many opportunities as he can and promotes him as much as he can. That is the case now with Jason Maguire. Jason is his rider, and it wouldn't matter if I or another more experienced jockey were available to ride the Gold Cup favourite for him. Jason is his jockey, and as long as he is available, he will ride Jim's horses. I have my commitments to David Johnson now, and I wouldn't expect Jim to jock Jason off any time I was available to ride for him. Fitzy's first commitment is and was to Nicky Henderson. He won the Triumph Hurdle on Katarino for him that year. But because Nicky had nothing in the Gold Cup or the Champion Chase, Nicholls snapped Fitzy up and jocked Joe Tizzard off. As hard as it was for me to see Call Equiname and See More Business going in in two of the three championship races at the festival, it must have been really sickening for Joe. Hardly good for morale or team spirit. So maybe I wouldn't have been on all the Nicholls horses at Cheltenham at all. It's a fickle business.

But it hadn't been a bad season for me. Another job lost, another one acquired. Nothing out of the ordinary, then. Even so, when I looked back on my season that summer, I could point to 73 winners including a winner at the Cheltenham Festival. It wasn't so bad for a fellow who had lost his job halfway through. That was the greatest number of winners I had ridden in a season since I went to England. In fact, up to that point I had improved on the previous season's tally each year: 26, 28, 60, 73. So I was in good enough shape heading into the autumn of 1999. But things were about to get a little tougher.

I had started to ride out for Mark Pitman as well towards the end of the 1998/99 season. Mark is, of course, the son of BBC presenter and ex-jockey Richard Pitman and Grand National- and Gold Cup-winning trainer Jenny Pitman. He had started out as a trainer on his own just a couple of years earlier after a hugely successful riding career, the highlight of which was victory in the 1991 Gold Cup on Garrison Savannah.

He moved into his mother's old yard, Weathercock House, from Saxon House in September 1999 with 85 horses, one of the largest teams in the country, including some real potential stars. Monsignor, the horse who won the bumper on the day I rode my four-timer at Sandown, had won the Cheltenham Bumper the previous March and looked like a real monster. Incidentally, Monsignor's owner, Malcolm Denmark, went into partnership with Mark in order that the pair could buy Weathercock House. Brendan Powell had desperate luck with Monsignor. He had given him a great ride to win the Cheltenham Bumper the previous season as an unconsidered 50–1 shot, but he was on the sidelines with a punctured lung when the horse made his debut over hurdles, and Malcolm Denmark got Norman Williamson to ride him. Brendan never got the ride back, and Norman partnered him to all five of his hurdle race wins that season.

Ashley Park was also at Pitman's at the time. He had won the Derrinstown Stud Derby Trial at Leopardstown for Charles and Vincent O'Brien as a three-year-old, and I had ridden him to an impressive victory in his novice hurdle the previous February. He was a bit fragile, but talk of the Champion Hurdle did not appear to be too far-fetched. Hitman was there too, straight from Henry Cecil's yard and rated 110 on the Flat, as was Smarty, a decent handicap chaser, and Bank Avenue, who was being prepared for a tilt at the Charisma Gold Cup. And, of course, Ever Blessed, who had won three on the bounce the previous spring and who had fallen when travelling like a winner in a Grade 2 novice chase at Aintree in April. One of Ever Blessed's owners was John Skull, a top-class physio who looked after me and a lot of the other jockeys when necessity dictated. So it all looked very promising, with the rides set to be split between me, Carl Llewellyn and Mark's conditional rider, Liam Corcoran. I was dividing my time anyway between Mark and Jim, and I was also riding a bit for other trainers, including Simon Sherwood, Karl Burke and David Gandolfo.

It was at Pitman's that I met Dawn. She was working for Mark as a stable lass, riding out and mucking out, and we just hit it off from the start. She had come from the apprentice school in Newmarket and was with Mark before I ever started riding for him. I just asked her out one night and we started going out together. We had great craic together, though it was all fairly new to me. She was really only my second long-term girlfriend after Kay.

The first time I rode Ever Blessed in a race was in the Mercedes Benz Chase at Chepstow in early October 1999. This is the meeting that traditionally marks the real start of the National Hunt season. Before SIS and all the racing channels came along, it was the first meeting of the season that you were able to see on television, as the BBC always used to show the Mercedes Benz and two other races. I remember when I was a kid watching this meeting at home in the sitting room. You wouldn't have seen a horse jumping a fence on television since the Galway Festival in July, and it would put you in good form just knowing that the National Hunt season was about to crank into action.

The Mercedes Benz is often won by a young chaser, often a second-season chaser who is ahead of the handicapper. As a seven-year-old progressive horse, Ever Blessed fitted that description, and they backed him into favouritism to win it, which he promptly did. Chepstow is a tricky track, up and down hills with some tricky fences, so I just hunted him around out the back in the early stages and concentrated on getting him jumping before asking him to improve at the end of the back straight. We took it up from Rodney Farrant on Star Traveller before the second last, and he stayed on well.

Natasha, Mark's wife, said afterwards that he would go for the Charisma Gold Cup at Kempton if he was OK after the race, but he wasn't ready on time, so the plan after that was to go straight to the Hennessy. He had loads of problems, and Mark did a fantastic job with him even to get him to Newbury. He had terrible trouble with his shoulder, and Mark had acupuncturist Chris Day down to see him regularly before the Hennessy, and again after the Hennessy. Everything went right before the race itself, though. Mark was agonising over whether or not he should run him on ground that looked like it would be faster than he liked. The last thing you want to do with a horse that has a shoulder problem is run him on fast ground. But the rain came the night before the Hennessy, a third of an inch of it, and turned the ground to good to soft, so there was no decision to be made.

The other concern was that, with Suny Bay in the race compressing the weights, Ever Blessed was going to have to run from ten pounds out of the handicap. Here's the science bit. Ever Blessed was rated 126 and Suny Bay was rated 160, which meant that in a handicap, Suny Bay would have to carry 34 pounds more than Ever Blessed. However, as the top weight in the Hennessy had to be 11st 10lb, and the bottom weight could carry no less than ten stone, Suny Bay could carry only a maximum of 24 pounds more than Ever Blessed. In spite of this, they backed Ever Blessed from 6–1 down to 9–2 favourite.

People used to say that Ever Blessed was a great jumper. Let me put the record straight. He wasn't. He really wasn't. And he was keen, so you always had to drop him in and get him to settle. There were only thirteen runners in the Hennessy that year, which is small for a Hennessy, probably because Suny Bay was keeping the weights down: if you weren't rated 136 or more you were going to have to compete from out of the handicap. So it made it easier to make ground from the back than if there had been a big field.

I dropped him in for a circuit and just crept around, until we got to the back straight on the final circuit when I pulled him wide in order to try to make some ground. He jumped really well down the back straight and got himself back into contention. In fact, going to the cross fence, the fifth last, he was one of only four horses who could win it, the other three being Earthmover, trained by Paul Nicholls with Joe Tizzard up; Spendid, who had won the Grade 2 race at Aintree in which Ever Blessed had fallen, so we had a score to settle there; and Fiddling the Facts, with Mick Fitzgerald up. Earthmover tried to take the cross fence home with him, he absolutely clobbered it, so that effectively ended his chance. I sat on Ever Blessed and didn't ask him to do too much early in the home straight. It's a long way home at Newbury, over four fences, from the top of the home straight to the line, and many a race is lost on the run-in by going on too early. Ever Blessed was staying on and staying on, and we took it up at the third last, but then he started hanging to his left and jumping to his left, so I had to try to straighten him up as well as ask him to go forward. He made a mistake at the last, but he ran on well to beat Spendid by about four lengths in the end.

I got a hell of a kick out of that. Everybody did. It was Mark's biggest success as a trainer, and it was a hell of a training performance given how many problems Ever Blessed had had. On top of everything, I didn't know it at the time but he had pulled a shoe off somewhere during the race, which possibly explained his tendency to hang to his left up the home straight. It was also a big win for me. I needed all the exposure I could get, and the Hennessy is the biggest race on the landscape by far between the November meeting at Cheltenham and Christmas. Ever Blessed was quoted at as short as 20–1 for the Gold Cup and Grand National after that, but, alas, his problems got the better of him. He didn't run again until the 2000 Gold Cup itself, in which he was never travelling and I had to pull him up. He never reached his Hennessy level of performance again, but he had had his day in the sun, and he had provided us with ours.

In spite of the exposure the Hennessy win afforded me, I didn't notice a huge surge in demand for my services. When you are a freelance, or associated with a relatively small stable, you have to wait for the spare rides to come up. Of course you never wish any misfortune to befall any of your fellow jockeys. National Hunt jockeys are a very close-knit bunch; we all look out for each other. I suppose we have to, given that calamity lurks over the next open ditch. While everyone is a competitor, and we compete against each other, we are also colleagues, and very close colleagues at that. There aren't many professions in which you face as much danger every day. It makes us closer as a group, probably closer as a group than Flat race jockeys. You notice the different atmosphere between the Flat jockeys on days when we share the weigh room, like on Betfred Gold Cup day at Sandown, when you have Flat and jumps races. Anyway, while you don't wish for any of your colleagues to get injured or suspended, the reality is that that is how the spare rides come up. Jim Old had only about 45 horses so I wasn't riding for him in every race. You're also waiting for the big days, when there are a lot of meetings on and the big yards have runners at more than one meeting.

But Jim was great and Mark was great. Mark suffered a bit of a setback in the middle of that season when Robert Hitchins, who owned a host of horses with Mark's mother, including Princeful and Toby Tobias, and had been one of Mark's main owners, took all his horses away. But Mark didn't let it affect him. He just put his head down and drove on. His business partner, Malcolm Denmark, increased the number of horses in which he was involved to fourteen, and everybody worked hard.

I loved riding for Mark and Jim. They didn't tie me to instructions too much and I didn't feel like I was under huge pressure. I was allowed to ride as I wanted to ride. I enjoyed the flexibility to be able to ride a horse as I found him, not to have to have him handy if I felt that he wasn't able to go the early pace. I was allowed to ride my own race. I enjoyed it more, and I'm sure that we had more success that way. There was no 'This'll win'. You weren't riding to have to win, you were riding to get the best out of your horse and achieve the best possible finishing position, and often the best possible finishing position was first place. They weren't all odds-on shots that were expected to win. When you ride a favourite or an odds-on shot, you are on a hiding to nothing. There's the pressure. If you win, you have achieved no more than was expected; if you lose, questions are asked. It's back to the penalty analogy. When you ride an odds-on shot, you are the penalty taker; when you ride a horse that is odds against or not favourite, you are the goalkeeper. No pressure. It was a different frame of mind for me. Of course I wanted to win and I rode to win, but I didn't feel like I had to force it. Better to just let it happen. Ride the horse to his strengths and position him to win. There was more craft in that, more guile; it was more of a test of your ability as a jockey, as a horseman. More use your judgement, less stick to these instructions. If it doesn't happen today, it will happen tomorrow. Make sure there's another day.

I had a pretty quiet Cheltenham Festival in 2000. I rode Ashley Park for Mark in the Champion Hurdle and he ran a remarkable race to finish fourth behind Istabraq. He had terrible trouble with his legs. As a result, that was his first race in over a year and only his second hurdle race ever. Again, it was a hell of a training performance by Mark to get him to Cheltenham as well as he was. We were hoping to run him at Aintree, but his problems resurfaced and we didn't get him there. In fact, he only ran once more, in the Christmas Hurdle at Kempton the following December. He would have won but I felt him go wrong on the run-in and just nursed him home. We ended up getting beaten by Geos by a head.

That Ashley Park ride was about as close as I got to a winner at Cheltenham that year. I got fairly close, I suppose, to winning the Sun Alliance Hurdle as Monsignor won it, but, like I said, he was Norman's mount. I'm not sure how close I came to getting the ride, but I suppose I could have had no complaints. Norman was riding a lot for Monsignor's owner, Malcolm Denmark, and he probably wanted someone with Norman's experience. In truth, there was hardly a better National Hunt rider in the weigh room at the time than Norman. As I said, it was far rougher on Brendan Powell than it was on me. I was delighted for Norman and for the yard. I actually finished last in the race on Romero for John Akehurst. Monsignor would have made a smashing chaser but, sadly, problems beset him after that and he never raced again.

I rode The Outback Way for Venetia Williams in the Champion Chase. Norman was riding most of Venetia's horses, but he got off The Outback Way to ride Direct Route for Howard Johnson. That was the race in which Direct Route and Edredon Bleu went head to head up the entire run-in and all the way to the line. Nobody knew who had won. Even the freeze frame on the line wasn't conclusive. In the end, Norman came out the wrong side of the photo, and it was another festival winner for McCoy. I also rode Alta for Nigel Twiston-Davies in the Coral Cup, Zaffre Noir in the Bumper, Count Campioni in the Stayers' Hurdle, Ever Blessed in the Gold Cup and Browjoshy in the SunAlliance Chase for Mark, and Kattegat for Jim in the Triumph Hurdle. All out with the washing. I almost salvaged the meeting in the last race, the County Hurdle, on Danegold for Mick Channon. We were third last jumping two from home, but he fairly took off up the hill and failed by just a neck to catch Master Tern and Tony Dobbin.

It was a blank Cheltenham, then, which capped a moderate season. Jim Old had had a terrible year. Most of his horses were just out of sorts. That's the way the game goes. It wasn't great for me, but I was lucky in that I had Mark Pitman and other trainers to fall back on. Jim just had to grin and bear it as best he could, and ride out the storm. I had 64 winners that season, down nine on my previous season's total – the first time that had happened since arriving in England. I suppose it wasn't so bad, however, considering that Jim had such a bad year and I was basically just picking up rides for others outside Jim's.

The 2000/01 season wasn't any better for me. In fact, things got decidedly worse. Mark had a lot of horses, but no real stars. Ever Blessed was gone and Ashley Park would only race once. There was also Monsignor, who wouldn't race again, and Patriarch, but he was owned by Malcolm Denmark and was Norman's ride. Jameson, Cruise The Fairway, Hitman, Jet Tabs, Smarty, and a nice young horse Mark's father Richard had bought from Tom Costello called Too Forward were there but it didn't look very promising.

There weren't many highlights for me that season. I rode Mac's Supreme to win the Kerry National for Ferdy Murphy at Listowel in September 2000. I had never before ridden for Ferdy, but Adrian Maguire, who was riding most of Ferdy's horses at the time, was out injured, and he suggested to Ferdy that I should ride. The prize money in Ireland was just beginning to increase around that time, and there was a fair pot for winning that, about IR£40,000. In September, Listowel is the only jumps game in town, and the Kerry National is the feature race of the festival, so that was a good one to win.

I also won the Badger Beer Chase at Wincanton – I realise we're scraping a little for highlights when we're talking about the Badger Beer Chase at Wincanton, but there is a significance to this one – on Flaked Oats for Paul Nicholls. I wasn't back in favour with Nicholls especially; this was just a spare. Mick Fitzgerald rode the stable's first choice, Ad

Hoc, in the race, and was just about to challenge me when he fell at the last. I thought I had the race in the bag after I saw him go down, and eased up on the run-in, only for King's Road to come with a late run and almost do me. That was a long photo finish, and it would have been disastrous if it had gone the wrong way, both from the point of view of my relationship with Nicholls and his owners, and due to the altogether more pragmatic fact that I would have been suspended for a minimum of 28 days for easing up prematurely and getting beaten. Fortunately, the short head verdict went in our favour. But Ad Hoc was Nicholls' Hennessy horse that season, and I think he was more disappointed about his fall than he was happy about Flaked Oats' win.

Ironically, I rode Ad Hoc in the Hennessy three weeks later. Mick was out injured and Joe rode Nicholls' other runner, the 33–1 shot Norski Lad. I don't really know why Joe, the stable jockey, was on the 33–1 shot and I was on the stable's number one. Anyway, Ad Hoc was travelling really well turning out of the back straight and I was just beginning to think that I could land back-to-back Hennessys on two different horses when we met the fifth last, the cross fence, all wrong and came crashing down. In another ironic twist – isn't this game full of them? – the race was won by King's Road, the horse that had almost got up to beat me and Flaked Oats in the Badger Beer Chase three weeks earlier.

I won the Warwickshire Gold Cup for Mark on Browjoshy, who looked like he might join Smarty in the Grand National, but he suffered a setback in March 2001 and National plans had to be scrapped. And there were other lowlights. Plenty of them. Ashley Park's injury was one. He definitely would have beaten Geos in the Christmas Hurdle that year had he not gone lame just before the line, and we really thought we had a chance of beating Istabraq in the Champion Hurdle that season. He was a classy horse, but his legs were like glass. It was a near-fore ligament that had given him trouble in the past, but it was his off-fore fetlock that went at Kempton. We had to constantly tread on eggshells with him, but unfortunately, after that the eggshells just couldn't stand up to the pressure any more.

As it happened, even if we had managed to get him back on time it would have been all for nothing that year. There was no Champion Hurdle, no Gold Cup, no Cheltenham Festival. The outbreak of foot and mouth disease scuppered it for the lot of us. It was a largely frustrating time for everybody connected with racing. At least I didn't have anything that had a huge chance of winning at Cheltenham. I couldn't imagine how Charlie Swan, Aidan O'Brien or J. P. McManus felt. It would have taken something extraordinary to stop Istabraq winning an historic fourth Champion Hurdle that year. Enter foot and mouth – something extraordinary. And Henrietta Knight was looking forward to her exciting novice chaser Best Mate lining up in the Arkle. Alas, he would have to wait until the following year to taste Cheltenham Festival success. Once he did, he couldn't get enough of it. The Willie Mullins-trained Florida Pearl was gearing up for the Gold Cup, as was Nicky Henderson's Marlborough. As Henderson's stable jockey, Mick Fitzgerald was committed to Marlborough, owned by Robert Ogden, which meant that Nicholls and Barber were looking for a new jockey for See More Business. Ironically, Robert Ogden had bought a share in See More Business by that stage as well. My name was in the pot, as were McCoy's and Johnson's. Eventually they asked Ruby Walsh to ride him. I wasn't too put out. I hadn't held out much hope anyway. And, of course, it was all irrelevant.

It was a difficult time for all of us. You didn't really know when racing was going to be on or off, and you couldn't go away because it could be back on at any time. You had to stick around, but you couldn't really plan anything. At least there was a good group of us around Faringdon, so we'd often do something together – a bit of karting, a bit of golf. It was basically a summer break in the middle of winter.

Off the track, there was a huge highlight: my son Shane was born in December 2000. He was amazing. They say there aren't any modern-day miracles. Well, Shane is one. Two arms, two legs, ten fingers, a head right in the middle of his shoulders, not too big, and all his bits where they should be. A proper little modern-day miracle. A little person, a new helpless little entry to the world, and he was my and Dawn's responsibility. I loved that he was there, but I have to admit that I hardly altered my lifestyle at all. I didn't neglect him, I thought the world of him, but I guess I just didn't think deeply enough about my responsibilities. Dawn did everything with him while I was out earning a living for all of us. Dawn and I had our moments, but I didn't invest enough in the relationship, and as a result she had a tough time with me. I just carried on as normal, going out on Saturday night, getting up late on Sunday, going down to the pub on Sunday afternoon and staying until late Sunday night. Then I'd be flat out during the week, riding work wherever I could, and every morning if I could, and going racing. Basically, I just carried on as if I was single. The fact that I should have been thinking about others now as well as myself when making plans didn't really register with me. Dawn had always been a poor third on my list of priorities after riding and drinking, and I'm sure that continued to frustrate the hell out of her.

But I was frustrated myself. This wasn't where I imagined I would be five years after leaving Ireland. I was supposed to be champion jockey by now, but I wasn't even close. Ashley Park was gone and, when I thought about it, while I was hugely disappointed that Cheltenham was called off, I couldn't point to a horse in any of the races and say, 'There, I would have won on that.' This wasn't where I should have been. I was a good rider. I was as good as these Williamsons, Maguires, Dunwoodys and McCoys. I should have had one of those top jobs. I should have had a plethora of good horses at my disposal. Good jockeys ride good horses, and I was a good jockey. Where were the good horses?

But I was missing the bigger picture. The truth was that I had been on a fast track to that destination, but I blew it. I had been on the fast track when I was at Bailey's, one of the top yards in the country at the time, but I blew that. I was lucky enough to get on track again with Nicholls, and I blew that as well. I must have been doing something right to get the jobs, but I had to have been doing something very wrong to lose them. That was the bit that I couldn't see. There was more to being a top rider than riding.

I was beginning to cop myself on a bit, though. I don't think I ever arrived at work at Jim Old's drunk or late, and I definitely didn't miss a day's work because I had been out the night before. I would often arrive in bad form. Jim said that I was unplayable. I would just be in bad form with myself and with the world, largely because I was frustrated with where I was. The number of good horses I was riding was limited and I couldn't see where they were going to come from.

I remember schooling a horse at Jim's one morning. He had just come back from injury and was a little bit fresh. Jim told me to take it handy with him as he was liable to try to run away with me, but he was a great jumper, so just get him settled and pop the three fences. Sure enough, the horse tried to take off with me as soon as he saw the line of fences. I couldn't hold one side of him. He was just so fresh and well and delighted with himself at being able to jump again. I'm not sure how I managed to stay on over the three fences. I was just a passenger. He wasn't heeding me at all.

I eventually managed to pull him up at the bottom of the school, and looked back down. Jim was almost falling off his old hack he was laughing so much. 'Right,' I thought, 'I'll teach this fellow a lesson.' I turned him round and headed back down the school in the wrong direction. Although schooling fences are smaller than the fences on the racecourse, they are built the same. There is an apron on the take-off side that helps horses to stand off the fence. The landing side is just sheer, a bank of birch. You are absolutely not supposed to jump them from the landing side. Fortunately, the horse managed to jump all three fences without doing serious damage to himself or me. Both he and Jim were a lot quieter when I got to the bottom. Jim should have read me the riot act. It was an absolutely stupid thing to do and it was lucky that neither I nor the horse was damaged irreparably. Don't try this at home. It didn't seem to do the horse any harm, however, as he went out and won a week later.

I was getting better with the whip. I was managing to contain my frustration a little better with animals that weren't doing it for me. The days when I would be suspended for using my whip with 'excessive frequency and force when out of contention' were becoming less and less commonplace. But I was banned for Easter 2001 for a ridiculous incident in a hurdle race at Ascot in April. I led over the third last on Romero and edged towards the inside where the rail runs out before you swing for home. Norman Williamson on Spring Margot came up on my outside before the home turn, kind of cutting me off, so I had to edge out otherwise I would have gone the wrong side of the rail that brings you into the home straight. The stewards gave me three days for overtaking on the inside. Overtaking on the inside, after I had been in front! I felt like I was banging my head off a wall with them. I didn't appeal. I didn't see the point.

Luckily, racing was back after the foot and mouth ban in time for the Aintree Grand National meeting. Smarty had had the National as his long-term plan since he won a handicap chase at Leicester the previous December, and he was in great shape leading up to the race. I had pulled him up at Uttoxeter on his previous start, but he hated Uttoxeter, especially when the ground was heavy. Heavy ground at Uttoxeter is unlike heavy ground anywhere else, so we weren't too worried about it. The prospect of very soft ground at Aintree was a bit of a concern, but he had won on it before and we were hopeful.

The 2001 Grand National is one of those Nationals that will always be remembered for the bizarreness of the race rather than for the actual result. The Devon Loch dive in 1956, Foinavon in 1967, the void race in 1993 and the quagmire that was 2001, where only four horses finished, two of them after being remounted. There was huge doubt over the race going ahead, even on the Saturday morning, the day of the race. We had had so much rain that the ground was almost unraceable. People said afterwards that it shouldn't have gone ahead, that the ground was too bad and it was just too much to ask horses to compete over four and a half miles and 30 of the biggest fences that can be found on any racecourse in the UK or Ireland on such ground. Perhaps it would have been abandoned or at least postponed if there had been no foot and mouth that

year and if Cheltenham had gone ahead. Perhaps not. I was delighted
that the race was run anyway.

Smarty and I were lucky to avoid the pile-up at the Canal Turn on the
first circuit when the blinkered and riderless Paddy's Return decided
not to jump the fence and inadvertently took with him the vast majority
of the horses that still had riders. We were left in third place after the
nineteenth fence, and when Beau got rid of Carl Llewellyn at the next, we
were second, behind what looked like Richard Guest on Red Marauder,
although it was difficult to know because his silks were almost black with
mud and rain. When I looked round I was amazed to see that there was
nothing else behind me with a rider on its back. I looked again just to be
sure. Yep, just loose horses and destruction behind. I concentrated on
what was ahead of me – Richard Guest and eight fences.

Red Marauder hit the last ditch so hard that I was sure he couldn't
have survived. As Smarty and I went on, I was almost certain that we had
to be the only ones left standing. Then, going to the second last, Red
Marauder loomed back upsides us again. Even so, I thought for a split
second that we might win it, the Grand National that I had won so many
times in the field out the back of the house. But it was only for a split
second. Smarty hardly had an ounce of energy left in him and Red
Marauder looked to be travelling OK. He went on before the second last,
when Smarty had nothing left to give. I left him off and just concentrated
on getting Smarty over the last two and home. He managed to negotiate
them OK and came home in second place, a distance behind Red
Marauder – probably the worst jumper ever to win the Grand National.

There is often an element of disappointment when you finish second.
You wonder if you'd done something differently whether you'd have
been able to make up the deficit. But I had no such thoughts after the 2001
Grand National. There was nothing I could have done differently.

I was delighted for the owner, Tracy Brown. She also owned Ashley
Park, and she deserved a little bit of luck that year. I was also delighted
for Mark. It was his first ever runner in the Grand National. Of course, his
family is synonymous with the race. It was his father Richard who rode

the joint-favourite Crisp in the 1973 renewal and led almost all the way until about twenty yards from the line when a young whipper-snapper eight-year-old with 10st 5lb on his back, Red Rum, got up to do him. And Mark's mother Jenny, of course, was the first woman ever to train the winner of the Grand National, when Corbiere staved off the late challenge of Greasepaint. Mark himself came close on his mother's Garrison Savannah in 1991, landing clear over the last only to be caught on the run-in by Seagram. He was second again now as a trainer, but he was delighted with that.

Meanwhile, in Ireland, the racing calendar was all over the place that year. People were extremely diligent in their efforts to keep the country foot and mouth free, and all animal-related activity was severely disrupted as a result. Everything to do with horses – racing, point-to-pointing, show jumping, breeding, sales – and everything to do with farming was affected. And on top of all that, Punchestown had their own problems with mole drains on the racecourse that year. They closed the track in December with the intention of having it ready in time for the festival in April, but they didn't make it. A little controversially, the Turf Club declared the track unfit for racing. So we lost the Irish Grand National meeting at Fairyhouse over Easter due to foot an mouth and Punchestown wasn't able to stage its festival. The authorities did a fair job of rescheduling the meetings, however, so we had this unusual situation where the first three days of the Punchestown Festival were run at Fairyhouse at the end of April, with the final day being run at Leopardstown, and the Fairyhouse Easter meeting, including the Irish Grand National, being run three weeks later, also at Fairyhouse.

Ireland was fairly well wrapped up by the home jockeys and it was difficult for an English-based jockey, even an Irish English-based jockey, to get rides in Ireland in those days. I used to go over during the summer a bit to try to pick up spares, especially lightweights in handicaps when Ruby Walsh or Barry Geraghty or some of the top guys wouldn't be getting down to do the weight. I could do ten stone no problem. Tony

My dad and I after riding out.

Robert Byrne and I taking time out at pony racing.

On board Bluebell at our local gymkhana.

*Posing for Mam before my first ride in a
point-to-point in Gowran Park.*

With Bluebell again, looking a little grumpy!

Competing in a point-to-point on a Michael Hourigan horse. I managed to stay on (somehow!) and went on to win.

Winning the Mitsubishi Shogun Trophy at Cheltenham on Call Equiname on my only ever ride on him in public.

Riding Smarty to finish second in the Grand National.

Winners enclosure with Valley Henry after the Telebet Novices Chase at Newbury.

Top: *Winning on Dawn Leader (left) the Aldaniti Novices Chase at Sandown.*

Westender wins at Cheltenham.

In the weighing room.

Riding Best Mate to victory at Exeter in what was to be his final win.

Aboard Davids Lad at Roscommon.

Being congratulated by the lads after Beef or Salmon had just won the Ericsson Chase at Leopardstown.

Celestial Gold wins the Melling Chase at Aintree

Beef or Salmon wins the Heineken Gold Cup at Punchestown

With Michael Hourigan and Hi Cloy

With Mark Pitman and his wife Natasha with Ever Blessed after winning the Hennessy Gold Cup at Newbury.

Above: *Henrietta Knight walks alongside me on board Racing Demon, who won his race the day Best Mate died.*

Left: *Teeing off at a charity golf day. Not sure where the ball ended up.*

On board Celestial Gold, on the way to winning the Paddy Power Gold Cup.

With David Johnson, Martin Pipe and the Paddy Power Gold Cup trophy.

Being presented with my 'Lester' by Sir Peter O'Sullevan.

Martin (Harvey, they call him) asked me if I would ride Davids Lad for him in a handicap chase on the third day of the Punchestown Festival, at Fairyhouse, if you follow. Harvey had been preparing him for a crack at the Kim Muir at Cheltenham, but obviously that plan had to be scotched. He reckoned that my riding style would suit Davids Lad. He liked to be ridden nice and quietly out the back, and that was how I liked to do things.

I came over for just two rides at the festival, both of them on the same day, both of them for Harvey. I finished well down the field in the novices' hurdle on Simply Honest, but I won the handicap chase on Davids Lad. The race just went like clockwork for me. They went off too fast and I settled him out the back. He jumped well and just carried me there. I was surprised that we won by twenty lengths, but they had gone off so fast that the margin probably flattered him. Surely the handicapper would understand. Harvey didn't. He was a bit annoyed that I'd let him win by so far. The handicapper would hammer him, he told me. How was he going to win the Irish Grand National now? In spite of this, he asked me to ride him in the Irish National three weeks later.

There was something surreal about the Irish National being run on 6 May, but we got on with it anyway. And the handicapper did hammer Davids Lad. He raised him sixteen pounds for winning at Fairyhouse, which I thought was really harsh given that the field had patently gone too quickly in the early stages and the leaders just died away. However, the good news was that he still got to carry bottom weight of ten stone. In fact, he was three pounds out of the handicap. As it turned out, then, it was just as well that we did win that handicap by as far as we did, otherwise we might not even have got a run in the Irish National. Perhaps the fact that he was on ten stone influenced Harvey's decision to ask me to ride him again. Commanche Court carried top weight of twelve stone, which meant that the weights were kept well down. The second highest weight was 10st 13lb, so if Commanche Court hadn't run, the weights would have gone up by a stone and a pound. Just as well he did run.

The Irish National panned out even better for me than the handicap chase had three weeks earlier. It was one of those races in which everything just went right. In fact, I would go so far as to say that it was the best ride I have ever given a horse. Everything just flowed. There was no take a tug here, no ask him to quicken there, no ride him into this fence or shorten him up at that one. Everything just worked out as smooth as silk. Poetry. He took me where I wanted to go in the race. When I wanted him to cruise, he cruised; when I wanted him to move forward, the gaps just opened up and he took me there. It was like driving a Ferrari around Silverstone among a load of Trabants. We joined Rathbawn Prince going to the last, pinged the fence like we had all 22 others, and just quickened away nicely to win cosily. I'd say I had a smug smile on my face for weeks afterwards.

So the 2000/01 season didn't end too badly. My total of 54 winners in the UK was my lowest haul in four years, but at least I could blame foot and mouth for some of it. I had ended the season on a high by riding the second in the Aintree National and the winner of the Irish National, and I had ridden as close to the perfect race as you could imagine in the latter. I didn't know it at the time, but there was a development afoot that would give my career another turbo boost. Be careful how and when you ascend, however, because what goes up must, at some point, succumb to gravity.

If you had plotted a graph of my career at that point, you would have had more sharp peaks and deep troughs than a lie-detector machine attached to a politician. There was another peak around the corner, as high as any I had scaled before. Somewhat appropriately, however, there was also a trough as deep as any I had ever before experienced or witnessed, or even imagined. It was a trough out of which it would be extremely difficult to clamber.

CHAPTER ELEVEN

MAJOR LEAGUE

Broady rang me one morning in May 2001. 'Bad news, Timmy. Nicholls wants you back.'

It wasn't a total surprise. There had been rumblings about Nicholls and Barber not being too happy with Joe Tizzard. I'm not sure that Joe did anything really wrong, but he was quite young and inexperienced for such a big job, and they just got to thinking that he wasn't up to it, that he hadn't grown with the yard or into the job. The racecourse rumour was that Joe wasn't going to be stable jockey for 2001/02, and it is rare that these racecourse rumours are not spot on the money.

It was tough on Joe. He had been thrown into the role as a teenager, pitched into the deep end as stable jockey for one of the biggest trainers in the country, with all the pressure that brings. I'm not sure he wasn't able for it. Like I say, he didn't really do anything wrong, but the word was that Nicholls' owners wanted a big-name jockey.

Actually, the jockey situation at Nicholls' was all a bit messy at the time. Joe was there, ostensibly stable jockey, but he wasn't riding the top horses in the top races if they could help it. Fitzy was actually riding as first jockey whenever he was available, but he was also first jockey to Nicky Henderson, another of the big trainers in the country, so the likelihood was that Fitzy would be committed to something else in the big races. Henderson didn't have a runner in the Gold Cup in 2000, which meant that Fitzy was free to partner See More Business, but he had Marlborough gearing up for 2001, which meant that Fitzy wasn't free for See More. But they didn't want Joe. Not in the Gold Cup.

Enter Ruby Walsh. He was all set to partner See More Business in the

Gold Cup before The Cheltenham Festival was abandoned, and he rode for them a little bit that spring. He rode Fadalko to win the Melling Chase at Aintree, and he rode him again when he was beaten a short head by Edredon Bleu in the two-mile Championship Chase at Sandown's Whitbread meeting. Then he went and rode Ad Hoc to win the Whitbread itself by half the track. Word was that Ruby had been offered the job as first jockey to Nicholls, but that he had turned it down. He would have been giving up too much if he had left Ireland, as he was riding for Willie Mullins and for his dad, Ted, who had some cracking horses at the time, including Papillon and Commanche Court. So it looked like I was holding the parcel when the music stopped.

Nicholls had rung Broady a couple of times even before that. Broady would tell me. I'm sure Nicholls knew that he would, so perhaps it was his way of letting me know that things weren't working and I might be able to get my old job back. Who knows. Paul Barber had told Jim Old that he had heard Murphy was a changed man, and had congratulated Jim on what a wonderful job he had done in turning me around. Jim laughed to himself. He had done feck all to turn me around, he reckoned, and he wasn't even sure if I had turned around. He just smiled at Barber and nodded. 'He's got the most natural talent of any jockey I have ever seen.'

Joe Tizzard won the Aon Chase on Shotgun Willy, beating First Gold, and Nicholls came out in support of him, saying that he was a really good rider and a great team player, and that he hoped that more owners would appreciate his ability and use him. When it came to the big races, however, Joe just wasn't wanted. He was jocked off Earthmover, who was second favourite at the time and whom they really fancied, in the Grand National in order to make way for Fitzy, in spite of the fact that Joe had ridden the horse in fifteen of his eighteen races, including when he won the Foxhunter at Cheltenham, and Fitzy had only ridden him once. Owners again. Joe was set to ride Mister One for his father, Colin, until Henderson claimed Fitzy for Esprit De Cotte and Joe was back on Earthmover again.

I was led to believe that it was the owners who were putting pressure on Nicholls, but I don't know how he coped with all the shenanigans about the jockey situation. It must have been a full-time job managing the different owners' jockey demands. John Keighley wanted Tizzard, Paul Barber wanted Fitzy, and Robert Ogden wanted Fitzy, and if not he wanted Ruby, but Fitzy and Ruby had their own commitments. It must have been a nightmare. You have to get on with owners, but surely there comes a point when you put your foot down. I'm sure it would have been difficult to say that to owners like Paul Barber and Robert Ogden, but Nicholls was one of the top trainers in the country and he probably didn't fully realise the strength of his bargaining position. It is true the fact that Barber was his landlord added an extra complication, and Nicholls blinked first.

Nicholls says that letting Joe know that he wouldn't be first jockey any more was one of the most difficult things he has had to do in his career, and I believe him. He says that he was nearly crying telling him. Joe had been so good, so loyal, such a great team player, and he put so much into his job, but at the end of the day the main owners in the yard wanted a higher-profile jockey, a name jockey.

So I was asked to enter this world again. It was a strange one. I had gone from being the yard's number one rider, with Joe as number two, to being used by the yard when Joe wasn't available, to being used when Fitzy or Ruby or any of the other top lads or Joe weren't available, to being asked to be stable jockey again. There was some talk about Fitzy riding all the Ogden horses in the yard, which included Fadalko and Ad Hoc. More messing. I asked Broady what he thought I should do. From his perspective, as my agent, it was a no-brainer. I would be riding good horses in good races, with a real chance of winning lots of prize money. As a jockey's agent is remunerated in proportion to the prize money his jockey wins, it would be a great deal for Broady. And he'd have less work to do, in theory. I would be riding for Nicholls in a set number of races every day, so he wouldn't have to go haring after a lot of smaller trainers all the time. But Chris is a friend as well as an agent, and he considered my situation, the type of job it would be, the pressure I would be under, and the job satisfaction, and he still thought I should take it. Why they wanted me was the next question. They're not happy with Joe; the owners aren't happy with Joe. We didn't know that Ruby had turned it down at the time. It wouldn't have mattered anyway.

I spoke to Jim and Mark. They were great, just like Jeff King had been great when I joined Nicholls the first time. That's why I still get on so well with the three of them. They totally understood. Nicholls had one of the strongest stables of horses in the country, second only to Martin Pipe. Indeed, he had finished second in the trainers' championship to Pipe in each of the last three seasons. He was a young, ambitious trainer who had owners with money to spend on horses and he was probably only going to get better. It was a great job, and both Jim and Mark told me as much. They didn't have the horses to be able to compete with what Nicholls could offer me. I'd be mad not to take it.

So I went down to Nicholls' place in Ditcheat and we talked through the role. I told him I would be delighted to join him again, but that I would want a retainer. He told me a retainer wouldn't be a problem, but that they didn't do written contracts or anything, so we'd just agree a retainer. I didn't ask for a lot. I should have asked for £50,000, but I only asked for £30,000, and they said sure, no problem. But I never got it. I just started riding, and I started riding winners, so I didn't think about the retainer really. Everybody was happy when the winners were going in. Like I've said before, success can paper over a lot of cracks. I suppose I thought it might be a little ungracious of me to go looking for my retainer when they were providing me with all these winners. Perhaps I thought I would get it at the end of the season. But nobody could have envisaged the way that season was to end. A £30,000 retainer that was outstanding was the last thing on anybody's mind.

We got off to a flyer straight away. You usually don't get good horses running during the summer, but Nicholls had about 25 horses specifically for the summer and we had winners at Stratford, Worcester, Market Rasen and a lot of those summer jumping fixtures. I even got some time to hop over to Ireland for the Tralee Festival and ride a couple of winners there. I also continued to ride for Mark, Jim and David Gandolfo, but Nicholls had so many horses that there was no guarantee I would be available for them when they needed me.

It was great. Horses like Ad Hoc, Fadalko, Cenkos, Valley Henry, Azertyuiop, Vol Solitaire, Kadarann and, of course, See More, although he was getting towards the dusk of his career. This was more like it. This was very close to what I wanted. These were the types of horses I needed to ride. No more sitting on the substitutes' bench, waiting for some ill to befall one of my colleagues so that I could get a chance of a decent spare ride. I was now in pole position in one of the strongest yards in the country, and it felt right.

I remember riding Armaturk in a hurdle race at Kempton that October against Jair Du Cochet, the new French kid on the block, a four-year-old that looked like a monster, and Impek, trained by Henrietta Knight. Paul told me to nick what I could out of the gate and go as fast as I could for the two miles. This horse was fit and we might catch them napping. So I did. I went as fast as I dared the whole way and held on to win by a neck from Impek. Paul told me afterwards that it was a great ride. I think he forgot himself for a second.

But I now had a better understanding with Paul, or rather he had a better understanding of me. He knew I wasn't one for the all-singing, all-dancing 'this horse is really great, honestly, he just looks useless, but when he gets a bit of good ground, or when he goes over a trip, you'll see a different horse' routine with the owners in the unsaddling area, so he kind of kept me away from that. He did most of the communicating with the owners and left the riding to me, with instructions, but not as inflexible as they had been three years earlier.

Other things started to go right. Chris thought it would be a good idea if I gave up drink for a year, to coincide with my return to Nicholls'. 'Just give it a go, Timmy. Just see if you can do it. It might do you good. You might feel better for it.' I'm not sure if he thought I was drinking too much or if he just wanted to ensure that I didn't blow the Nicholls job again. 'Of course I can do it,' I thought. 'I'll tell you what,' I said to him, 'I'll give it up till Christmas.' And I did. I managed to get to Christmas, though I have to admit I was dying for Christmas to come round that year, and soon I was back drinking as good or as bad as ever, depending on your perspective. I had succeeded in giving it up for four months in total, though, and I had proved to Broady and to myself that I could do it. Nothing to it. I didn't particularly enjoy not drinking, however, and I didn't think that it did me any good really. I was just delighted to be able to have a drink again at Christmas. After Christmas I went drinking and partied hard. So much for responsibilities.

While my whip-happy days weren't completely behind me, I was a lot better about it than I had ever been. It was a combination of a more settled frame of mind and the fact that I was riding better horses. I got done for three days at Taunton for hitting Lady Vienna, who really wasn't much good, with undue frequency when out of contention in the selling hurdle. That annoyed me because it ruled me out of the Peterborough Chase meeting at Huntingdon and the Becher Chase at Aintree, in which I was due to ride Smarty. I considered appealing, but I would have been appealing out of frustration at missing such a good weekend for a misdemeanour in a selling hurdle at Taunton, so I figured there wasn't really any point. You couldn't make this stuff up. Norman Williamson ended up riding Smarty in the Becher Chase and he finished second to Amberleigh House.

I had ridden 50 winners by November. That was my fastest 50 ever by a long way. I was third in the jockeys' table, and I wasn't losing that many days due to injury or suspension. I took a pretty bad fall at Fairyhouse in January 2002 when the horse I was riding, Darbys Bridge, fell and caused an eight-horse pile-up. The poor horse was killed instantly and I suffered bruising to my lower back, concussion and a cut lip, for which I had to get stitches. I was taken away to Blanchardstown Hospital feeling pretty shaken, and I was out of action for almost two weeks. Then I got a shoulder injury in February that just wouldn't get better. I'm sure I tried to rush back too quickly. When I thought it was nearly better I'd be off riding again, but I would only aggravate it and it kept me out of action on and off for a couple of weeks. In fact, it nearly kept me out of the Cheltenham Festival, as I had only three days' racing between the time I injured it at Plumpton on 7 February and the Wincanton meeting the week before the festival, a month later. I rode a double from three rides at that Wincanton meeting, thus dispelling any doubts that anyone had about my fitness.

Nicholls had a good team lined up for the 2002 Cheltenham Festival. I hadn't ridden a winner for him at the festival before, but I was sure I would that year. Alas, I didn't. I finished third on Armaturk in the Arkle on the first day behind Moscow Flyer and Seebald, so no real disgrace there. It would have been a fair leap of faith to think that we could have beaten Seebald, given that he had kicked us off the park in the Grade 2 novice chase run over the same course and distance the previous November. Cenkos had no right to beat Flagship Uberalles, Edredon Bleu or Tiutchev in the Champion Chase the following day, but when we rounded the home turn in front I thought we were going to. It had rained the night before and the ground was riding a little on the slow side, which wouldn't have suited any of the big guns except Flagship Uberalles. I had looked round at the top of the hill and seen that he wasn't travelling so well, until he came round the home turn and faced up to the last. At that point Cenkos and I went for home, the headlines already going through our heads, but it wasn't to be. Flagship Uberalles, having left Nicholls for Philip Hobbs and now being ridden by Richard Johnson, sailed past us on the run to the last, and we were also overhauled by Conor O'Dwyer on Native Upmanship just before the line. Still, third place in a Champion Chase wasn't so bad, especially given that Cenkos was a 66–1 shot.

But that was as close as we got to a winner that year. Valley Henry fell in the SunAlliance Chase. I was disgusted with that one. He fell at the first fence down the back straight first time. It's actually the third fence in the race, and the ground runs away from you a little on the landing side. He just clipped the top of it and landed too steeply – a real novice's fall. Thisthatandtother was fourth in the Bumper, behind Pizarro, Rhinestone Cowboy and Back in Front. Again, not a bad trio to succumb to, but I was very disappointed at the time. Of course I didn't know how good those three would turn out to be, but I had thought that Thisthatandtother was my best chance of success at that year's festival. He had all the attributes you looked for in a Cheltenham Bumper winner: he travelled well, he stayed further than two miles, he was tough and he was a six-year-old. We took it up about half a mile out, but just couldn't find the reserves of energy to hold the others off up the home straight.

I rode Sir Talbot for Jim in the Stayers' Hurdle, but he took a real crashing fall early on. Fortunately I was able to pick myself up and ride Shotgun Willy in the Gold Cup. It didn't really matter, though, as he was never travelling and I ended up pulling him up a long way out. Irony of ironies, Joe Tizzard finished third behind Best Mate and Commanche Court on the 40–1 shot, twelve-year-old See More Business. He actually looked like winning it at one stage. Now that would have been some story. Sometimes it's stranger than fiction this game.

I was third on Davids Lad in the Cathcart, but at no point in the race did I think I was going to get in a blow at Royal Auclair, who led all the way under McCoy. Until that race I'd had something in common with McCoy in that neither of us had ridden a winner at that year's festival. I was on my own after that. Earthmover pulled up in the William Hill, Barba Papa pulled up in the Pertemps Final, Iverain pulled up in the SunAlliance Hurdle, Asador pulled up in the Grand Annual, Exit to Wave finished in mid-division in the Mildmay of Flete, and not even my old friend the County Hurdle could get me off the mark, as I finished fourth on Benbyas for Les Eyre in that.

I rode Davids Lad in the Grand National the following month. Paul had two runners in the race, Murt's Man, a 66–1 shot that really had no chance, and Ad Hoc, who was owned by Robert Ogden. Paul Carberry was on a retainer to ride all Ogden's horses at this stage, so Ad Hoc was never going to be my ride, but Paul Nicholls very fairly allowed me to get off Murt's Man in order that I could ride Davids Lad. And it was all going so well. I hunted him round out the back on the first circuit and gradually allowed him to creep into contention. He seemed to be enjoying the place and coping with the fences no problem. Then, going up the far side for the final time, before we got to the Melling Road where you cross the intersection and rejoin the Mildmay track, we met the fourth last fence wrong. He didn't have time to adjust his stride, he clouted the fence, and the two of us came crashing down. Ad Hoc, who had been tracking us, landed almost on top of us and came down as well. Looking at the replay, not to take anything away from the winner, Bindaree, but there is every chance that both Davids Lad and Ad Hoc would have been involved in the finish. We'll never know. I was hugely disappointed as Davids Lad was travelling so well. But it's hard to win a National (ask AP) or even complete one (ask Jonjo).

By the middle of April 2002 I had taken my total number of winners for the season to 98. My best season ever already by far, and there were still two weeks to go. Barring injury or something unforeseen, I would ride my first century. That was something to think about. Another milestone. A hundred winners in a season.

It wasn't to be, however. Something unforeseen was on the horizon – quite literally, as it turned out. There are those who will tell you that it wasn't completely unforeseen, that the way I was going something was going to happen. The way I was going there was going to be some major event in my life, and how I dealt with it was going to determine if it would turn out to be a good thing or a bad thing. It was around that time that Glenn Tormey, a fellow jockey and a mate, told Chris Broad that he was sure that at some time in the future, and not too far into it, they would be visiting me either in a prison or in a mental institution. He couldn't have known how correct his prophecy would prove to be, or how soon it would come true.

CHAPTER TWELVE

CALAMITY

The Nakayama Grand Jump is the richest steeplechase race in the world by some way. I didn't know too much about it before the spring of 2002, but when Paul told me that he thought Cenkos would be an ideal type for the race, and that there was over £400,000 up for grabs for winning the thing, I began to take interest. To put that type of money into context, Flagship Uberalles won £127,000 for winning the Champion Chase that year, Best Mate won £174,000 for winning the Gold Cup. This was a race to which it was well worth paying attention.

As the field is limited to sixteen, overseas runners have to be invited before they can run in the race. You let the Japan Racing Association know that you are interested in running, and then it is up to them whether they think you are good enough to receive an invitation. The Venetia Williams-trained The Outback Way had been invited to the inaugural running of the race in 2000 after finishing fourth in the Champion Chase, and he had acquitted himself very well by finishing third. Given that Cenkos had finished third in the Champion Chase that year, we figured there was every chance he would get an invitation. He did, as did two other British-trained horses, Banker Count, trained by Venetia Williams, and Exit Swinger, trained by Martin Pipe.

Andy Stewart, Cenkos's owner, very generously paid for Paul and me to travel first class with him to Japan with Virgin Airways. The other horses' connections were just behind the curtain in normal class. There was Banker Count's trainer and jockey Venetia Williams and Norman Williamson, as well as Martin Pipe and Rodi Greene, trainer and rider of Exit Swinger. You could walk around the first-class section or sit up at the bar in the middle of the cabin. The bar was free, and I took full advantage. A couple of the others came up and joined us for a glass of champagne during the nine-and-a-half-hour flight as well, and the craic was good. Paul thought that I wasn't drinking. He had heard that I was off the drink and he had assured Andy that it was orange juice or tonic water that I was drinking. By the time we landed, however, they had figured out that what I'd been drinking was slightly stronger.

I left my passport on the plane. That was the beginning of it. I didn't realise I didn't have it until I got to immigration, and it is a hell of a job to get back from immigration at Narita airport to the plane to get your passport. It was all we could do to get them to let me into the country. Actually, it would have been a whole different story if they hadn't.

Paul wasn't happy. When we got to the hotel, he told me to go to my room, dry out, and stay there until the race. This was Thursday, two days before the race on the Saturday. Stay in the hotel for two days? He was serious. He told me that if he saw me having a drink between then and the race, I would not ride Cenkos.

As Norman and Venetia had been there two years earlier with The Outback Way, they were the ones with the local knowledge. The last time they had been out, they had schooled the horse over some of the fences at Nakayama on the day they arrived, and that was what they planned to do this time as well. A bus brought us from the airport to our hotel, and another bus came to bring us back to the racecourse later that day. I didn't go. I was too busy sleeping off my excesses.

Everything we did was under the supervision of the JRA. The jockeys weren't allowed to leave the hotel before the race without being accompanied by someone from the JRA. We were brought to Nakayama racecourse on the Friday morning and I was blown away by it. It could have been a football stadium. The stands were unbelievable, accommodating, as they do, 180,000 people, and they are apparently filled to capacity on Arima Kinen day and Japanese 2,000 Guineas day. About five different levels, more luxurious the further up you go. The chairs on the top floor were more comfortable than most beds.

The racecourse itself was in great condition, although the ground was fairly fast. The jumps track is inside the main racecourse, and the course itself is quite tricky, a bit like the cross-country track at Cheltenham with all its turns and twists. I got to school Cenkos over a couple of fences on the track that morning, and he seemed very well. The fences there are, of course, different to our fences. You could brush through the top of them. If you jumped out over them, you were jumping them too big.

Cenkos ran well in the race itself the following day. I just hunted him round in midfield in the early stages, just to let him warm to the task, but when I wanted him to go forward he just couldn't make up the ground. It was all so new to him. He jumped the fences bigger than he needed to and he never really figured out that he could brush through the top. The ground was on the fast side for him and the distance of two miles five and a half furlongs was further than he wanted to go, but he stuck on well to finish fifth, about fifteen lengths behind the winner, St Steven, trained by the New Zealander John Wheeler and ridden by Craig Thornton. St Steven was Australian Jumper of the Year in 2001 and had had a run at Nakayama in the Pegasus Jump Stakes the previous week, so he had the edge on us in terms of experience of the course and acclimatisation. If you were to do it again, you would have to consider running in that race as a prelude to the Grand Jump, although that would mean missing Cheltenham. It would be a big sacrifice, but if you had the right horse, it might be a sacrifice worth making.

Paul and Andy were fairly happy. Cenkos had run well, he was the best of the English horses – Banker Count finished ninth and Exit Swinger finished last of the fifteen runners – and he had picked up £42,000 for finishing fifth. When he went back to Sandown two weeks later and beat Flagship Uberalles in the Queen Mother Celebration Chase – which was a hell of an achievement for a horse that had been halfway round the world – he picked up just £44,000.

We had dinner in the hotel that evening and then a few drinks. There was a good crew from the UK there. As well as the horses' connections, Phil Smith, the BHB handicapper, was there, as was Anthony Bromley, the bloodstock agent. Actually, we had quite a lot of drinks. Well, I did anyway. I know we left the hotel at some stage and went into Tokyo for the night. As is the case with a lot of my big nights out in Faringdon, I don't remember a great deal about it. I do remember being back in my room at about four o'clock in the morning, looking for more drink, and Anthony Bromley scarpering out of the room in his underpants because he wanted to get some sleep. I think he ended up crashing in with Phil Smith. I ended up in Norman's room, fully clothed, in my suit, so that when the call came to get up to go to the airport, all I had to do was stand up and I was ready to go.

At the airport, Norman and I went to buy cigarettes in duty free while everyone else went to the first-class lounge with Andy. Norman and I just sat at a bar in the airport. He had a coffee, I had an orange juice. Just an orange juice. I was beginning to sober up at this stage and I wasn't too far off being fully sober by the time we got on the plane.

I remember the plane taking off and I remember getting out of my seat, which was directly behind Paul Nicholls, and going up to the bar. I sat there with Martin Pipe and Norman Williamson, having a vodka and orange, and just having a bit of craic with them. Then another vodka and orange, and another. The next thing I can remember is waking up in Heathrow airport, and all the commotion. That's genuine. If the flight had actually passed off as innocuously, things would be very different for me today, that's for sure. I am deeply ashamed of my behaviour on board that flight, and I have apologised unequivocally to everybody who was there. But I can't turn back the clock. And though it pains me to do it here, I have done my best to piece together the events as best I can.

Apparently, as I was sitting at the bar, I was getting progressively boisterous. I suppose my boisterousness was in direct proportion to the amount of alcohol I was consuming. The usual. Pipey and Norman left the bar and returned to their seats – I probably wasn't great company – but I stayed there, drinking more and getting progressively louder and more cantankerous. Eventually the hostess came up to me and asked me to return to my seat, which I did, just behind Paul, but I didn't stop giving out. Andy was beside Paul and was getting more and more annoyed with me. Paul kept asking me to be quiet, but it took me a while to calm down. Eventually I did, and I fell asleep.

We were more or less in the same seats as we had been in on the flight out. Norman says that at one point he saw me come through the curtain from first class. Most people were asleep and the plane was in semi-darkness, but Norman couldn't sleep. He watched me as I walked all the way down the aisle, down to the back of the plane, stopped, head-butted the back of the plane, and walked all the way back up and disappeared behind the curtain again. He said that I looked completely out of it. I could hardly put one foot in front of the other. He told me afterwards that I looked like a man who was spaced out, more than just drunk. Perhaps it was the altitude mixed with alcohol, perhaps I had taken sleeping tablets. I can't remember.

The real trouble started when the crew began to come round again and woke me up. I got up out of my seat and went up to the bar, but they wouldn't serve me any more alcohol. Of course they were right not to, but I wasn't happy about it. I began to get out of control. Apparently there were people on the plane who were genuinely frightened, and you can't blame them. We weren't too long after 9/11 and any commotion on a plane was bound to frighten even the most seasoned travellers.

Paul went and got Norman and asked him to look after me, so Norman came up into first class, got me to sit back down in my seat and sat beside me, in the aisle seat, so that I couldn't get out without jumping over him. He says that he grabbed me by the shoulder to get me to sit down and that my shoulder felt like jelly. He had seen me drunk before, but he had never seen me like this. I was completely spaced out. After a little while, one of the stewards came up to Norman and told him that he couldn't sit there as he wasn't a first-class passenger, so, despite his protests, he had to return to his seat.

As soon as Norman had gone, I was up again. I started banging on the door of the cockpit, apparently thinking it was the toilet. I had wet my seat. When they didn't open the door I urinated up against the fuselage. It was at this time that the incident with the air stewardess apparently happened as well. They got hold of me and were going to put me in a straitjacket, but they didn't. Instead, they got Norman to come back up and sit beside me again.

I'm not sure exactly what happened with the air stewardess. She says that I put my hand up her skirt. I can't dispute it. It's her word against the word of a drunk who can't remember a thing. If I did it, I am deeply remorseful, and I have expressed as much. It's not me. I'm not like that. But then, Timmy Murphy with twenty vodkas inside him isn't me either.

I was asleep as we came in to land, ten hours after we had left Narita. I woke up just after the plane touched down and looked out the window. This I remember. As we taxied to a halt I noticed that there were three or four police cars on the tarmac. I turned to Paul Nicholls and asked him why there were police cars outside. 'I think they're here for you, Timmy.'

It didn't hit home with me. I just kind of wondered, 'Why are the police here for me?' I was somewhere between asleep and awake, drunk and sober. That quasi-slumber you go through when you are coming out of a deep sleep. Not in the fullness of my faculties. Sufficiently aware to wonder why the police were there for me, but not lucid enough to appreciate the gravity of what was going on.

Nobody was allowed to move when the plane stopped. The door was opened and a couple of armed officers got on. I sat up in my seat, still trying to wake up properly. They came down to my row and they took me out of my seat. It is still all very hazy. They asked me if I was Timmy Murphy. When I said I was, they told me that I was being arrested for assaulting a flight attendant.

I was mesmerised. Rabbit in the headlights. Assaulting a flight attendant? I wondered what I had done. They took me up to the top of the plane, down the steps and into the waiting police car. I was stunned. Could this really be happening? Was I really in the back of a police car on the way to a police station? This was nothing like those Sunday mornings when I used to wake up and think, 'Jesus, what did I do last night?' or

'What did I say to your man?' This was a whole different league. My heart was going about a hundred miles an hour.

I was questioned by the police for a couple of hours. What do you remember about the flight? I couldn't remember a thing, that was all I could tell them. I remembered getting on the plane, having a drink up at the bar, and landing at Heathrow. That was it. Of course by that time I'd realised the seriousness of the situation. If anyone did anything on a plane at that time, like now, they were severely punished. I knew even that evening, in police custody, that there was a good chance I would go to prison for this. How would I cope with prison? Me, behind bars. It was unimaginable, absolutely unfathomable.

By the time I was released from custody, everybody had gone. The Lester Awards were on that evening, and they were all going. I was supposed to be there. What a laugh. Before I left for Japan I was wondering if I would be back in time for the Lesters. That was usually a good night. Amazing the way things work out, the way things that you think are important can suddenly become so irrelevant that you wonder how they ever figured on your radar. I hadn't expected anyone to hang around for me, and what would I have said to them anyway? What would they have said to me? All right now, Timmy?

It was dark as I travelled home, my mind racing. What now? What would I do? How would I face my friends, my family? How would my Mam and Dad deal with it at home? What would Shane think of his father? It would probably be the talk of the Lesters that evening, and it would probably be all over the papers in the morning. There was a hole in my gut the size of Hyde Park. Alcohol had got me into some real situations in the past, but this made all the others look like tiny specks. I concluded that my life would be so much better, so much easier, without it than it was with it. For the first time, right there on my way home from Heathrow, I realised that I had a problem with alcohol, and that I needed to face up to it.

CHAPTER THIRTEEN

MY NAME IS TIMMY MURPHY

I woke up from my half-slumber early the following morning with a feeling in my stomach that was so hollow it was painful, as if someone had reached deep down into the pit of my belly and pulled out my intestines. My head was spinning. What now? What would I do? What should I do? Usually when faced with a crisis I'd have a drink, even when that crisis was caused by drink. But not this time.

I was a wreck. I had hardly slept. I didn't know what I felt. Shame, worry, fear, confusion. I felt like I was lost, out of control, not in charge of my own destiny, and it was my own doing. I had placed my fate in someone else's hands through my stupidity, my brashness, my drinking.

Then the phone rang. It was the first time it had rung. It would have rung all night, I'm sure, had I not taken it off the hook. What could I possibly say to anyone? If it was the press, what was I going to tell them? If it was a friend, enquiring about my well-being, what was I going to say? I'm fine? I wasn't. I closed the curtains on all the windows, locked the doors and closed myself off to the world. It was difficult telling Dawn what had happened. I wasn't sure how she would react. Well, she was great. But the papers weren't. I didn't read them that morning, but I had a fair idea what they would say. I just ignored them. Ignored the outside world. In my house I wasn't a part of that world. I could hide away, for now anyway. I couldn't hide for ever, but I could for now, and I wanted to.

Seanie Curran came round later that day. He had brought my tuxedo to the Lesters the evening before, the thinking being that I would go straight from Heathrow to the Hilton Hotel and meet him there. When I hadn't shown up, he thought I had just been delayed, until he saw Norman there and the Nicholls team. He went up to Norman and asked him where I was, and Norman told him, quietly, discreetly.

Actually, they had decided that they wouldn't tell anyone at the Lesters about the incident. They figured people would find out in their own time, or maybe they wouldn't, and if they went around telling everyone about it at the Lesters it would be the talk of the evening. That's what happens. These stories are like bush fires in the outback at the height of summer. Adrian Maguire met Norman in the toilets and he asked him where I was. He was on the plane with you, is he not at the Lesters? Norman shrugged his shoulders. He didn't know. But later in the evening, someone else came up to Norman and asked him if it was true that I had been arrested. It's a little village, this racing world.

Like Dawn, Seanie was great that day too. He is one of the world's great talkers, but that day he just listened. I told him what I could remember about the plane journey, and he just nodded at the appropriate times. What else could he do? Even then I thought there was a very real possibility I would end up in jail. Plane incidents just weren't being tolerated any more.

Ironically, when Seanie was leaving Wincanton a couple of days before the Japan trip, on his way to his car he saw Paul Nicholls across the way. 'Look after Timmy now in Japan, won't you?' he shouted across to him, half-joking, half-serious. He knew what I was like. Nicholls didn't respond. Seanie's not sure if he even heard him, or if he smiled, or if he just chose to ignore him, or if he thought I was big enough to look after himself. If he had, he would have been right. I should have been.

I remember my last phone call with my Mam before I left for Japan. It's amazing the things you remember. If Japan had passed without incident – or rather, if the journey home had passed without incident – there is no way I would have remembered that. It's like, if you are in a traffic accident, or if something unexpectedly bad or good happens to you, you remember every little thing that happened in the lead-up to the incident. Every little detail. The minutiae take on a whole new relevance.

I remember Mam telling me to be careful with my drinking in Japan. She would sporadically tell me to be careful with my drinking, even though she knew the reaction her words of advice would provoke. Mam was never one for confrontation, so it was a fairly big deal for her to say anything. She must have been more concerned than usual for me, perhaps because I was going to a different country, a different culture, whose appreciation for and tolerance of alcohol weren't fully known here. She got the reaction she would have expected: 'Ah Mam, for feck sake. I'm well able to handle that.'

Mam was going through a tough time of her own then. She was off work sick for six months around that time and was in and out of hospital a lot. I'd say a lot of it was caused by stress, and a lot of the stress was caused by me. She used to come over to England to see me about once every year, and she'd stay with me. Of course I wouldn't change my lifestyle much when she was over. I think she was shocked at the drink culture, much more prevalent than in Ireland, and the amount I used to drink. If she said anything to me, I would flare up. 'It's not like I'm drinking every day! It's not like I'm not doing my job! I only drink at weekends!' And other justifications. I'd make sure she was OK when she came over, but I'd still go out drinking. She would come racing with me sometimes, or if one or two of the lads weren't racing and I was, I'd get them to take her shopping. It was a good community like that. We'd all look after each other. Seanie, Johnny Kavanagh, Jim Culloty and Glenn Tormey. They'd be delighted when Mam would be coming over. 'Oh, Mrs Murphy is coming, that means there'll be dinners.' I'd ring Mam on my way home from the races.

'Mam, how many are you cooking for this evening?'

'Eight.'

'You couldn't stick two more in the pot, could you?'

She loved that. She loved looking after all the lads, but she just couldn't get over the amount we drank. I didn't know this at the time, but she used to go home quite upset, just knowing how big a part alcohol was playing in my life. She always thought something was going to have to happen to me to make me see sense, and she wasn't alone.

I thought of my Mam and Dad that day in my house, 15 April 2002, with the curtains drawn and the phone off the hook, a recluse, cut off from the world. They couldn't hibernate. They couldn't retreat into their shells. Kilcullen is a small community where everyone knows everyone and everyone knows everyone else's business. They would nearly all know Mam and Dad. I thought of my parents going about their daily business among the whispering classes. No hiding place. They would have to carry the shame I had brought on the family. They would be huge sufferers in this and they had done nothing wrong. I hadn't seen the papers, but that didn't mean nobody else had.

They didn't tell my Mam that morning. Her friends didn't tell her. I don't know why. Maybe they thought it would be too much for her given her illness, but they bought all the papers and they brought them down to her at home. They just gave her the papers and said that she should read them and then left. It was a bit strange. She has some very good friends, but it was a strange thing to do. Maybe they just couldn't tell her to her face. Who wants to be the bearer of bad tidings? Obviously they thought that was the best way to tell her.

The news floored her. I knew it would. Of course it would. One of the papers had managed to get an interview with one of the passengers who had said that the champagne had been flowing and that Murphy had got out of hand. It was against everything my Mam stood for. Being drunk on board an aircraft was bad, being arrested was worse, but the charge of indecent assault on an air hostess was just as bad as it could be in my Mam's eyes. She went to bed and stayed there for two days. Then she thought, 'Why not? Why not go out?' She would go into Kilcullen and she would see little groups of people, just chatting, and she would think they were talking about me. 'There's Helen Murphy there, Timmy Murphy's mother, the jockey, the fellow who was arrested for assaulting an air hostess. And they seemed like such a decent family.' They were saying whatever her imagination allowed them say.

But then there were her real friends who came to see her every morning, and stayed and chatted with her, and had coffee, and invited her to their houses for meals and things. They were good friends. And there were other people who would come in to the shop where Mam worked and didn't know what to say, but just put their hand on her shoulder as if to say, 'We understand your pain, we can only imagine what you're going through.' That was nice as well. But they were transient comforts. Mam would go out every morning those days with her head held high and a smile on her face, but when she got home she would cry. Every single night, she would cry.

I don't know how my Dad dealt with the news. He had his horses. In times of joy and in times of crisis, it didn't matter, he always had his horses. As I have said before, we weren't and aren't the best at discussing things together, me and my Dad. We would talk all day about horses, but get off the subject of horses and we were struggling together. It is quite remarkable, but to this day I haven't discussed the incident with Dad. We haven't discussed the plane journey, the court case, even my time in prison. Three months of my life, one of the most impactful things ever to have happened to me, and it has never ever been discussed between me and my Dad.

I phoned Broady, and he said he would talk to Michael Caulfield. Michael would know what to do. He was the chief executive of the Jockeys' Association at the time, and he had helped me when I was up in front of the stewards in Portman Square on whip offences. Lots of whip offences, lots of dealings with Michael. This wasn't a whip offence, but at least he would be able to advise me.

I was sitting behind locked doors and closed curtains when Michael arrived. We just sat there in the sitting room. Dawn was upstairs. I remember staring down at my shoes and just saying to him, 'Can you help me?' I was as low as I had ever been before. I didn't want anyone to know I existed. Michael was great. He knew what I was going through with alcohol having experienced it himself. He checked that I had private health insurance, which I did, and then he called the alcohol rehab centre in Southampton, The Priory, and booked me in. He said it would help to keep me out of prison. I told him I would go down for a day but that I didn't want to stay there. That place was for addicts and people with serious problems. I wasn't an addict. I just drank too much sometimes, and this time I had gone too far. He said, 'Fine, you don't have to stay, but stick your toothbrush in your pocket just in case.' Michael also organised some legal representation: Chalk, Smith and Brooks, who were the Jockeys' Association's retained solicitors at the time, and my barrister, Robin Leach. Actually, Andrew Chalk is Michael's brother-in-law. I was due to appear at Uxbridge Magistrates' Court that Friday and I needed to get things together before then.

Michael came with me and my solicitors and barrister to Uxbridge, as did Seanie, who was an absolute star through all of this. The hearing lasted only about five minutes. I confirmed my name and address, and Robin Leach did the rest of the talking. There wasn't that much to say, and the hearing was set for 2 May, less than two weeks later. I was remanded on bail and they kept my passport. Where would I have been going?

I decided that I wasn't going to ride until everything got cleared up, whenever that would be. I wanted to hide from the world and get this to pass as quickly as possible. I was embarrassed. I would have found it difficult to go racing at that time. I hated the thought of going into the weigh room, facing the lads, the slagging, facing trainers, owners, the press. I just thought it would be better to keep my head down, answer the case, accept the punishment, whatever it would be, and move on.

I did stay at The Priory. Michael said it would help my case, make the judge more sympathetic towards me if I was seen to be doing something to try to help myself. That made sense to me. Of course, I wasn't an alcoholic. I chose when I drank and when I didn't drink, it was just that I liked drinking at the weekends, and sometimes I drank too much. Doesn't everybody? The commitment I made to myself on my way home from Heathrow that I wouldn't drink again was already beginning to wane, my resolve weakening. It wasn't that I needed never to drink again, I just needed to be more careful when I drank. But I certainly wasn't going to drink until this court case was over, that was for sure, and if doing a four-week course at The Priory would help my cause, then a four-week course at The Priory it would be. If it kept me out of prison, it would be four weeks very well spent.

It was hard work at The Priory. You had to write your life history from your first memory to the present day: when you first had a drink, how you felt, what you did, who you were with. That was hard for me. They just kept digging and digging until they found something. I think they found me a little tricky in the beginning. I wasn't a great communicator and I don't think they could really figure out what was going on in my head. I'm not sure I knew, so it would have been difficult for them to figure it out. It was the hardest mental work I've ever done in my life by far. Irish with Mrs Stewart was a doddle by comparison. Just thinking and writing, all the time. You had to go back through your memories and write down everything, innermost feelings you probably hadn't fully even come to terms with yourself at the time. When you got your first kick out of alcohol, how you thought it affected you, how you felt afterwards. So you did all your work during the day, and then at night time you had to write stuff on what you had done during the day. You were ready for bed when you were finished, that was for sure. And then you had to go to your meetings after that. They packed a lot into the course.

I didn't believe in it at the start. I was only there because Michael Caulfield suggested I should go there. I was only there so that the judge would be lenient on me, so that I might stay out of prison. I didn't belong there, not among these people, not among these alcoholics. I was just playing the part, acting it out, playing along with everyone so that I would be seen to fit in, but I knew that I didn't.

We were put into groups. There were four or five in our group in the beginning, which grew to eight or nine in the end. That was the way it worked. People would come and join the group and learn from the people who were already in it. You sit in a circle and just discuss things. You read out the work you did the previous evening, charting your actions, feelings and motivations, and people pick holes in it. They want you to be open and honest, and if you are not, they can see it immediately. They pounce on you. People would be presenting nice pictures of their lives – oh, I had a drink there, that was a good night; or, I'd had a bad time of it so I had a drink – and you start ripping into them, trying to get to the bottom of it. Why did you have a drink? How did you feel? How did it help? The whole group does it. They'd get you to draw a picture which you would then give to someone else in your group and they'd interpret it. If you drew trees or something, they might go, 'Why are your trees so small?' or 'Why are your trees so different to each other?' And they'd read into it, saying that you were a loner, or you didn't function well in groups. All the while they'd encourage you to look for the similarities between you and the other people; it's very easy to see the differences. And it was remarkable. Once you stopped focusing on the differences and began to look for the similarities, you could find them. 'Oh yeah, I've done that,' or, 'That rings a bell.' The similarities were uncanny, and then you begin to realise, then it clicks. I didn't start to look for the similarities until three weeks into the course, but when I did I was blown away.

You see, you don't know that you have a problem. You don't see that if you go out to get drunk you have a problem. People have to point it out to you, show you exactly where you are going wrong, why you are doing something, how it's affecting you and those around you. They show you examples of other people, how they started off similar to you, and then you go to your AA classes and just listen. It was good to hear other people's stories. Everyone has a different story, but it's the same topic, and ultimately the same conclusion. You start sliding down the slippery slope until you've lost yourself. You don't think you're doing anything wrong, you don't see any problems, but it starts to eat away at you gradually, so that you don't notice it. It affects your work and your performance, and it affects the people around you, and suddenly you wake up one morning and it's all gone. Your job, your family, your friends. All you have is your bottle. People go on about hitting rock bottom, but that's not rock bottom. Rock bottom is when you're dead. If you are still breathing, then you still have a chance.

My name is Timmy Murphy. I'm an alcoholic.

It took me more than three weeks, but I got there. There were only a few days left of my course, so I decided to stay an extra week to make sure that I got the most out of it. It had taken me nearly a month to admit that I had a problem, and a few days wasn't enough once the realisation had dawned. If I was going to drink then I might as well forget about my career, and I'd probably end up losing my family and everything I valued, so I decided to knuckle down and work at getting it right.

I had huge difficulties with the idea that I wasn't going to drink again. That was scary. But they told me not to think of it like that. You can't think like that. You don't know what's going to happen tomorrow, so just do it for today. It's only today that you have control over. If you don't drink today, that's fine. Nobody is asking you to say that you won't drink next week, or next month. Just today. But I couldn't get my head around it at first. That's crap, I thought, saying you're not going to drink today when you know you're really never going to drink again. But never is too long a time. You can't say never about anything and know that you're right. You can't say 'I'm never going to drive a car', or 'I'm never going to eat a donut', and know with 100 per cent certainty that you won't. It's just too long a time to get your head around. But you can say 'I'm not going to drive a car today', or 'I'm not going to eat a donut today', and mean it, and know that you won't. Same with drinking. 'I'm not going to drink today.' Right, that's manageable. Just until I go to bed tonight. Tomorrow we'll worry about tomorrow. Or if a day is too long, just say, 'I'm not going to have a drink in the next hour, or in the next half-hour.' You can only manage the present.

I learnt so much at The Priory. You learn to talk. If something is bothering you, share it. And it helps, it really does. It makes it easier. It's still difficult for me to talk to people, but it's not as difficult as it used to be. That was the main thing I learnt, and that was huge for me. Just tell someone about it. If you're feeling lousy, just talk to someone and the reason why you're feeling lousy will come out whether you know it or not. You just feel better as a result. Before I went to The Priory I didn't want to burden anyone with my problems. I didn't know what was going on myself so I didn't even know what to talk about. I just knew that I felt bad, but I didn't really know why. I was all tangled up. But now, if I'm feeling low, I just tell someone I'm feeling low. At the very least it's a conversation starter. They'll ask you why, and then you can try to tell them. Beforehand, I would just curl up and go out drinking. The solution to all ills.

You learn about how depressed you get after drinking. You think it's just a hangover but it drags you down and you feel like shit. Then you're eating because you think you're hungry, but it's a false hunger. Then you put on weight and you have to sweat it off, and that makes you even more depressed. And everything builds up until one day someone says something to you, something innocuous, after a race or something, and your head explodes. You're just waiting to explode instead of thinking things through.

I wouldn't have been able to give up drinking without The Priory, that's for sure. I had done it for four months before, but this was a whole different ball game. I had decided that I wasn't going to drink again on my way back from Heathrow that night, but within a couple of days I was already reconsidering. I needed some external force to strengthen my resolve. The Priory was that external force, and even then I knew it wasn't going to be easy.

After I finished in The Priory, I decided that I would go back riding again. My case had been put back and I was due to appear at Uxbridge again on 13 June for a committal hearing to send the case to the Crown Court. It would probably take another month to go to trial, so what was I going to do in the interim? There was nothing more I could do for myself. Best thing would be to get back to riding and prepare as well as I could for the case. Who knew what was going to happen? It was out of my control anyway.

It was really good to get back into the weigh room at Stratford on 1 June. The lads were great. Nobody spoke about the incident, they just welcomed me back. There were a few members of the press around, but it wasn't a high-profile meeting so they left me alone in the main, which was good. I was bowled over by the reception I got from the normal racegoers when walking into the parade ring and walking around the ring before going out. It really was a huge lift for me.

I was supposed to ride Firestone for Tony Carroll in the handicap hurdle, but he was a late scratching, so my first ride back was on Khatani for David Gandolfo in the two-mile-five-furlong handicap chase. It was amazing just to be back race-riding. For those six minutes, you forget about everything else. You are only aware of your immediate environment, the horse pounding the ground beneath you, sticking his neck out, trying for you. You concentrate on keeping him balanced, helping him to meet his fences on a stride, getting a position, holding it, asking him to go forward before rounding the home turn, and all as smoothly as you can, all in unison with the horse. We finished third, but I was thrilled. It was just great to be back.

I had to wait eight days for my next ride. That was on Torn Silk for Paul Nicholls in a handicap chase at Worcester. I didn't talk to Paul about the incident on the plane. Not at all. We didn't talk about my job or my retainer, which remained unpaid, or what we would do going forward. That was my way. I wasn't one to bring things up, and I hated talking about the incident anyway, and Paul didn't broach the subject with me. Ruby Walsh was riding a lot of Paul's horses when his commitments in Ireland allowed him, and I still had the court case hanging over me, so there was no point in talking about it until I knew if I was going to be free to ride – or even just if I was going to be free. Torn Silk hadn't run since the previous October, so we were both a bit rusty, but he stuck at it well to win by a head. That was great. Back in the winner's enclosure. All smiles and joy. You could have been forgiven for thinking that everything was normal. Just another jockey riding another winner.

I was only five minutes at Uxbridge Magistrates' Court on 13 June, but it was long enough for a charge of being drunk on board an aircraft to be added to the charge of indecently assaulting an air stewardess. It was a bit of a reality check for me. It was all well and good riding horses and riding winners, but this wasn't going to go away until I faced up to it, and the sooner I could get to trial and just get it over with, the better. It was eating me up inside, occupying almost all of my thoughts when I wasn't sitting on a horse. Because it doesn't go away. It's always there. It doesn't matter how much you laugh it off or pretend that it doesn't affect you or play on your mind, because it does. It's there when you go to bed at night and it's there again when you wake up in the morning. It's there until you deal with it, until you face up to it.

A plea and directions hearing was set for 23 July. I was supposed to ride Jupon Vert for Nicholls at Newton Abbott on the evening of 13 July, but I didn't. Robbie McNally rode him instead. I wasn't too disappointed. In early July, Nicholls announced that Ruby would ride for him for the 2002/03 season whenever he was available. I wasn't too disappointed with that either. My mind was focused elsewhere.

I didn't get too involved in the preparation of my case. I left that up to the solicitors. They were the experts, they knew what they were doing, so I just figured I'd leave them to it and do whatever they told me to do. About a week before the trial, however, Chris Broad and David Gandolfo thought that the preparation wasn't thorough enough. They thought that the solicitors weren't speaking to the right people and that they weren't making the progress they should be making. They thought that people who had offered to give character references weren't being chased up, so they tried to get involved in order to speed things up and construct the best possible case for my defence. In reality, we didn't have a lot of time before the trial, so we needed to work quickly. It led to a little bit of tension, which we didn't need. I remember Michael Caulfield asking David Gandolfo to let the solicitors get on with their job.

'How about I go up and train your horses for you?' said Michael.

'Come on,' said David, 'you don't know the first thing about training horses!'

'Exactly.'

It was, however, a little disappointing that people like Norman Williamson and Adrian Maguire weren't called to be character witnesses.

My solicitors didn't speak to Paul Nicholls, Andy Stewart, Venetia Williams or other people who were in our group on the plane either. But they had Mark Pitman, Mick Fitzgerald, Dean Gallagher and Michael Caulfield as character witnesses. They also had David Knott, my counsellor. So they had a good cross-section of people, and to be honest, I don't think the judge's patience would have lasted too much longer than it did. And they advised me to plead guilty, even though Chris asked them how I could plead guilty to something I didn't remember doing.

Isleworth Crown Court is a dark old building. Maybe it just appeared to me to be dark that day, but I felt that even if there had been floodlights in it, it would still have been dark. Going in was like going through customs at an airport, all the security and beepers. Everyone was dressed in a suit and they were all sitting in different places with their solicitors all round this little square corridor. The courtroom was also dark, small and dark, with very few redeeming features. There were only about twenty people there. There was my legal team, the prosecution, my character witnesses, Seanie Curran, Jim Old, David Gandolfo, Mick Fitzgerald, a couple of press people – not too many, for which I was thankful – a couple of others and my three uncles who had come over from Shanballymore, Mick, Pat and John. Mam and Dad didn't come over. I was actually happy that they weren't there. I don't know if I could have handled facing them. My Mam was too ill to travel and my Dad, I think, was just sticking his head in the sand. If he didn't acknowledge it, then maybe it didn't happen.

I didn't have a good feeling from the start. My solicitor, Andrew Chalk, told me to be prepared. 'Just be aware that this might not go our way.' So I started thinking, 'What if this doesn't go my way? What's going to happen? I'm going to prison. Well, get that into your head for a start. If you're prepared for that, anything else will be a result.' There had been a high-profile case the previous month in which the REM guitarist Peter Buck had been acquitted of the charges of being drunk on an aircraft and two charges of assaulting an air steward, also at Isleworth Crown Court. The verdict had provoked outrage among the airline's unions. Not that it should have had any bearing on my case, but it was worth bearing in mind.

The hearing lasted about three hours. It was tough to stand there and listen to it all, to relive the horror. The prosecuting barrister, a fellow called Simon Connolly, presented the case against me. He said that I was seen drinking vodka and orange before boarding the flight and that I then spent two hours at the bar on the plane drinking wine. He said that during my first encounter with the stewardess I called her a 'fucking whinger' and then, when she was passing by my seat later on, I grabbed her leg and moved my hand up her skirt. He said that the stewardess was in tears, and that she informed her supervisor immediately, who informed the captain. It was after that that I urinated against the flight deck door and walls, he said.

As I said, I couldn't refute any of it. I couldn't remember. It was frustrating as hell just standing there in the dock, unable to answer back, unable to do anything. I do know, however, that I was drinking orange juice before getting on the flight, not vodka and orange. They just assumed that there was vodka in it. That was frustrating, but I guess it would have been a pretty weak defence. 'It wasn't vodka and orange, your honour, it was only orange. But I can't remember the rest of it.'

My barrister, Robin Leach, said that I acknowledged that my behaviour was inappropriate, which I absolutely did, but that it was not the act of a serial sex offender. He said that I had received counselling for my alcohol problem. But nothing he or any of my character witnesses could say – and they all spoke very highly of me, and I am hugely indebted to them for that – would sway the judge.

Just as he was about to pass sentence, the phone belonging to Richard Brooks (of Chalk, Smith and Brooks) went off. It was one of those really annoying long shrill tones that tells you you have received a text message. Richard was mortified. The judge went berserk and threw him out of the courtroom. I just shook my head. For fuck's sake. It was the last in a litany of things that went against us. I am not so naive as to think that the judge decided to impose a more penal sentence just because my solicitor's phone went off, but it certainly didn't help. Things generally just hadn't gone smoothly. The chemistry was never right between people like Broady, Gandi and Jim Old, who were all batting for me as hard as they could, and my legal team. The lads wanted to see more effort. I have no doubt that my solicitors were working as hard as they could. Perhaps they just didn't have the experience or the knowledge to be able to deal competently with something of this nature, or perhaps the lads were wrong. Perhaps nobody would have done any better. Seanie thought they were fine defending you against a whip ban, but that this was a whole new ball game for them. They seemed to be more nervous than I was. Whatever the reason, while they were all trying to pull together and they all had the same goal, they were never in harmony. I never once felt it was going our way during the court case. The judge's demeanour was always negative. He had a blank stare throughout, as if he had made up his mind beforehand. At no point did I think we had him on our side.

I listened as he began his judgment. He was speaking to me, only me, in the middle of a crowded courtroom. It was a weird sensation. He was talking to me, you this and you that, looking directly at me, but actually his words weren't only for me. His words were for everybody who was there in the courtroom, listening, fearing for me, everyone who would listen to the radio or watch the television that evening, everyone who would read the newspapers the following morning.

My head was spinning. I had one of those out-of-body experiences where things seem like they're further away than they are, like your world goes into four dimensions. I heard the judge's words louder now than they had been, even though the volume hadn't gone up. I caught some of them. Past records, drink driving, a man in your position, should know better.

And then he said it. Six months. It took a second or two for it to register. Six months. It was like when your car goes out of control and you know you are going to crash. You know there is going to be a collision. You brace yourself. You expect the impact. You are powerless to do anything about it. And then it happens. Wham! It doesn't fully register with you for a couple of seconds. Your world pauses for a fraction of a second as you try to come to terms with what has just happened. That was me as I stood in the dock. Wham! Dazed. Reality suspended.

CHAPTER FOURTEEN

LIFE INSIDE

I stood there, stunned. Gobsmacked. I didn't know where to look, what to do. I thought I had prepared myself for the worst, but now that the worst had happened I wasn't sure I was that well prepared after all. Prison. Six months. I tried to get my head around it. Half a year. And the judge was still talking. Six months for indecent assault and three months for being drunk on an airplane, to run concurrently. What did that mean? Was that nine months? And something about the sex offenders' register. It just didn't hit home with me. I was still trying to get my head around the fact that I was going to prison. Then the gavel dropped and a policeman took me by the arm.

It was a strange feeling, being led away. You are sentenced, the gavel drops, and that's it. No hugs or kisses with family members or friends, no tears, no meaningful glances, nothing like you see on television. You're going to prison, and you're going to prison now. More Monopoly than *LA Law*. I had a few minutes with my solicitor Andrew Chalk before I was led away. He confirmed to me that it was six months in total, because the three- and six-month sentences would effectively be running at the same time, but that I would be out in three if I behaved myself.

I was put in the prison van with about twenty others. Lads roaring and shouting and abusing the police. At least you had your own little cell in the van, but it was still fairly scary. I don't know how long it took us to get to Wormwood Scrubs. Twenty minutes maybe. That was the other thing. This was Wormwood Scrubs, not Fluffy Bunny Open Prison. Lester Piggott had done his time in an open prison, so I was thinking that, if it came to it and I was sent to jail, perhaps it would be to an open prison as well. Not so. Cases from Heathrow are heard at Isleworth, and convicts from Isleworth are sent to Wormwood Scrubs. That's the way it usually works. To tell the truth, I don't really know what I was expecting. I had never been inside a prison before.

I'm not sure my friends and family around me fully appreciated what lay in store. I didn't, so it's unlikely they did either. Seanie was shocked. He says he caught my eye as I was led away and tried to say to me, 'Be as strong as you can.' I don't remember, I was in a daze. Dawn was distraught. Others were just taken aback. Seanie had my mobile phone, which rang later on that evening.

'Hello?'

'How're ye, Timmy? Tony Martin here. Jesus, I just heard the news.'

'Tony, eh, this is Sean Curran. I have Timmy's phone. He's gone to prison.'

'Yeah, I heard. Does he not have his phone with him?'

When we got to Wormwood we were all put into a holding cell. Some people were asking what others were in for. You don't know who you're talking to, you don't know what to say or to whom you should tell what. I just kept my head down. It was the same feeling I had when I went into the weigh room at Kilmuckridge point-to-point. You don't know anybody, you feel scared, nervous. You don't want to do or say the wrong thing.

Your name is called and you go and have your photograph taken. They then take all your belongings from you, you take off all your clothes, and you put on the prison uniform. They took me to the hospital wing as they didn't have a cell for me that night. It was a bit scary there as there were six lads in the room with me and you weren't sure who they were or what they were in for. It was a bit tricky going to sleep that night, so I didn't really, I just stayed alert.

The problem was that, because of the judge's error which would later come to light, I was down as a sex offender. I was placed on the sex offenders' register for five years, so they were going to put me in with other sex offenders on that wing. I was thinking, 'That can't be right. I'm not a sex offender. I'm not a rapist or a child molester.' Yet I was classed in the same category. The fact that the error would later be remedied was of no help to me at the time. It was only when I got to prison that I realised the implications of being on the register. That type of thing doesn't go down well, which is why the sex offenders have their own wing. The prison officers had some sympathy for me. They told me that if I went on to that wing I'd be labelled, so I said I'd go on to the normal wing. It was a bit of a risk. I would be in among normal convicts, and if they found out I was in as a sex offender, rightly or wrongly, I could get into a lot of trouble. I was willing to take my chances.

I was put into a cell with another fellow on the second day. He was all right, in for blackmail or something. I didn't delve too deeply into why he was in and I didn't want to divulge too much about myself, but even at that, during the first couple of days, there were lads coming up and banging on my cell door telling me that they knew who I was, calling me a rapist and telling me that they were going to get me. 'As soon as you come out of your cell we're going to do you in, we're going to stab you.' They had seen the newspapers. They had read that I was convicted as a sex offender and that I was in Wormwood Scrubs. 'Hey up, there's one of them lads in here.' And, of course, my picture was all over the newspapers. I just kept on denying it. 'You've got the wrong person.'

I was afraid of my life to move outside my cell. The worst thing was, I wasn't supposed to be on that register. I kept thinking to myself, 'That's a mistake, I shouldn't be on it.' A couple of the prison guards were racing fans from the north of England, and they kept an eye on me, asking me if everything was all right. Strange question. How long do you have? One of the long-termers was also big into his racing and he knew who I was. He used to keep an eye out for me as well. He was moving out of the block and he said that he'd put in a good word for me, to get me moved to the bottom floor, the main prison floor. He said that I would be better off down there. There were better cells down there. They had what they called an en suite, which was a bit of a laugh: it just meant that you had a toilet in your cell so there was no slopping out.

That first week inside was hell, the worst week of my life without question. I hardly slept at all. You couldn't sleep. You couldn't trust anybody. I didn't know anybody, didn't know what to say to anybody. You'd be afraid that you'd say the wrong thing to the wrong person. Think of your first day at school, or your first day in a new job, when you are on your own and everyone else there knows everyone else. You are the only one there who doesn't know how things work, what time you should take your lunch, where the toilets are. Think how alone you feel. Now, add in the fact that all the other people there, all the other people who know each other, are criminals, and half of them are telling you that they're going to stab you when they get the chance, just you wait. Now think how you would feel. There was a lad there who hanged himself during that week, and there were a couple of stabbings. It's a rough prison.

And as well as the worry for your own safety there were still the feelings of guilt and shame. The embarrassment I was to my family. How bad are they feeling? They are a good, straight, honest family. They go to mass every Sunday. And here I was, Jimmy and Helen Murphy's lad, banged up in prison for assaulting an air stewardess. I felt really terrible for them, thoroughly ashamed. I had let myself down and I had let my family down. Those feelings didn't go away just because you were in prison. If anything, they grew stronger. You had more time to think about them. And those early days were very, very long. There was nothing you could do to fill them. You were just there, alone, with your thoughts, your fears and your sadness. I could have cried, but what good would that have done?

Seanie and Dawn came to see me after a week there. That was tough. It was difficult even speaking to them, but we didn't need to say too much. I knew they were there for me. They were both great during this whole time. Dawn didn't bring Shane, I didn't want him coming near the place, and that was tough, not seeing him.

We were allowed out for one hour a day for exercise, but I didn't go. It was difficult to bring myself to leave the cell during the day when I had lads banging on the door at night time telling me they were going to get me in the morning. After about a week, however, things got a bit better. The racing guy was true to his word, and he got me moved downstairs to a better cell and a slightly safer environment. I was put in with a big guy who looked a bit like Mike Tyson to me. He was in for armed robbery and grievous bodily harm, and I think he had been shot as well. He just said to me, 'If you don't annoy me or get in my way, we'll get on fine.'

'Right,' I said.

'I've had it on good authority that you're all right,' he added, 'so just make sure that you are.'

'Right,' I said again. I didn't feel like I was in a strong negotiating position.

There is a pecking order among the prisoners, as there is in any walk of life, and this guy was high up on it. He looked out for me and I felt safe with him. He was also in charge of the kitchen, which was a position of fair responsibility in there. You had to sign for your dinner, to say that you wanted a dinner each day. Sometimes fellows wouldn't sign and they'd just get whatever was left over, the dregs, and there would often be a row in the kitchen with fellows going, 'I'm not eating that shit,' and all hell would break loose. And there was no eating area in the kitchen. You'd queue up with your tray, show your card, get your food and go back to your cell to eat it. Unsurprisingly, it wasn't the type of food you'd be rushing back to your cell to eat.

I thought a bit about what I would do after I got out. I couldn't ride in the UK again, that was for certain. I thought there was no way they would have me back. No trainer would want me, no owner would want me to ride their horse, not after all this. I probably wouldn't even get my licence back. I couldn't go to the States as I wouldn't get a visa with a criminal record. I couldn't ride in Ireland, no way – I wouldn't be able to handle the embarrassment. So I definitely couldn't go back to being a jockey again, not in England or Ireland. And I didn't want to go back riding anyway. Better to keep my head down and maintain a low profile. I couldn't be in the news, in the newspapers, riding on television. I didn't want to be in a high-profile position any more. I wanted to be away from the limelight, away from the public glare. Maybe I could get a trade, become a plumber, a builder or a carpenter. But who would give me an apprenticeship? I really hadn't a clue what I would do.

Then the letters began to arrive. One from Seanie, one from Dawn, one from my Mam. A trickle at first, then more. Seanie had asked all the lads in the weigh room to write to me. 'It doesn't matter what you say, just write to him. Just let him know you are thinking about him. It will mean a lot to him where he is.' Graham Lee wrote a lot, as did Tony Dobbin, Jim Old, Mark Pitman, Kay Hourigan, Norman Williamson and John Osborne. Seanie and Dawn wrote every week, and I began to get letters from people I hadn't heard from in a long time, people I hadn't spoken to in years, people I didn't know but who knew friends of mine, and people who didn't know me or know anything about me but who were racing fans and wanted to give me some encouragement.

And it worked. To tell the truth, I was bowled over. You wouldn't believe how much a letter means to someone in prison until you are in a situation like that yourself. When you receive one you rip it open, dying to read it, dying to see who it is from, what news they have, what they want to tell you. It didn't matter if it was only a couple of lines, a couple of words, just the fact that they were thinking about you meant everything. The highlight of every day was that time just after dinner when they gave out the mail. You would read every one slowly, making it last as long as possible, cherishing every word, savouring every syllable, and when you were finished, before you put it back into its envelope you would go back to the beginning and read it again.

I replied to every letter. I figured that if this person had taken the trouble to write to me, then I was damned if I was going to throw their effort in their face or let them down by not responding. It was the very least I could do. It wasn't as if I didn't have the time. I responded to every letter that had an address on it, whether it was from someone I knew or someone I didn't know. Apart from anything else, I found it hugely therapeutic. Reading the letters I received and writing back allowed me to escape from prison life, even if it was only for a short while. It enabled me to experience feelings of warmth, happiness, hope and excitement – feelings I rarely experienced inside.

It was because of those letters that, gradually, I came round to the notion that maybe I would ride again after all. People can be so kind, so generous with their words. I hadn't appreciated how much people thought of me as a rider or as a person until I read those letters. Perhaps some of them were exaggerating their thoughts, but it didn't matter. The point was that almost every single letter was one of encouragement – stick it out, chin up, be strong, hurry up and get back riding, your skills in the saddle are missed on the racecourse, your wit is missed in the weigh room. All encouraging. And I thought, 'Maybe there is something out there for me after all of this.' I'd ring Broady and he'd tell me that there were loads of trainers ringing him, promising to support me when I got out. Mark Pitman said that he would support me; David Gandolfo did likewise; Paul Nicholls said that Armaturk was still my ride. And there were others. So maybe things weren't so grim.

I kept every one of those letters, every single one. They are all in a box under my bed in my house in Shrivenham now. If ever I am going through a bad patch, or if ever I think that life is tough, or if little things are getting me down, I open up the box and take out a bunch of them. It doesn't take long to appreciate what you have when you realise what you didn't have not so long ago.

I started eating more. I had lost an awful lot of weight in my first week. Basically, I hadn't felt like eating at all. I'd just stopped caring, I had just given up. Nothing seemed to matter too much. But when things began to look up, I began to look after myself a little. I did sit-ups and press-ups in my cell, and just started to feel a little more positive about everything.

About two weeks into my sentence I got word that I had been taken off the sex offenders' register. I was delighted to be off it, but if anything it made it even more infuriating that I had been put on it in the first place, with all the grief it had caused me. The judge had accepted that he had made a mistake in law and had withdrawn that part of my sentence. That was big of him. A mistake in law. A judge had made a mistake in law. That would be like a doctor making a mistake in medicine. But it wasn't a big deal, it appeared. Just amend that part of his sentence. Well, it was a big deal, actually. It was a huge deal. As well as the fact that it made my life hell for my first week in prison, there were also the headlines when I was sentenced. Timmy Murphy, sex offender. No headlines when I was taken off the register, of course. No trumpet blast. Just a couple of lines in the *Racing Post*.

I got a job as a painter inside. I think one of the prison guards got it for me, the guy who was into racing. There was me and these two South African guys, who were pretty sound, although they were always having a go at me for going too quickly. 'You'll be out of here and we won't have a job!' I had my own little system, in the same way as I had a system when I'd be raking the yard at Halford's, or when I'd be preparing a horse to go racing. A couple of others came and went, but we were the main three. The others wouldn't really bother, they wouldn't really do any work, so they were just taken off the job and put back in their cells. We painted our whole block in three months, all four storeys of it.

After a few weeks I was told that there was a chance I could be moved to an open prison if I wanted. I thought about it. It would have been good to move to a place for prisoners who were low-risk, where you had more freedom, where there was no lock-down, where you were more or less free to ramble around, where you'd have your job, working outside, cutting grass or sowing vegetables or building, basically like being in college except that you wouldn't be allowed to go outside the perimeter. But I decided no. I knew the run of the place by that stage, and I had a fair idea who I could talk to and who I couldn't. Better the devil you know. I might have been crazy to turn down a potential move to an open prison, but I did.

A couple of days after that I was told that I could be released on a tagging system, and I went for that. But it was the worst thing that could have happened for my frame of mind. I spent the whole week looking forward to the end of the week when I would know if I was going to get put on the system, and at the end of the week they told me that they didn't know yet. They wouldn't know until the following week. This went on for six weeks, and it wrecked my head. Every week you'd be thinking that you might be out at the end of it, and every week you weren't. On the sixth week they told me that I wasn't getting on to the system. At least I knew where I stood then.

So I settled into a routine, the same routine every day except Sunday. There weren't as many prison guards working on Sunday, so you were locked up for most of the day. Up in the morning at about seven, have your tea. The people with jobs would be allowed out first, and I'd be painting by eight o'clock. Have a break, get your lunch, then there would be a lock-down for two hours. The doors would be open again around three, work again for about two hours, then wash up for dinner. Come back, have your dinner, get your mail. My cellmate would be working in the kitchen so he would be last man back, and if there were any goodies he'd bring them back and we'd share them. It was lights out at nine, but we had lights in our cell, so I could stay up reading or writing if I wanted. There were a couple of nights when the Jamaicans had Bob Marley playing as loudly as they could, and I swear to God, you'd want to have heard the racket. You would have thought there was a riot going on, but it was only the Jamaicans, banging on beds and kicking doors just because they were singing songs with Bob Marley in full swing. There were loads of Jamaicans in there, mainly for doing drugs. Fellows would come over with drugs and they would be arrested at the airport. But there were drugs in prison. Actually, there was everything in prison. It was amazing. When the judge was passing sentence, I remember him saying, 'Well, it will be easy for you to stay off the drink where you're going.' Not so. It would have been the easiest thing in the world to get my hands on alcohol in prison, or to get my hands on whatever I wanted.

I read the Seabiscuit book which was a gift sent to me by a trainer while I was in prison. I wouldn't be a big reader, but I enjoyed that book. The rest of the time I was either painting, writing or reading letters. There was a library in the prison so I could have read all day, but I preferred to be painting. I got £9 a week as wages for it, and I'd spend it on newspapers, some goodies and phone cards. Mainly on phone cards, but they never lasted as long as I wanted them to. People couldn't ring me, so if I wanted to talk to anyone on the phone I had to use up my card. And everyone would be asking you for your card. Of course, if you ever gave it to them you wouldn't see it again, so you quickly learnt not to. In fact, if you ever gave anything to anybody, it was rare that you would see it again. This fellow asked me for our toilet roll one day, so I gave it to him and told him to bring it back. Bring it back! My cellmate went mad with me. 'Don't ever give anything to anyone! That fellow who took your toilet roll, he's a lifer.'

To be honest, I would have painted for nothing. It's amazing how the time went by so much more quickly when I was working. And you settle into a routine then. The human mind is an amazing thing. When you are in a situation you deal with it as best you can. My way was to keep busy and keep my routine. You settle into your own little lifestyle, your own little cocoon, and you have a completely different set of values to what you have in the outside world. Like, as I said, a letter is the most important thing in the world. Ordering your dinner is huge. A piece of chocolate, talking to someone on the phone, a newspaper that is two days old. Remarkable.

Thursday was visiting day. It wasn't like visiting day in a hospital, mind you, or visiting day in boarding school. You had to apply for permission for people to come to see you a week in advance, you had to name them, and you were only allowed three visitors per week. Seanie and Dawn came every week. Every single week. It didn't matter what else was going on in their lives, they dropped it all and came to see me. Adrian Maguire also came to see me, as did Johnny Kavanagh, Seamus Durack, Jim Culloty and Andy Thornton. I didn't have much to say to any of them, but I really appreciated them making the effort. Andy, as I mentioned before, wouldn't let anyone take my space in the weigh room. There is an order in the weigh room. The longer you've been riding, the closer you get to the door. There's Seanie, Robert 'Chocolate' Thornton (no relation to Andy), Andy Thornton, then me. Andy wouldn't allow anyone to use my peg. That's his nature. I suppose it was the least he could do after taking my place on See More Business and winning the King George.

You'd look forward to visiting day. You'd be transported across to another part of the prison where you'd go into a waiting room and wait for your name to be called. Then you'd be searched and you'd go and get your half-hour with whoever was there, though it never felt that long. It was never long enough, and everyone would be upset when time was up and you'd be led away again. Until next week.

Seanie used to bring a newspaper every week, but not the *Racing Post*. He didn't want to be upsetting me, getting me thinking about racing. He needn't have worried. I was able to keep up with what was going on on the telly, although it was all Flat racing at the time, no real jumps, so I was only half interested.

Dawn and I probably grew closer when I was inside. It was strange. I suppose I wasn't out drinking all the time or away riding, so I had more time to think about her and Shane. She must have gone through hell and back with me, but she was strong. She had to be, for her and Shane. And Seanie was a great crutch for her.

So I coped. Only just, but I did. I could manage if I stuck to my routine and concentrated on just getting to the end, ticking off the days, waiting for the three months to be up. If they had come along at the end of the three months and said, 'Actually, you have to do the full six,' I'm not sure what I would have done. It would have been devastating. My spirits began to rise a bit as my final week approached, but I tried not to get too excited about it just in case some fellow did take it into his head to make it difficult for me. By this stage I couldn't wait to get back on a horse again. I missed riding. It was the longest period I had ever gone without sitting on a horse since I was able to sit upright on my own. Even with injuries and suspensions, I had never been off for more than six weeks. And then I began to think, 'I wonder if I'll still be able to ride?' That might sound a bit silly now, but I just wanted to go and do it straight away just to prove that I could still could.

I thought a lot about what I would do immediately after I got out. I wanted to be around horses, I wanted to ride, but I wanted to be away from England, away from the media glare. I had been writing to Kay Hourigan, and one evening I thought, 'That's it, I'll go to the Hourigans', if they'll have me.' I had lost touch with Mike along the way a bit since moving to England, but I never felt that I couldn't pick up the phone to him if ever I was in trouble. He's a real father figure to me, Mike, and his wife Anne is fantastic, and Kay and the whole family. They are a great family. I thought I would be made welcome there and I hoped I would be able to ride out a bit.

I spoke to Broady about it and he thought it was a good idea. Get out of England for a little while, spend some time with the Hourigans, get fit again. There was a gym in the prison, but I only actually got to go to it once. You had to apply to use it. I applied during my first couple of weeks there, but by the time my application came through I was in my final week.

Kay answered when Broady phoned the Hourigans' house, about a week before I got out. Mike and Anne were on holiday in Marbella. When he put it to Kay about me coming over to stay with them for a little while when I got out, she was delighted. 'Absolutely, brilliant, tell him we'd be delighted.' She phoned Mike in Marbella to tell him. I felt excited when Broady told me. It felt like I was going home.

I counted down the days, then the hours, but I was still very cautious. I swear to God I was sure that something else was going to come up that would keep me inside for a while longer, so I tried not to think about it too much. Then, one day, the guard came in the door and said, 'Right, let's go.'

It seemed to take for ever to get out. I had to complete all the formalities, all the administration, collect my belongings and put on my clothes, and all the while freedom was getting more and more real, so close I could almost grab it in my hands and splash it all over my face. Seanie and Dawn would be out there, ready to collect me. What would I do? I couldn't very well go legging it down the road to them in the car, like a school kid. I'd probably walk, cool as you like, as my heart leapt for joy. No more would I have to ask for everything. No more would I be told when to get up, when to go to bed, when to go to the toilet, when to eat. There is no doubt about it: you don't appreciate your basic liberty until it is taken away from you. If I was a different person at that moment to the person I had been back in April, I hoped that I was a better one. I hoped that I had learnt to appreciate life a little more. It may have been easy to think it then, standing there with my bag of belongings and my big black sack full of letters, ready to leave, but while I regretted what I had done I didn't regret paying the penalty for it. I am a firm believer in things happening for a reason. If I could learn from this experience, it might even turn out to be a positive thing. It may have been for the best. Who knew? Time would tell.

I looked up at the calendar on the wall, which read 22 October 2002. I would remember this date for the rest of my life. Eighty-four days of hell, and here I was about to go out on to the other side. They opened the gate that stood between me and the world, and I walked through it. A new beginning.

CHAPTER FIFTEEN

PRODIGAL SON

Fresh air is an amazing thing. I could almost taste it. I had only been outside once in the previous three months, and I was so much on tenterhooks in the exercise yard that day that I didn't appreciate it. I stood for a second outside the prison and took a couple of gulps, filled my lungs, then went home with Seanie and Dawn and had a meal. A real meal.

It was great to spend time with Seanie and Dawn without a guard standing there watching every hand movement and listening to everything you were saying, without looking at the clock and knowing that your time with them was going to be up soon, without knowing that you would be sleeping on a hard bed that evening in a room that had bars on the window. And it really was fantastic to see Shane again. He was about twice as big as he was when I had gone in. They do a lot of growing in three months. But to sit on a horse again – that was what I really wanted to do.

Seanie was riding for Martin Bosley at the time, and he had arranged for the two of us to go over to Martin's the following morning to ride out. It was like a little get-out-of-jail present for me, like your brother might arrange for you to have flying lessons as your Christmas present. I was a little nervous to begin with. Would I be able to do it? Would I have forgotten how? I was, and I hadn't. It was amazing. Just to sit up on a horse again, tuck my feet into the irons, feel him breathe beneath me. The first canter was fantastic. To feel his body move up and down rhythmically beneath mine, smoothly, easily; to squeeze my legs together a little so that he picked up for me, willingly, enthusiastically. It was an amazing feeling, and one that I had missed desperately.

A couple of days later I was on a plane to Shannon. There was no problem with me flying. I hadn't even thought there might have been until Mike mentioned it to me when I got to Hourigan's. It was funny going back to Lisaleen Stables, where it had all begun for me the best part of a decade earlier. So much had changed in the meantime. I had been through so much, and Mike had done a lot of building around the place – he must have spent some of that money he was saving up – but he was still the same Mike. He and Anne welcomed me into their home like I was their prodigal son.

I rode out three lots the first morning and it nearly killed me. I pushed myself because I wanted to get fit again. Mike didn't force me. He told me there were horses there to be ridden if I wanted to, but to see how I felt myself. So I just rode out, ate and slept. I didn't do a whole lot else. I probably had about three months' sleep to catch up on, and about two and a half months' worth of nutrition. I was less than nine stone when I came out of prison. Mike said that I looked gaunt, ill even, but that I still had my talent. Now, drop your irons!

I didn't talk much, and that must have been difficult for Mike and Anne, but they were brilliant, they didn't push me to do anything. If I wanted to talk, they were there to listen, and I knew that. Mike used to go swimming every evening up in the Woodlands Hotel, and I used to go with him sometimes. He'd be doing his lengths away on one side as I'd be pounding the water on the other, nowhere near as smooth as Mike but much more aggressive. It was a mixture of my frustrations coming out and the fact that I just wanted to push myself to get fit as quickly as possible.

I built up my muscles gradually. You use muscles when you are riding that you hardly ever use when you are not, and all mine were weak. I rode five lots one morning and I had to go and lie down for the rest of the day. But I was getting there. I was getting stronger. Anne was feeding me well, and I was sleeping well. I'd come up to the main house after riding out and then they might not see me for the rest of the day. I would just go up to my room or into the sitting room and crash, sleep for most of the afternoon. Then I might go for a swim with Mike in the evening.

Nearly a week after I had arrived I was sitting in the sauna with Mike in the Woodlands, just the two of us, and I just started to talk. I started to tell him about prison: what it was like, what I did, how I filled my days, what I thought. It just seemed like the right thing to do. I just felt like telling him. It was nothing too deep, no real opening up or baring of my soul; we were just sitting there, the two of us, and it just felt like the right thing to do. He seemed genuinely interested, and he listened to me.

Broady was anxious for me to go back to England as soon as possible. He told me that he still had all these trainers ringing him up, wanting to support me, offering me rides, so that made me feel good. I still wanted to stay away from the public glare, but I had my hearing with the Jockey Club at Portman Square to get my licence back on 30 October, and I knew that if I wanted to get my career back on track I would have to return to England. A lot of the trainers were great. People like Mark Pitman, David Gandolfo, Jim Old and a host of others. Barry Marshall, who owned Armaturk, was reported as saying that he wanted me to ride his horse in the Haldon Gold Cup at Exeter on the Tuesday, just two weeks after I had been released from prison. I suppose the Jockey Club could have refused me a licence, but they didn't, so I was eligible to ride in the UK again. I schooled a few for Mark Pitman and I rode out for David Gandolfo the following day, as all the while I counted down to what would be my first ride back: Fireball Macnamara for Mark in a novice chase at Wetherby on Friday, 1 November.

It was great to be back in the weigh room that Friday. To see the lads again and take my place beside Andy Thornton, the place that had been vacant for more than three months. To smell the leather and the Deep Heat, to put on my boots and silks, to weigh out and walk into the parade ring. People were great. People around the parade ring were supporting me, applauding me and telling me that it was great to have me back. I felt like I was wanted, that I wasn't cast away, that I wasn't forgotten. And it felt great.

I finished second on Fireball Macnamara in the two-mile novice chase. It was his first ever steeplechase race and he didn't jump very well, so he did well enough. I felt fairly good though. Of course there is no substitute for match practice, and you can ride out and school as many times as you like but you will still not get to the level of sharpness you will if you are race-riding regularly. But that would come with time. For a first effort after being cooped up for three months, it wasn't so bad. Interestingly, it was a horse of Paul Nicholls', Epervier D'Or, under Mick Fitzgerald, that won the race.

The press were actually OK with me. A couple of them had phoned Seanie while I was at Hourigan's, asking him where I was. Seanie just said he didn't know. A few of the better informed ones had phoned Mike.

'I hear Timmy Murphy is with you at the moment. Is that true?'

'He is not,' Mike told them. 'But when you get to talk to him, tell him that he still owes me a few weeks' rent.'

I did my couple of interviews and it was all the same kind of thing: how do you feel, what do you think. It went on for bloody ages though. Every time my name came up they always had to mention the jail term. They couldn't just say 'Timmy Murphy', or 'jockey Timmy Murphy', it always had to be 'Timmy Murphy, who has only recently been released from prison after serving three months for indecently assaulting an air stewardess'. They must all have used the same template. Still, at least they were writing about me and talking about me a little, so that wasn't a bad thing.

Things built up gradually. I had a few rides the following day at Ascot, the Saturday. I finished third on Colombian Green for David Gandolfo in the two-mile handicap hurdle, I finished fourth on Briar for Mark Pitman in the juvenile hurdle, and I finished second on Infrasonique in the three-mile handicap chase for Lavinia Taylor. That one nearly killed me. Chasing McCoy on one of Pipe's around Ascot in a three-mile chase on soft ground when you are less than match-fit is just not what you really want to be doing, but I was able to ride a finish and I hope I repaid Lavinia's faith in me.

I returned to Ireland on the Sunday for one ride, Royal County Buck for Tony Martin, in the beginners' chase at Navan. He was a 14–1 shot and didn't have much of a chance, but I didn't care. I was grateful to Tony for putting me up and we both came home intact, even if we were about 50 lengths behind the winner. I met Jennifer Walsh (daughter of Ted, sister of Ruby) at Navan that day and I asked her if I could stay with her that night, as I needed to get to the airport in the morning in order to get back to England. Fair play to Jennifer, she put me up no problem and drove me to the airport the following day. In fact, over the next four or five months I stayed with Jennifer a lot whenever I was in Ireland. The way it began to work out, I would ride in England during the week and go back to Ireland at weekends. A lot of the good racing in Ireland took place on Sundays, and Sundays in England were only really getting going then.

As it turned out I didn't get to ride Armaturk in the Haldon Gold Cup. Ruby Walsh was riding all Paul Nicholls' horses when he was available, and he came over to take the ride. I was a bit disappointed, given that he was one of the horses I had most been looking forward to riding during my time in prison, but Paul and Ruby had their arrangement in my absence, so I couldn't complain.

Ruby's place in the weigh room was right beside me during the winter. The Walsh family have always been very good to me throughout my career. I have often looked for advice from Ted in the past, and I am sure to do so again in the future. They are always willing to help someone out. I'm not sure if Ruby felt a little uncomfortable coming over to ride for Nicholls and sitting beside me, given that I had been riding for Nicholls before him. If he did feel uncomfortable, he needn't have. I didn't feel any animosity or jealousy, or anything like that. In fact I was delighted to help Ruby out whenever I could: advice on riding for Paul, horses whose little idiosyncrasies I knew, what Paul would expect, or how this owner or that owner was. You are in the unusual situation when you are a jockey that your sporting rivals are also your work colleagues. While we are all against each other on the track, off it we are probably as close a group as you will get anywhere. The camaraderie among jump jockeys is second to none, and we help each other out whenever we can. Ruby is a good friend and a top-class rider. He has struck up a hugely fruitful relationship with Paul, and I'm delighted for him.

I actually did get to ride in the Haldon Gold Cup though. Nicholas Butterly, who was involved with Davids Lad, the horse on whom I had won the Irish Grand National, had a horse called Ichi Beau in training with Ferdy Murphy and he wanted to support me, so he very generously asked me to ride his horse. He was a 33–1 shot, eleven pounds out of the handicap, but I was still grateful to the owner for offering me the ride. I needed as many rides as I could get, and the Haldon Gold Cup is one of the most high-profile races at that time of the season. We finished last of the six runners and Armaturk finished third. The race was won by Edredon Bleu, ten years old and 10–1.

It was about ten days and twenty rides before I rode my first winner back, Santenay, trained by Paul Nicholls, in a valuable hurdle race at Wincanton in which we just got up on the line. It was a great feeling to be led back to the winner's enclosure with all the lads there. I have to say, the crowd at Wincanton that day were superb. They gave me a really warm reception as I was led back in, and I thought, 'This is a great game. This is what I missed.' Paul Nicholls put me up a bit in those days when Ruby wasn't available. Joe Tizzard was injured and Fitzy was obviously still committed to Henderson, so there were a couple of rides going. I got back on Armaturk in a good two-mile handicap chase at the Cheltenham November meeting, and I rode Poliantas for Paul to finish second to Cyfor Malta in the Thomas Pink (now the Paddy Power) Gold Cup on the Saturday. Cyfor Malta was a remarkable horse. He had won the race four years earlier as a five-year-old and here he was coming back to win it again as a nine-year-old under Barry Geraghty, with McCoy on the stable's selected Chicuelo. Later that month I rode Poliantas to win a decent chase at Wincanton.

On 19 November I won on Cresswell Quay for Peter Bowen at Newton Abbot, and I rode him again at Warwick a week later in a three-and-a-quarter-mile handicap chase. I used to love riding Cresswell Quay.

He was one of those horses who would give you his all. He didn't have any great gears, he would just keep galloping, and he would often get there on the line. It was as if he knew where the winning post was. The trick was not to panic on him. The ground was so soft at Warwick that day that three fences had to be omitted. Cresswell Quay was favourite, and there was the weight of expectation that that brings, but I kicked him off out the back of the thirteen-runner field anyway, and we popped away. Down the back straight for the final time we began to creep closer, but he got in too tight to the fourth last and lost momentum. I didn't do too much on him, there was plenty of time yet. I just allowed him time to gather himself and he began to pick up again. He just lobbed along, making gradual progress, picking up his rivals one by one. I took him between horses going to the last, but he made a mistake there again and lost more ground. Still no panic. I allowed him to gather himself again and then asked him for his effort, which he duly gave me, and which was sufficient to get us home by two and a half lengths from Young Thruster. I was really chuffed when, at the end of the season, *Racing Post* readers voted that ride as the best National Hunt ride of the year.

Still, it wasn't easy to build my career back up again. I was still trying to eke out an existence and build up momentum, riding out for Mark Pitman, David Gandolfo and Jim Old in England and coming over to Ireland at the weekend to ride for Tony Martin and Mike Hourigan, staying with Mike or with Jennifer. I was extremely grateful to all those trainers who stood by me, and Jennifer was great company and was always willing to listen to me. I was a bit of a nomad. It can't have been easy for her having me living in her house, with my occasional moods and my frequent surliness. She was working for Irish Racing Services at the time. She therefore went racing in Ireland whenever there was racing on, so she didn't have to go out of her way to bring me racing, but still, it can't have been easy having me in the car with her all the time, although she'd never admit it.

I remember one evening getting home from the races with Jennifer, turning on the television, and the film *The Green Mile* was on, about a big black guy who is on Death Row. I didn't mind, but Jennifer got a little embarrassed, so she decided to switch channels. Fine by me, but not fine by her when the programme to which she switched was about a girl who was burying diamonds outside the grounds of Wormwood Scrubs! Poor Jennifer. I didn't mind at all, but she was mortified.

Nothing was happening too quickly for me. In fact, it was like going back to the start again. I began to question the way I was riding, if I was still as capable as I had been before my spell in prison, and that was assuming I was even semi-capable then. Was my balance as good, my judgement of pace, my ability to present a horse to a fence? I wasn't riding that many winners, but maybe I wasn't getting on horses that could win. Then again, maybe I had lost it. I didn't think that I had lost it, but how do you know?

I had a conversation with Mike one evening.

'What are you going to do, Timmy?' he asked me.

'I'm not sure what I'm going to do,' I told him, 'but I'll tell you what I'm not going to do. I'm not going to end up riding the odd horse here and the odd horse there. I'm not going to just be a survivor. I'm desperate to get back riding good horses, and I'm going to do whatever I need to do in order to make that happen.'

Mike looked at me pensively for a few seconds. 'Well, I just might have the right horse for you here,' he said carefully. 'Maybe I can get you to ride him. He'll put you back on the map.'

I had ridden Beef or Salmon in a couple of pieces of work, and he hadn't really felt like anything special. He felt like a nice horse, now, but just like a lot of other nice horses I had sat on. Nothing exceptional. He had won a couple of bumpers, a hurdle race and a qualified riders' race on the Flat, and he had finished third in a November Handicap at that stage. Paul Carberry rode him in his first ever chase, the Morris Oil Chase, a Grade 2 race in which he was competing against experienced chasers, and he had beaten them hands down. But Paul was with Noel Meade, so he couldn't commit to riding Salmon.

I rode him in the Hilly Way Chase at Cork in early December. I wasn't too certain of the wisdom of running him in a two-mile chase, a horse that was supposed to be a three-miler, but he showed remarkable pace to win comfortably in the end from River Clodagh and Fadoudal Du Cochet, who had won the Grand Annual Chase at Cheltenham the previous March. Mike asked me what I thought afterwards, and I told him, 'If this fellow is a three-miler with that pace over two, he's some tool.'

We would find out in the Ericsson Chase at Leopardstown's Christmas Festival. It was only a seven-horse race, but these were the best staying chasers in the country – Harbour Pilot, Colonel Braxton and Rince Ri, and First Gold was coming over from France. It was difficult to believe that Salmon was only a novice, competing in only the third steeplechase race of his life. I just hunted him round at the back, giving him time and space at his fences. The fact that there were so few runners and the ground was heavy was in his favour as it meant that they didn't go a fast gallop and I was able to just get him popping over his fences. I kept him to the outside and on the better ground, giving away ground but giving him a clear sight of his fences. I didn't start asking him to go faster until going to three out, and even then I didn't put the gun to his head, I just squeezed my legs together a little. The response was impressive. How fast do you want me to go? One by one we picked them up. Over the second last and around the home turn towards the final fence. We met the last on a perfect stride just behind Colonel Braxton, winged it, and pulled right away up the run-in.

I got a hell of a kick out of that. I always get a kick out of riding good horses, and this fellow was one of them. He was a freak. He was never bred to be any good, by Cajetano. Who was Cajetano? Nobody had ever heard of Cajetano before Salmon came along. And he was pretty ugly, to be fair to him. He had a big arse on him, a ratty little head and a tail that never grew, and he was always miserable in his box. But he had an engine and he had speed. He had a nice low action I always thought would be more effective on good ground than soft, and he has proved that he can go on good or fast ground, but he was also one of those unusual horses who could use his speed on soft ground just as easily.

Mike was on a hiding to nothing running him in all these big races. It was an amazing programme of races for a horse who had never jumped a fence in public before that season: Morris Oil Chase, Hilly Way Chase, Ericsson. People said that he was off his head running him in the Ericsson, a novice having only his third ever chase. If he had got beaten in that, the I-told-you-so merchants would have been out in force. They were also waiting for him after the Hennessy, but after winning the Ericsson you had to go for the Hennessy. It was the only race you could really go for after the Ericsson. It was only natural that there would be talk of the Gold Cup after the Ericsson, but we figured we'd get the Hennessy out of the way first before committing.

Beef or Salmon aside, I was back to being a journeyman jockey, just riding what I could in England and Ireland. I made about the same amount of money and had about the same number of rides in each country during that time, going over and back usually twice a week. I picked up a hell of a spare on Marlborough in the King George at Kempton on St Stephen's Day. Fitzy chose to ride Henderson's other horse, Bacchanal, in the race, and we finished second and third to Best Mate. I thought turning for home that we had a hell of a chance of winning it, but Best Mate was just too good and we went down by just over a length.

Beef or Salmon and Marlborough were the exceptions, however. In spite of the promise I had made to myself, I did end up riding a lot of no-hopers. Don't get me wrong, I was glad to be riding anything, delighted to be back in the saddle, and I was really appreciative of the fact that a lot of owners and trainers had enough faith in me to put me up. But it's like everything: the more you get the more you want. Once I'd got back riding, I wanted to be riding winners. I had no major yard behind me – though I suppose there are only a few major yards – so I had to take what I was given. I don't want to sound disrespectful to anyone with an average horse – I was delighted to ride it; I'd bite their hand off to ride it – but at the same time, as much as you appreciate getting the ride, you probably know it's not much good. You still want to win, so you kill yourself to try to get it to run faster, but it just can't. It gets you down a bit. Broady used to apologise for booking me on some of the horses he put me on. Novice chasers that couldn't jump, and suchlike. I'd come in afterwards, almost always in one piece, and give him a bollicking. 'What did you put me on that for? It had never seen a fence before!' But there were so many trainers, small trainers mainly, ringing him up wanting me to ride their horses, wanting to support me, wanting to give me an opportunity to ride a winner, that it made me feel good at the same time.

In the back of my mind I knew I probably shouldn't be doing as well as I was doing. I probably shouldn't be back riding at all. Think of your first week in prison, Timmy. If you had been told that you'd be back riding regularly in Ireland and England with the support of a lot of good people and good trainers who were putting you up, how big a lift would that have given you? How difficult would it have been to believe that at the time? But I still wanted to win, and when you don't win on a regular basis it kind of gets you down. That was why I got such a kick out of winning the Ericsson on Beef or Salmon. This was Concorde compared to the other light aircraft I was riding.

You can't do it without the horse. Nobody can. I'm sure Paul Carberry was a bit gutted that Harbour Pilot was around at that time. If Noel Meade hadn't had a high-class staying chaser at the time, who knows? Paul might have ridden Salmon in the Ericsson, I may never have got to ride him, and the Timmy Murphy story might be completely different to the one it is today. Because, not for the first time, Michael Hourigan's prophecy proved to be spot on the money: this horse did put me back on the map. For a horse like Beef or Salmon to come along at any stage in your career is rare. But for him to come along just at that time, when I really needed a horse to carry me and my flagging career back into the limelight, was just unbelievable. You need horses to put you in the headlines. Otherwise you're just another jockey. 'Well, he rode good winners there at one time, but what has he done since he came out of prison? He's not the same jockey.' It took a while for people to stop talking about prison and start talking about my riding, and Beef or Salmon was the main instigator of that.

Brendan O'Rourke has always said that Beef or Salmon saved my career. Brendan is a son-in-law of Dermot O'Rourke, who was a director of the National Stud, who bought the late Lord Howard de Walden's Plantation Stud last year, and who has been a friend of my Dad's for years. I moved in with Brendan and his girlfriend (now wife) Diane in January 2003. I figured that Jennifer had had enough of me and I didn't want to overstay my welcome. Brendan lived very close to my parents, so that was good, and Jennifer often still collected me from Brendan's house when I needed a lift to the races.

I was fairly down in myself when I got to Brendan's. I was wrecked from all the travelling across to England and back, just to ride, just to keep my name up there. Brendan used to sit me down at the kitchen table and try to perk me up. One night I sat there with him from seven o'clock in the evening until four o'clock the following morning, just talking. He was great. He'd try to make me feel good about myself and good about my riding. Your talent doesn't go away just because you haven't ridden for three months. Have you forgotten how to swim, or how to ride a bike? 'Beef or Salmon,' he'd say, 'that's your ticket.' Every second day we used to talk about Beef or Salmon. I loved talking about Beef or Salmon. He was the one horse who could potentially carry me back into the limelight, and, thanks to Mike and to the owners Joe Craig and Dan McLarnon, he was my ride.

At the same Leopardstown Christmas meeting at which Beef or Salmon carried me to victory in the Ericsson, I also rode Hi Cloy for Mike to win a maiden hurdle. Then I rode him to win a decent novice hurdle at Leopardstown in January, and they started talking about letting him take his chance in the SunAlliance Hurdle at Cheltenham. He was another string to my bow. Were it not for him and Beef or Salmon, it would have been a whole lot more difficult to get up in the mornings than it was. And it still wasn't easy.

I cut down on riding out a bit. My body just couldn't take it. I was going around absolutely wrecked half the time as it was, looking terrible, and I'm sure it wasn't doing my riding any good. Of course I wasn't drinking, so I wasn't going out that much. I tried to avoid going out in the beginning, and I was probably a grumpy old bugger as a result. I remember being in Kiely's pub in Donnybrook in Dublin one night with Jennifer and a lot of her mates. I just got pissed off with it all. Everyone was getting progressively more drunk and nobody was making any sense. Eventually, I'd had enough. I caught Jennifer's eye. She knew I wasn't enjoying myself, so she suggested we head home. She was great like that, always looking out for me even if it meant cutting her night short.

I had some difficult times then, psychologically difficult times. Sometimes it was like I was back at Noel Chance's or Dermot Weld's: I just couldn't really see from where the breaks were going to come. But so many people were good to me. Mike and Anne used to pick me up from Shannon airport, and Brendan or Jennifer would bring me to Dublin airport or pick me up from it. I'd say Brendan's car could have found its way to the airport on its own.

All of my travelling expenses were coming out of my own pocket. I was doing it because I knew I had to. I never really got to a point where I said, 'Feck this, I can't do this any longer, there is no light at the end of this tunnel.' I just kept plugging away. But it was hard. I didn't want to be just a journeyman jockey for the rest of my life. Of course, as I said, there were days when I realised how lucky I was even to have been given another chance, when I savoured being able to ride the likes of Beef or Salmon, but those days were few compared to the days when I felt down and washed up. But Brendan kept encouraging me. He kept telling me to take the money. Worst-case scenario it's a job, it's a good job; you love riding horses and it pays better than being a plumber or a carpenter. Of course he was right, it was just that sometimes I couldn't see it.

The Hennessy Cognac Gold Cup that February was almost a carbon copy of the Ericsson. Same course, same distance, almost identical rivals. I tried not to think of it as a big race, a high-profile race with thousands there and thousands more watching on television in both England and Ireland. I tried not to worry about the big occasion. Just ride your race. Because the pressure was on this time. Already they were talking about Salmon as a possible usurper of Best Mate's Gold Cup crown. In the Ericsson he was a 5–1 shot, just a novice who would be up against it to beat these seasoned campaigners, but in the Hennessy he was the even-money favourite and a real live Gold Cup aspirant.

I hunted Salmon round out the back, got him jumping, stalked the leaders, produced him at the last and ran away up the run-in. I got a huge kick out of that. You get a great deal of satisfaction from achieving your goal when the pressure is on. I smiled as Salmon and I careered away from Colonel Braxton and Harbour Pilot (again) up the hill to the line. It was at those moments when I thought, 'I might be back after all.'

It was fantastic to win the Hennessy, probably the most prestigious conditions steeplechase on the Irish racing calendar, and it was great for me, both from the point of view of building my confidence and for heightening my profile. People seemed to notice it more than they noticed the Ericsson. I'm not really sure why. Perhaps there is so much going on at Christmas, so much racing, that it all gets a bit diluted. But this was the middle of February when all of racing's eyes and ears in the UK and Ireland were focused on the Hennessy and on this new horse, a novice, that they were talking of as a Gold Cup pretender. Beef or Salmon was the new steed on the block, and Murphy was on him. That's Timmy Murphy, is it? The fellow who was in jail? Yep, apparently he's back.

They cut Salmon to 4–1 second favourite for the Gold Cup after that, and they were probably right to do so. It was difficult to see anything else bar him or Best Mate winning the thing. They were billing it as the Irish against the English (don't they bill everything as the Irish against the English at Cheltenham?), Arkle against Mill House, L'Escargot against Red Rum. Alas, it wasn't to be. It was a big pity because I really thought he had a chance of winning that Gold Cup. Although his two big wins had been on soft ground, I always thought he would be a better horse on good ground. He has this nice low action, as I said, and he has speed. I always thought he wanted good ground. He didn't get beyond the landing side of the third fence. I hate that fence, the first fence in the back straight. Valley Henry had fallen with me there the previous year in the SunAlliance Chase. The ground kind of runs away from you on the landing side and it can catch a horse out. Salmon just clipped the top of it and landed too steeply. It was a novicey fall, I suppose, and some people were giving out afterwards, saying that Mike shouldn't have run him in the Gold Cup when he was still a novice. They didn't know what they were talking about. What was Mike supposed to do? He had won the Ericsson and the Hennessy, and he was second favourite for the Gold Cup. Mike would have looked like an eejit if he hadn't allowed him to go for the Gold Cup. Of course, these were the people who had said in December that he shouldn't be running in the Ericsson but who were very quiet after the race, and who were also very quiet after the Hennessy. They had found their voices again.

I had a pretty quiet Cheltenham apart from that. I had about ten rides but they were all 33–1 and 50–1 shots, and I didn't even get close. Hi Cloy did run in the SunAlliance Hurdle, but he was a 50–1 shot and he fell at halfway. Besides Salmon, the Tony Martin-trained Ross Moff was by far my best chance. He started favourite for the Grand Annual, but at ten years of age he just wasn't fast enough to be competitive over two miles and he finished fifth.

I'm not sure that Salmon was ever really the same horse after that fall. His back problems since then have been well documented, and Mike and Liz Kent have performed miracles even to be able to get him back on to a racecourse. He has now won eight Grade 1 races, but he rarely gave me the same feel again.

Davids Lad was supposed to be my Aintree horse that year. He had fallen at the fourth last when travelling really well in the 2002 Grand National, and Tony Martin had been preparing him for the 2003 renewal all season, and was considering running him in the Mildmay of Flete Chase at the Cheltenham Festival. I rode him in the Newlands Chase at Naas at the end of February in what was to be his last race before

Cheltenham. He wasn't given much chance by the bookmakers, being put in as the 14–1 outsider of the eight runners. I rode him out the back, which is how he liked to be ridden, the intention being that I would creep closer as the race developed. But he was never travelling. He just couldn't pick up out of the sticky ground they had that day. I didn't punish the horse. Perhaps I should have been a little more forceful, or made it look like I was being a little more forceful, but what are you to do? He was struggling so much on that ground that he wouldn't have finished any closer even if I had been hard on him. The horse blew for about twenty minutes after the race, and I was glad I looked after him as well as I could.

Still the stewards went to town on us. They banned me for seven days, fined Tony €1,000 and banned the horse for 42 days. It was ridiculous. It meant that the horse couldn't run at either Cheltenham or Aintree. There was nothing to be gained from not trying with the horse. The weights were already out for the Grand National so it wasn't as if he would be handicapped any more favourably if he ran poorly. It sparked a series of appeals. The first one to the Appeals and Referrals Committee of the Turf Club was unsuccessful, but then the owners, Nicky Butterly, Eddie and Jimmy Moran and Mattie Lynch, took the case to the High Court, which granted a stay against the ban, which would have meant that the horse could have run in the National. But the Turf Club appealed against the granting of the stay and won, which meant that the ban was in force again. Finally, the owners brought the case to the Supreme Court, which ruled in favour of the Turf Club. It was a situation that should never have arisen, and it really was an awful shame that the horse didn't get to run at Aintree. He ran a cracker to finish fourth behind Timbera in the Irish National, beaten just four lengths, under top weight of twelve stone.

It was very similar to the Harringay case at Towcester in November 2005. The mare, whom I was riding for Henrietta Knight in a novices' hurdle, had had a wind operation. She had made a noise before, and she made a noise again during the race, so I wasn't going to kill her. Again, it may have looked bad, but I was only minding the mare. She was doing as much as she could do with me. How can you get a horse to go faster when it can't breathe? The stewards obviously thought it did look bad as they fined Hen £1,000, banned the mare from racing for 40 days and suspended me for a fortnight. It seemed to be a case of appearances being more important than what was actually happening, perception more important than reality, and again it was crazy. Hen said afterwards that she was not in the habit of being dishonest. She asked why would she use the racecourse as a schooling ground when she had a perfectly good one at home. She had to go home and think about what to do as she had never been in the situation before. She was desperately upset about the whole affair, coming, as it did, just a couple of days after Best Mate had died. Anyway, we both appealed and we both won. My ban was rescinded, Hen's fine was quashed, and the mare was allowed to run again. My legal representative, Rory MacNeice, got into a bit of hot water for having a go at the stewards when he suggested that the RSPCA might be interested in stewards' secretary Paul Barton's views on how Harringay should have been ridden. But we did get a very fair hearing. The panel saw where we were coming from.

In 2003 there wasn't much summer jump racing in England, and in Ireland it was patchy. I was trying to keep my weight down so that I could ride anything, and that was difficult. I was so afraid of missing a ride, of missing an opportunity. I even had a ride on the Flat at 9st 2lb, which obviously wasn't doing my body any good. There are a lot of mixed cards in Ireland with two or three jumps races and a bumper mixed in with half a Flat card, and of course there are a lot of Flat-only cards at the weekends. So I spent my time going to the Kilbeggans and the Clonmels of the world, riding mainly for Mike, and a bit for Mick Halford, Tony Martin, Pat Hughes and a couple of others. In England, Mark was my main yard, but Hughie Morrison and Henrietta Knight were also very good to me.

When Brendan decided that he had had enough of driving me to the airport, he insured me in his car, his BMW. That was a huge deal. Brendan was very good to me always, very giving of his time, his space, anything he had really. He'd give me his car sometimes to go racing, which meant that he had to make his own way, get a lift or take Diane's car, but he didn't mind. That was just the way he is.

I'm sure I wasn't easy to be around. I think Diane found me tough going. I think she found me a little too quiet, like she wouldn't know what to say to me, or if she should even say anything to me. Some days I would work away without even saying hello, which was probably seen as being a bit rude, but I wasn't intending to be rude, that was just my way. I am quite happy to potter away in silence, but I realise that most people don't feel comfortable with that. However, Diane was great as well. She ironed my shirts and cooked my dinners.

Central Billing carried me through that summer. He was quite an incredible horse of Mike's. I rode him in six races between May and September 2003, and he won all six. Tipperary, Gowran, Tralee, Galway, Kilbeggan, Listowel – four handicap chases and two handicap hurdles, and all over three miles. The bizarre thing was that he didn't win any of the six races by more than three quarters of a length. He was one of those characters who only did just enough and kept as much for himself as possible. The time I won on him at Kilbeggan, Brendan told me that if I rode a double he'd give me his car for a week. I said, 'How am I going to ride a double? They're all goats I'm riding.' Anyway, two of the goats won, so I was fully mobile for a week.

That race at Kilbeggan – the Joe Cooney Memorial Handicap Chase, just an ordinary handicap chase – rocked the whole world of racing to its very foundation. That was the race in which jockey Kieran Kelly suffered fatal injuries when his mount, Balmy Native, fell at the fifth last fence. I was coming along behind Kieran on Central Billing when he fell. I saw his horse falling in front of me and managed to avoid them. We see so many falls on our journeys as National Hunt jockeys. You see some bad-looking ones and some easy-looking ones, but it is often the easy-looking ones that can do the most damage, as was the case with Kieran. It was desperately sad. We didn't know he had suffered fatal injuries at the time, but we knew it wasn't good. There was a cloud over the weigh room the whole evening, and that cloud covered the whole of the world of racing for a long time afterwards.

Kieran was a top rider, a top man. Just the week before that day in Kilbeggan I had taken quite a nasty fall at Galway, and it was Kieran who drove me home. It was quite incredible. One week he was looking after me, the next week he was gone. He was only just beginning to break into the big time as well, and I have no doubt that he would have made it. He was such a talented rider. Dessie Hughes had shown enough faith in him to allow him to keep the ride on Hardy Eustace in the SunAlliance Hurdle at Cheltenham just the previous March, and Kieran had repaid that faith by riding with every sinew of energy and no little guile to get Hardy home from Coolnagorna and Pizarro. His death was truly a tragedy.

When something like that happens, you stop and think for a moment. You know horse racing is a dangerous game, but you don't really think of the perils until something tragic happens. Shane Broderick, Chris Kinane, J. P. McNamara, Scott Taylor, Tom Halliday, Sean Cleary, Dary Cullen, Richard Dais … there are far too many serious injuries and deaths in this game. It was also desperately sad when Vince Slattery's little boy Jonty died just last year from a blood disorder. He was often in the weigh room during the summer months and all the lads got to know him well. Vince is one of the great characters of the weigh room. He was the only one who would go up to Dunwoody and mess with him if he was having a bad day. The rest of us would be cowering in the corner, but Vince would go up to him and tell him a joke or something. Everyone tried to help raise money for him. You always do what you can to raise funds for good causes. Under normal circumstances you wouldn't catch me doing a parachute jump or playing golf, but you want to do your little bit. You know your fellow jockeys would do the same if roles were reversed.

The early part of the following season, 2003/04, was a quiet enough time for me. Beef or Salmon was never right during that season. We won the John Durkan Chase at Punchestown and we won the Hilly Way Chase again, but it always felt like there was something niggling him. It wasn't until we got beaten by Best Mate in the Ericsson that they discovered the problems with the muscles in his back. After that, they had only about six weeks to get him ready for another crack at the Gold Cup.

I won a Grade 2 novice chase on Hi Cloy at Limerick on St Stephen's Day, and finished third on him behind Pizarro in the Grade 1 novice chase at Leopardstown two days later. At the Easter Festival at Fairyhouse later that season, we beat Kicking King in the Powers Gold Cup. I was delighted with my ride on him that day. I held him up and held him up as long as I dared and produced him on the line to win by half a length. I was disgusted with myself two weeks later at Punchestown, however, when we got mugged by Lord Sam in the Ellier Developments Chase. Mike just said something to me on the way out, something that put a little bit of doubt into my mind. Something like, 'Don't leave it too late now.' So I didn't. Lord Sam kicked every fence out of the ground that day, so swinging for home I had a look over at Jim Culloty, hard at work on him, and thought, 'Right, he's beaten anyway.' So I rode to beat Nil Desperandum and Sum Leader, which I did, and took it up on the run to the last, only for Lord Sam to get going again on the stands side and get up to do us by a neck.

Cheltenham was good in 2004. Beef or Salmon was a staying-on fourth behind Best Mate in the Gold Cup, which was a remarkable performance given how little time Mike had to prepare him for it. But I had two winners that year, Tikram in the Mildmay of Flete, and Creon in the Pertemps Final. It is great to ride a winner at Cheltenham, but two in the same week was fantastic, and it doubled my Cheltenham Festival tally. Creon was a 50–1 shot, owned by J. P. McManus. It meant a lot just to have a ride for JP, Ireland's most successful owner, but to ride a winner for him at Cheltenham was just unbelievable. JP was delighted, but he didn't have a penny on him. He said that if Creon had been a 500–1 shot he still wouldn't have backed him.

But one of the most significant things to happen to me that season happened in February, when Martin Pipe's office phoned Chris to ask if I could ride a horse for them in the Reynoldstown Chase at Ascot. McCoy was out with a fractured cheekbone and they needed a replacement. Of course I would. I had ridden for Pipe on occasion, a second or a third string at Cheltenham, usually after McCoy and Richard Johnson had had their picks, or at a lesser meeting if I was there and McCoy was at the main meeting. But this was a great one to get. This was a Grade 2 novice chase, £20,000 to the winner, and Our Vic was going to be a warm favourite for it.

I met Martin in the parade ring with the owner, David Johnson. I didn't have too much time with them, just exchanged pleasantries. There weren't many instructions, just a reminder that he had never been beyond two and a half miles before, so don't make too much use of him, just get him settled and get him jumping. I didn't do anything special on the horse, he was a really nice horse, but he jumped to his left a bit, which is not ideal at right-handed Ascot. I just kept him between the wings, but, to be honest, he could have gone around the hurdle track that day and still won. I was quoted in the papers the following day saying that I thought this was one of the nicest horses I had ever ridden, and that I thought he would have a great chance in the SunAlliance Chase. That was the truth. He gave me a really good feel and he had easily beaten some decent novices. I got off him in the winner's enclosure, told Martin and David what I thought, thanked them for the ride, and I was off. It was a brief encounter, but it was a significant one for all of us.

CHAPTER SIXTEEN

DAVID JOHNSON

When David Johnson was growing up, he was as likely to enter the world of racing as I was to enter the world of aeronautical engineering. His father was a docker who lived with his mother in a prefab on the east side of London, ordinary working-class folk with no interest in or connection with racing. In fact, David's dad was absolutely opposed to betting on horses. He figured, he had to work so hard for his money that he definitely wasn't going to throw it away gambling. Wise man.

That didn't stop David though. In fact, it may have encouraged him. There is often one black sheep in a family – spot the one in the Murphy household and David reckons he was it in his. He started off betting with his pocket money, just a sixpence each-way yankee on a Saturday, very low key, just a bit of fun. As he grew up and became a successful businessman and had a few more pounds around him, however, he began opening betting accounts with a couple of bookmakers. Suddenly he found that he was being invited by bookmakers to lunches and dinners. After initially feeling chuffed at making the invitation lists, he gradually realised that he was only being invited to these functions because he was losing money.

At one of them, he met a fellow called Robert Williams, a Newmarket trainer, who suggested to David that he should have a horse in training. It sounded great, but he didn't have the type of money that would be required, so he got three or four others and they all clubbed together, just a couple of grand each, and bought a cheap horse. That horse turned out to be Mister Majestic, who went and won the 1986 Middle Park Stakes at Newmarket, one of the most prestigious races for two-year-old colts on the racing calendar. The fuse was lit.

They sold Mister Majestic and bought a couple of other Flat horses. But David liked a punt, and he was becoming a little frustrated, mainly due to the fact that when he went to Redcar, Nottingham or Thirsk to have a few quid on one of his, he would invariably come up against one of Stoute's, Cecil's or Dunlop's, a Sheikh Mohammed horse or a Sheikh Hamdan horse that probably cost about twenty times what his had cost. It was just too difficult to compete on the Flat with the type of horses he could afford to buy.

He happened to be talking to somebody who introduced himself as Peter Scudamore after one of his horses had finished second one day. Scudamore suggested that his horse would do well over hurdles, and that he could introduce him to a good trainer of hurdlers if he liked. Of course, Scudamore was riding for Martin Pipe at the time. The following week, not only had the horse gone into training with Pipe, but David had also become the owner of a new French-bred horse of Martin's called As Du Trefle.

Strange, the twists life takes. That was in January 1993, and As Du Trefle racked up three wins before he got a leg and had to be put on the easy list. Four years later he came back. That's Martin Pipe for you. He won a novice chase at Southwell and started favourite for the Mildmay of Flete at the Cheltenham Festival with McCoy on board. That was the race in which I rode Pipe's second string, Terao, for Brian Kilpatrick, which, as I have mentioned, was sent off at 20–1 and provided me with my first Cheltenham Festival victory.

Of course, David and Martin went on to forge an unbelievably successful partnership, aided and abetted by the ubiquitous McCoy. But when the announcement came in April 2004 that McCoy would leave Pipe in order to take on the role as retained rider to owner J. P. McManus, the racing world was less than surprised. There had been rumours going around for a couple of seasons that AP was going to join McManus. It really appeared as if it was only a matter of time. Like I have said before about these racecourse rumours, they are rarely without substance. So, while it was the talk of the place, and while people were having difficulty getting their heads around the fact that we would be seeing McCoy in JP's green and gold silks rather than in David's blue and green ones after an eight-year partnership with Martin and David that rewrote most National Hunt records, nobody was really that shocked.

AP had phoned Martin the previous morning and said that he wanted to come over and have a chat. Apparently he was in tears when he told him he was leaving. I'm not surprised. Martin was like a father to AP, still is, and AP is like a son to Martin. Martin asked him if there was any point in trying to keep him, and AP told him that there wasn't. The offer was just too good.

It was a tough one for Martin, and, by extension, as the biggest owner in the yard by some way, for David. David was away playing golf with some clients when Martin phoned him to tell him the news.

'Is there anything we can do to keep him?' asked David.

'No. The offer is too good.'

'Well, what will we do then?'

'Let's not panic for now,' said Martin. 'We have Jamie Moore, Tom Scudamore, Tom Malone and Rodi Greene here, and we can use Richard Johnson when he is available, so let's not do anything too hasty for now. Let's think about it for a little while.'

So they did. Before they went on holiday together the following week, they made an offer to Richard Johnson, but after some deliberation he decided that he would stay loyal to Philip Hobbs and his owners. There were a couple of others who were in the running. Ruby Walsh and Barry Geraghty were both under consideration. Both of them had ridden second strings for Pipe at Cheltenham before and beaten McCoy, Geraghty twice at the 2002 November meeting including when he rode Cyfor Malta to win in the Thomas Pink, and Walsh on Blowing Wind, who beat Lady Cricket in the 2002 Mildmay of Flete. Geraghty couldn't commit to England, however, and he was probably just a little bit heavier than was ideal, but David made a tentative approach to Ruby on Martin's behalf. He phoned Jennifer Walsh, Ruby's sister and agent, and my good friend of course, and just asked her if Ruby was happy with life in Ireland.

'David,' said Jennifer, 'he's unbelievably happy with life in Ireland. Thanks a million for phoning though. Ruby will really appreciate the enquiry, but you know, he is very happy at the moment.'

I was an interested observer of all of this, no more. The day after the news broke about McCoy leaving, I was busy riding Macs Joy for Jessica Harrington to win the Swinton Hurdle at Haydock. Barry Geraghty would have ridden him, of course, if top weight Westender (the mount of A. P. McCoy) hadn't run and the weights had gone up, but he did and they didn't, so Macs Joy was allotted ten stone dead, which I could do handily enough. He bounced off the fast ground that day and won doing handsprings. Although I was desperate for a big job, I never thought for a second that I would be in the running to take over McCoy's role. I'm just not a Martin Pipe type of jockey. I'm not a McCoy or a Scudamore. That's just not my style. So I didn't even put my name forward for it. I didn't think there was any point.

I was therefore surprised to see an article by Andrew King in the *Racing Post* on 9 May saying that there had been a flood of money for me to be named as Pipe's new stable jockey. And then there was all the talk. Everybody wanted to interview me, all the press, the television stations, everybody. I just said that I didn't know anything about it, which was the truth, but that I was flattered to be mentioned as a potential, which was also the truth.

David had apparently admired my riding from afar. He said that I always looked to be at one with the horse, that you would always be able to spot me in a race, and that you wouldn't want me looming upsides going to the last. I was flattered. I'd never had any real dealings with David. I had ridden a couple of horses for him, mainly second strings, but I was always booked through Martin, never through David, which is the norm. Even when I rode Eudipe for him to finish second to Teeton Mill in the 1998 Hennessy at Newbury, the only times I spoke to him were in the parade ring before the race and in the unsaddling area afterwards. It was the same when I rode Our Vic for him to win the Reynoldstown. After that race I was struck by his politeness. 'Thank you for riding for me,' he said to me. I was gobsmacked. You're thanking me? That's not right. It was a privilege to be asked.

When David asked Martin about me, Martin told him that I hadn't even applied for the job. They couldn't approach me if I hadn't applied for it, so David phoned Broady.

'Why hasn't Timmy applied for the job?' asked David.

'Well, he doesn't think he's a Pipe type of rider,' said Broady. 'And he wouldn't get it anyway, would he?'

'Just get him to put his hat in the ring, will you?'

So I did, although I was a little bemused by it all. I told Brendan O'Rourke about it, asked him what he thought. 'Yeah, that would be a good job,' he said. 'You'd have to consider it if you were offered it.' Actually, later he told me that inside he was going, 'You fecking eejit! That's a fantastic job! Are you off your head even thinking about it? Jump at it! Grab it with both hands!'

In the back of my mind, I was thinking about Beef or Salmon. If I took another job, any other job, I probably wouldn't be able to ride him.

David phoned me himself shortly after that and we arranged to meet at a hotel just outside Swindon. I brought Broady along with me. I was no good at this sort of thing, no good at discussions or negotiations, so it was good to have someone there with me. Also, I had fractured my collarbone in a fall and my arm was in a sling, so I needed someone to drive me. It was the first time I had ever sat down and had an in-depth discussion with David. He seemed like a nice guy, straight and genuine, no angles, no hidden agendas. You can generally tell what a person is like within the first five minutes of meeting them, and the feeling I got from David was a positive one. He said he would like me to ride his horses, just for a year, see how it goes. He was at pains to point out that I wouldn't be Martin Pipe's stable jockey, rather I would be riding for him as an owner. That made more sense to me, to be David's rider rather than Martin Pipe's stable jockey. David had told Martin that he was going to offer me the position, and Martin had said fine.

I was a bit blown away by David's approach, to tell the truth. The magnitude of what he was saying didn't really register with me until later. I would ride all his horses. I would ride all the horses for the guy who had been champion owner for the previous three seasons.

'I'd be delighted to ride your horses,' I said. 'But I ride the way I ride. I can't take the job if I'm expected to ride like AP rides.'

'I'm not asking you to ride like AP,' said David. 'I'm offering you the job because of the way you ride yourself.'

I was thrilled. Not only was I being offered one of the top jobs in National Hunt racing, but my riding was also receiving a vote of confidence from the champion owner. It didn't get much better.

The meeting was quite short actually. If I'm honest, I was quite shocked at how suddenly it ended. David just asked me how I felt about it, and I just said fine. I think he was a little disappointed at my lack of reaction, but that's me. Inside my head and my heart were doing overtime. Chris asked a lot of the questions, but really there was only one thing I needed to know: would I still be able to ride Beef or Salmon? I asked David. He didn't think so, not really. My heart sank. It wouldn't work. Sure, if there were no clashes, then fine, but he hoped that he would have runners in those top staying conditions chases in which Beef or Salmon would be running. If he let me ride Salmon, it would mean that he would have to go and find another jockey for those big races, and that wasn't on, given that I had agreed to ride all his horses. Why would you strike an agreement with someone and then let them go and work for the opposition on the biggest days of all? He wanted a top jockey, a team player, someone who would ride for him and think of the long term instead of just thinking of one race. He didn't want to be always scratching around for the best available because the best available are always snapped up on the big days. He was right, of course, but still I was a bit disappointed. It was the only thing that was wrong for me, but we shook hands on it.

I had phoned Michael Hourigan to tell him that I was meeting David. Mike was delighted for me, but he did say, 'Make sure you get a clause in your contract that allows you to ride Salmon.' It was tough telling Mike that I hadn't secured that, but I was still hopeful that I would be able to ride him whenever he was running. Hopefully there wouldn't be any clashes, not for a while anyway, if Mike would have me.

I phoned Brendan O'Rourke to tell him that I had been offered the job. He was thrilled for me.

'Yes, but Beef or Salmon,' I said, fishing for a reaction.

'Beef or Salmon is a top-class horse,' said Brendan, 'but he is only one horse. Anything could go wrong with him. With the Johnson job, you have your pick of 40 horses, 50 horses, most of whom are good and any of whom could be top class. This is a fantastic job. You deserve it, but grab it with both hands and make it work now.'

It was pretty quiet during the summer as David didn't have that many summer horses. I went down to Pipe's to ride out, which was fairly strange. Jonothan Lower was doing all the schooling and Pipe had his other lads there as well. I couldn't help feeling that I was a little bit of an outsider. I remember one evening towards the end of that summer when I was back in Ireland, sitting in Brendan O'Rourke's kitchen, feeling fairly sorry for myself.

'I'm not happy,' I said to Brendan.

'What do you mean you're not happy? Haven't you got one of the best jobs in racing?'

'Yeah, well, maybe I'm not cut out for this,' I said. 'Maybe I'm not cut out for one of the best jobs in racing. Every time I go down there they're talking about McCoy. I'm not McCoy.'

'Of course you're not McCoy.' Brendan was getting a bit agitated.

'I don't know if I can take much more of this,' I added hesitantly.

'Listen,' said Brendan, getting angry now. 'Of course you're not McCoy, but McCoy is not fucking Timmy Murphy. You have that job because you *are* Timmy Murphy. They want you to be Timmy Murphy, not to try to be like McCoy. If you throw in the towel now, you're a failure. All the work you've done, all the travelling, all the grafting was to get to where you are now. Don't be an idiot. Now, do you want a cup of tea or not?'

I rode Beef or Salmon that November in the James Nicholson Chase at Down Royal, and we beat Kicking King in what proved to be a messy enough race. It was a small field and they went no gallop early on, so there was a danger that Kicking King would do us for speed, but Salmon quickened up really well after the last to win going away. I'm not too sure that David was totally happy with me going. I asked him early in the week and he had said, OK. He had a few runners at Wincanton on the day, including Comply or Die, so it was a tough one for him. I think the fact that McCoy was available to ride at Wincanton for him swayed him into allowing me go. But he made it clear that I probably wouldn't be free to ride him much more. That was fair enough. It was good of him to let me go to Down Royal in the first place.

At Pipe's, everything was being geared up for the November meeting at Cheltenham, as usual. Pipe and Johnson are synonymous with this meeting, but I didn't fully appreciate how much effort they put into preparing for it until I joined the team. Effectively, I was on a hiding to nothing. If we had four or five winners, which was going to be a tough task, it would be nothing more than would have been expected. Don't they always have four or five winners at that meeting? However, if we had one or two, you could be certain that the fingers would be wagging. They always had four or five when McCoy was riding them. But I didn't feel the pressure. Not that year. I was just tipping away, riding horses, so I was looking forward to it. But I didn't really appreciate how massive it was for David and Martin. I actually felt under more pressure in 2005, when I did appreciate it.

There was a bit of talk before the 2004 meeting about Pipe not being happy with me. I don't think he was too happy with one or two rides I had given his horses during the summer. There were a couple he thought AP would have won on, a couple on which he thought I should have been a bit more aggressive. Martin used to say that I would get stuck in to horses when they were beaten, when they had no chance of winning, but that I wouldn't be hard on horses I needed to be hard on in order to get them up to win. That was going back to my whip-happy days when I used to beat horses up if I thought they weren't trying for me. It's a difficult one. You don't have to be seen to be aggressive in order to get the most out of horses. There are different ways. McCoy has his way, I have mine. Just like Scudamore had his way and Dunwoody had his. But that was always going to be the problem. That was what I meant when I told David that I didn't think I was a Pipe type of jockey. That was why I didn't apply for the job in the first place. There were also rumours around that time that McCoy wasn't completely happy at JP's, or at Jonjo O'Neill's place, Jackdaws Castle. Jonjo was training the vast majority of JP's horses in the UK. Put all of these things into the mix, together with the close relationship McCoy and Pipe still had, and still have, and you could see why people thought that my position was under threat going into that November meeting.

Actually, it wasn't. Not my position as David Johnson's rider. Provided I did what David asked of me, he was happy. As long as I did my best. If I made a mistake, too bad; learn from it and move on. We all make mistakes; as long as we learn from them they are not in themselves bad things. It was a refreshing attitude, and one under which I thrived.

We got off to the best possible start at that meeting. If I was feeling a little nervous before the meeting got underway – and I don't remember being any more nervous than I would have been before any big meeting with a couple of fancied rides – it was dispelled when I won the first race I rode in, the Grade 2 two-mile novices' hurdle, on Marcel. But just when things looked like they were going to pick up and soar, I got beaten by Armaturk (of all horses!) on Well Chief in the two-mile handicap chase. I was disgusted with myself, and Martin and David weren't too happy with me. I kicked him off last, he was slow over the first three fences, and we were always playing catch-up after that. We just got beaten a head, and on the face of it it wasn't a bad effort for a horse having his first run against seasoned campaigners. But we should have won. I should have won. He was the best horse in the race and he got beaten. To be honest, I thought he would show a little more speed than he did, but I should have been closer. I would know better next time.

From then on, however, it was all positive. Well, almost all. I won the very next race, the three-mile novices' chase, on Comply or Die, which was the last race in which I could ride on the Friday. Then on the Saturday, we cut loose. I won the opener on Over the Creek, I won the second race on Vodka Bleu, just getting the better of Ruby on Paul Nicholls' Mount Karinga in a thriller, I won the Paddy Power Gold Cup on Celestial Gold, and I won the race after that, the three-and-a-half-mile handicap chase, on Stormez. Of course it was fantastic to win the Paddy Power, especially when Celestial Gold was our second string after Our Vic had got injured in the lead-up to the race, but Stormez's win was particularly sweet. Martin didn't think I would suit him. He needed lots of riding and cajoling – a real McCoy-type ride. In fact, he bet me a tenner I wouldn't win on him. Apparently that wasn't a good bet for me to take on, even money about a 7–1 shot, but I did. Fortunately for us, five fences were omitted in that race because the low sun would be in the eyes of the horses as they were jumping them. Stormez is tiny and always found it difficult to clamber over his fences, so the three-furlong run-in played right into his hands, and we won going away. Martin came into the winner's enclosure with the £10 note held high above his head. I still have that note, framed, hanging up in my dining room at home. I'd say I'm one of very few who has managed to extricate a tenner from Martin Pipe.

All of those winners were for David. The next day, the Sunday, I won the second race on the card on Team Tassel, owned by Matt Archer and the late Jean Broadhurst. She was a lovely lady. Any time you won a race for her, you had to be prepared to leave the winner's enclosure with a big lipstick mark on your cheek.

There was a bit of a sting in the tail for me at that meeting, however. One of David's horses, Contraband, was well fancied for the Grade 2 two-mile novices' chase on the Sunday, but Martin suggested, as he'd done with Stormez, that I wouldn't suit him, that he was much more an AP ride than he was a Murphy ride. I had been beaten on him by River City at Aintree the previous month, so David went along with it, even though he wasn't happy about it. I said, 'Fine, if thats what you want.' It was a bit of a kick in the head though. You're riding for someone, you're in this job, but you're not considered good enough to ride one of the horses. But what could I say? There was nothing I could do. The decision was made. I wondered what would have happened if McCoy hadn't been suspended on the Saturday. Would I still have ridden Celestial Gold in the Paddy Power? Probably. Would I have ridden Stormez? That would have been an interesting one. Martin was so adamant that he wasn't my type of ride that there is every chance AP would have been on board had he been available. We'll never know. All of this was going through my head as I watched Contraband get beaten by Fundamentalist on the television in the weigh room.

Contraband's next race was the Henry VIII Chase at Sandown the following month. Martin wasn't there to take my saddle as he was off watching another runner at another meeting. I didn't get to talk to him before the race at all, so I said to Frankie, the girl who looks after Contraband and who was leading him up, 'I haven't spoken to anyone, Frankie, what do you think?'

'You do whatever you want to do, Timmy,' she replied. 'Just win.'

So I did. Contraband almost always made the running, but he always ran a bit too freely, so I thought I'd try to settle him in behind. He mightn't run so free that way and he might have more energy left for the finish. I took a lead from Tom Scudamore on The Last Cast down the back straight. Every time he'd go to start pulling for his head I'd just take a little tug. He loved it. He loved running in behind horses and then passing them. We arrived upsides at the last fence and won going away. It was the most impressive performance of his career up to that point.

I rode Beef or Salmon once more that season. That was on his next run, in the John Durkan Memorial Chase at Punchestown against Kicking King. David let me go and ride him because the race was on a Sunday and he had no reason to keep me in England. In fact it was the last time I rode Salmon until the Punchestown Gold Cup in April 2006. Unfortunately, it wasn't a happy send-off. He just didn't feel right. He had missed two weeks' work in the lead-up to the race and he didn't jump with any fluency. Kicking King was just too good on the day. It would have been a big ask to beat Kicking King over two and a half miles even if Salmon had been at the top of his game, but he wasn't, and he eventually finished a disappointing third.

But 2004/05 was a hell of a season for me. I rode Best Mate for Henrietta Knight and owner Jim Lewis to win the William Hill Chase at Exeter in November. We just got home by a short head from Seebald, giving him weight. Best Mate was such a lovely, lovely horse to sit on. So balanced, everything in proportion. He was never a flamboyant jumper, he was just very quick over his fences. He was never a horse you could fire at a fence. If you did that, he would actually be slower getting over it. You just had to leave him alone and let him do his own thing, because he was very good at doing his own thing. It was a great privilege to be asked to ride him.

As it turned out, the William Hill Chase at Exeter in November 2004 was to be the last race that Best Mate would win. He only ran in two more races in his life. That December he got beaten by Beef or Salmon in the Lexus Chase at Leopardstown. The ground was desperate that day and suited Salmon much better. Best Mate had also banged his head on the ferry on the way over to Ireland and raced with staples in his face. Hen was preparing him for the Gold Cup the following March, but he bled from the nose following a gallop a week before the race and missed out on his attempt to land a fourth consecutive Gold Cup. His only other run was in the Haldon Gold Cup back at Exeter the following November. Regrettably, that was to be his last act.

Celestial Gold followed up his Paddy Power Gold Cup win by winning the Hennessy at Newbury. I was delighted with the ride I gave him there. I just crept and crept, similar to Davids Lad in the Irish National, and got there at the last upsides Ollie Magern before going on to win by a length and a half. Unfortunately Celestial Gold went wrong after that and ran just once before the Gold Cup the following March, where he finished down the field behind Kicking King after a less than ideal preparation.

I wasn't out of the woods with the stewards either. In December I rode a horse called Semi Precious for Paul Keane in a lowly handicap chase at Plumpton. He fell with me at the fourth last. He hadn't been doing anything for me during the race and I was frustrated as hell. As he was galloping away from me, absolutely unharmed, I jumped to my feet, tried to catch him, failed, and just fired my whip after him. It may have brushed his backside or it may not have, I don't know. It was irrelevant. It looked bad, I was told. I was up in front of the stewards and was given a seven-day suspension for 'improper riding following misuse of the whip'. I was livid. Improper riding? Firstly, I wasn't riding at the time, and secondly, the horse was completely unharmed. But it was the image of racing they were concerned about. We can't be seen to condone this sort of thing. Sometimes people are more concerned with how things look than how they are.

The timing of the ban was such that it would have ruled me out from 26 December to 1 January, the whole of the Christmas period. That was just too much, I had to appeal. I did, and the ban was reduced to one day, which meant that I could serve it on a day when there wasn't a Grade 1 race on. Common sense prevailed in the end.

In February I was banned for another seven days for not making sufficient effort on Oasis Banus in a maiden hurdle at Ludlow. It was crazy. The horse hardly jumped a jump and hung to his right. I niggled him along to try to get closer down the back straight, but there was no response. There was no point in beating him up. I was dumbfounded when I was hauled in front of the stewards. It was as if they had a camera on me every time I rode, and if it looked like I even thought about doing anything that wasn't in the rule book they were doing me for it. Rory MacNeice, my legal representative, was convinced that I would win on appeal, but I decided not to. I didn't see the point.

But there were so many really good horses. Brendan O'Rourke was right. Marcel was brilliant for me that season. I won seven races on the bounce on him, from a novice hurdle at Kempton in October 2004 through that Grade 2 hurdle at the Cheltenham November meeting, taking in another Grade 2 event at Windsor, and culminating in a win from a high-class field of novices in the Grade 1 Tolworth Hurdle at Sandown. He started favourite for the Supreme Novices' Hurdle at the Cheltenham Festival the following March, but he just wasn't in the same form on the day as he had been earlier in the season.

Touch wood, I have been extremely lucky so far in my career to have avoided serious injury. Of course I have had broken arms and collar bones, but I haven't been on the sidelines for a protracted period of time due to injury. Like I say, I count myself extremely fortunate in this regard. You can't take anything for granted. But I did injure myself quite badly on Marcel at Stratford in August 2004. It was all very innocuous-looking. I was trying to anticipate the start. I thought the starter would let us go, but he decided not to, so I had to take Marcel back. When I did, the horse slipped and pulled me forward. Whatever way I wrenched myself, I felt this searing pain go through my back. We won the race, which was great, but when I cooled down afterwards I could feel the pain getting worse. The following morning I could hardly stand up. I spent about two weeks visiting different back specialists, but none of them could tell me exactly what was wrong. In desperation, I rang Stuart Pearce, the Manchester City manager. He had had horses in training with Mark Pitman, and I had got to know him as a result. He told me to come up that Saturday and he had the Manchester City physio take a look at me in the players' treatment room. He diagnosed it immediately – I had put my pelvis out of place – and recommended a guy in Reading, John Fern. John was brilliant, and I was right as rain again fairly quickly.

We had several other high-class horses and big wins that season. Medison won the Imperial Cup. Well Chief ran his heart out to finish third behind Moscow Flyer and Azertyuiop in the Tingle Creek Chase in December in one of the races of the decade. He fell with me when travelling like a winner in the Castleford Chase at Wetherby in early January, then, just when it looked like I might never get him right, he went and showed tremendous courage to win the Victor Chandler Chase at Cheltenham under top weight of 11st 10lb, giving a stone and six pounds to Thisthatandtother. Two weeks later he ran in the Game Spirit Chase at Newbury, where he got beaten by Azertyuiop, who was giving us four pounds. I was a bit disappointed with him there, he didn't jump as well as he can, but maybe the race came a little quickly after his Victor Chandler run. Then, in the Champion Chase at the Cheltenham Festival, he ran out of his skin to chase home Moscow Flyer, the pair of them well clear of Azertyuiop in third. We were always fighting a losing battle that day against Moscow, who put in one of the best performances of his career – and that's saying something. There was one point, on the run to the second last, when I thought we were going to get him, but Moscow just kept on finding more and beat us by two lengths. I'd say that had Well Chief found those two lengths from somewhere, Moscow would have found two more.

But we had two winners at the 2005 Cheltenham Festival, Contraband in the Arkle (yes, I held him up again) and Fontanesi in the finale, the County Hurdle. It was a hell of an Arkle in hindsight, with Ashley Brook, River City, Watson Lake and War of Attrition all in arrears. Then I went to Aintree and rode Al Eile for John Queally to get the better of World Hurdle winner Inglis Drever in the Aintree Hurdle.

The struggle between Martin Pipe and Paul Nicholls for the trainers' title went all the way to the wire. The Celebration Chase at the Betfred (ex-Whitbread) meeting at Sandown, with £58,000 to the winner, was going to have a huge impact on the destination of the title. They were both desperate to win it, so we had this quite unique situation where, in a nine-horse race, five were trained by Pipe and four were trained by Nicholls. Nicholls' four runners were spread across three different owners whereas of Pipe's five runners, only one of them wasn't owned by David. We barely had enough different coloured caps to go round. I wore the white cap with the green spots, rode Well Chief, and won the race in a cracker from Azertyuiop, thus securing the trainers' title for Martin.

David was champion owner with 111 winners and almost £1.8 million in total prize money, which was more prize money than anybody else. It was an incredible tally for an owner, and I had ridden over a hundred of them. David insisted that he shouldn't be winning the owners' championship, that he shouldn't be in the same league as JP, Trevor Hemmings or Paul Barber, he only a docker's son from the east end of London. And it had been an unbelievable season for me, way beyond what would have been my wildest expectations at the beginning of the season – if I had had expectations at the beginning of the season. I ended up with 143 winners, the first time I had broken through the century barrier and almost one and a half times as many as I had ridden in any season before that. Career-wise, things could hardly have been going better.

CHAPTER SEVENTEEN

FEET ON THE GROUND

It's strange the way this game never allows you to become complacent. If you ever get to feeling a bit smug, if you ever start to get a bit cocky, if you ever start to think you are great and that things are going well because you are great, and when you start forgetting about the perils of your profession, this game has a habit of providing you with a fairly stark reminder.

The 2005 Punchestown Festival began on Tuesday, 26 April, just three days after the last day of the British National Hunt season, when I had won the Celebration Chase at Sandown on Well Chief. I rode a nice novice chaser called Forget the Past for Michael O'Brien in the 3.45 that day, the Ellier Developments Novice Chase, and we won easily. We were all excited afterwards, as he was a lovely prospect. Talk of the 2006 Gold Cup was not misplaced, given that he ran out of his skin to finish third to War of Attrition in that contest the following March. A half an hour after I had dismounted in the winner's enclosure, however, I was fired into the ground on the far side of Punchestown when Emotional Article fell with me in the very next race, the handicap hurdle. Right back down to earth.

My arm was terribly painful, far too painful even to think about riding for the rest of the day. My Mam took me to Brendan O'Rourke's house, and Brendan brought me to Naas hospital where they told me what I already knew: my arm was broken. But they couldn't set it in Naas for some reason, so they sent me off to Blanchardstown Hospital on the north side of Dublin. When we got there, however, they told me to wait. Eventually I could wait no longer. I convinced Brendan that we should go, I went back to his place, slept there that night with a broken arm, and we went back to Blanchardstown the following day to get the arm set by their surgeon, Dr Kenny, who was excellent.

There was more pain in the early summer of 2005 when I finally split up with Dawn. These tough decisions are never easy to make, and believe me, this was a tough decision. It wasn't easy living together, but it wasn't easy splitting up either. The easiest thing in the world would have been to continue going as we were going, but it wasn't right. I certainly wasn't the easiest to live with at the time. I'm still not. If I had a bad day, everyone would suffer. And in racing you have a lot more bad days than you have good days.

It's so hard when you fall out of love. It wasn't right for any of the three of us – me, Dawn or Shane. It was tough on Shane, seeing his parents break up like that. He needs his Dad as well as his Mam, but it would have been tougher on him to see his parents arguing all the time, and I'm sure it was easier on him then, at the age of four, than it would have been at the age of ten or eleven.

Dawn moved into the house in Faringdon with Shane while I stayed in the house in Shrivenham, just about ten minutes away. As break-ups go, it was about as good as you'll get. We started getting on a lot better afterwards than we had been when we were living together, so that was good, and we worked it out so that I could see Shane regularly. All in all, it was a better state of affairs. It wasn't ideal for anyone, but I think we salvaged a lot from what could have been a very difficult situation, and I think the three of us are much happier now as a result.

Before the 2004/05 season ended, David asked me if I was happy with the same arrangement for the following season. Nonchalant as you like. He could have been asking me if I took milk in my coffee. I said I was, and again, that was that.

It was working well, and we had a good system. I would speak to David in the morning on my way to the races when he had runners, and go through all the horses, their chances, and how we thought the race would pan out. Then I would speak to him on the way home: how things went, what I thought, what I should have done, anything I would have done differently. Then I would phone Becky (Rebecca Ward) to file my report. Becky works at Carl Llewellyn's, but she also keeps me on the straight and narrow. She looks after everything for me. She tells me how much I can spend, how much I can't, where I can go, what engagements I have, when I am free. She's fantastic. I dictate my report to her on all the horses I ride for David, and she types them up and sends them to Pipe's. That's pretty much the system we still have going today. It seems to work well for everybody.

Jim Culloty retired that summer and there was a lot of talk about who was going to ride Best Mate. I was riding a little bit for Best Mate's trainer, Henrietta Knight, at the time, whenever my commitments to David allowed, so it was obvious that my name was going to be associated with her best horse. Hen was great to me, and I have learnt an awful lot from her and from her husband, former top rider Terry Biddlecombe. She likes the way I ride. There is nothing more important to Hen in the world – possibly with the exception of Terry, but only possibly! – than her horses. She is very sympathetic towards them and she knows I don't abuse them. But I was never going to be able to commit to riding Best Mate, for the same reason that I couldn't commit to riding Beef or Salmon. Hen wanted to use me whenever I was available though, so that was a great vote of confidence. Besides Best Mate, she also had a hugely exciting novice chaser, Racing Demon, who had finished second in the SunAlliance Hurdle and was being talked about as an Arkle candidate as early as October.

On 1 November, Hen sent both Racing Demon and Best Mate to Exeter. I couldn't ride Best Mate in the Haldon Gold Cup as I was riding Contraband for David in that, but I was free to ride Racing Demon in the two-mile novice chase. Paul Carberry rode Best Mate. I was never travelling on Contraband in behind; he wasn't jumping well and he never really felt like he would get competitive. I asked him to improve going to the fifth last. I remember going past Best Mate and thinking he wasn't travelling so well, but it wasn't until I pulled up after finishing fifth on

Contraband that I realised what had happened. Paul Carberry had pulled Best Mate up before the third last fence. As soon as he dismounted, the horse collapsed and died.

It was a desperately sad time for Hen and Terry, and for the horse's owner Jim Lewis, whose wife Valerie passed away just a couple of months later. Best Mate, triple Gold Cup winner, was a huge loss to racing, but it was just one of those things. Nothing Paul Carberry could have done and nothing Henrietta Knight could have done would have saved the horse on the day. Hen was in tears when she came to meet me as I pulled up on Racing Demon after winning the novice chase, the very next race. I just put my hand on her shoulder. What could I say? That's racing for you. That's life. One star fades, another begins to radiate brightly.

The 2005 Cheltenham November meeting was as you were. Just the usual five Pipe winners, then. It's quite incredible how Martin could prepare his horses for these races over those three days at Cheltenham. I didn't ride Martin and David's first winner, Getoutwhenyoucan, on the Friday in the amateur riders' race, obviously. In fact, I didn't ride any winners on the Friday. I was second on Buena Vista in the opener and on Celtic Son, who was beaten by Church Island, trained by Michael Hourigan and carrying the colours of Beef or Salmon's part-owner Joe Craig, in the three-mile novices' chase. But normal service was resumed on the Saturday. We kicked off by winning the novices handicap hurdle with Not Left Yet, followed that up with Standin Obligation in the long-distance handicap hurdle, and completed the set when Our Vic won the Paddy Power Gold Cup. If the monopolies commission ever investigated the Paddy Power Gold Cup in any of its recent incarnations (Mackeson, Murphy's, Thomas Pink, Paddy Power) Martin Pipe and David Johnson would be in serious trouble. The weekend was rounded off nicely when Bannow Strand easily carried me to victory in the two-and-a-half-mile handicap chase on the Sunday, beating the Philip Hobbs-trained Shalako into second place. Apparently, after that race Philip told Martin that he was disappointed Shalako got beaten as he thought he had about two stone in hand. 'Not enough,' said Martin. 'I had about three.'

I met Verity that year, Verity Green, daughter of Raymond and Anita Anderson Green who own quite a lot of horses in Scotland. Theirs are the green colours with the yellow sash that Sparky Gayle carried to victory in the 1997 Cathcart Chase. I ride for them whenever I can – nothing like putting added pressure on yourself! There was pressure on me to win on D J Flippance in a three-mile handicap chase at Ayr just before Christmas. Raymond expected him to win and, fortunately for me, he did. He just stayed on to beat Kerry Lads by a length and a quarter. It was quite possibly one of the most important winners I rode that season. And it made the journey home in the car a whole lot easier than it could have been.

Verity's brilliant. We just hit it off from the start. She used to work at Bangor racecourse. I'd seen her there but I never actually spoke to her until that summer. It was a strange weekend, another one of those what-is-meant-to-be-will-be scenarios. I was on my way to Andy Thornton's stag on the Friday in Blackpool. It was going to be a whole weekend – imagine, a gang of jockeys in Blackpool for the weekend. But I got stuck in a traffic jam on the M5, and, it took me about two and a half hours to go about twenty miles. So I said, 'Sod this.' I rang Chocolate Thornton, who lived close to where I was, and said, 'Let's go for something to eat, I'll stay with you, and I'll head up to Blackpool in the morning.'

Richard Burton was having a party to celebrate winning the amateur riders' title the following day, and Choc was going up to it. So he asked me to come along. It was up by Shrewsbury, it wasn't that far north from there to Blackpool, it would be good craic, so I said, 'Grand, I'll go.' It was at that party that I met Verity properly. I was standing in the corner on my own – I'm not really one to get stuck into the middle of a crowd at a party these days – texting or something on my mobile, when suddenly I heard this voice behind me.

'You know it's quite dull to be texting somebody when you are in the middle of a party.'

I was mad about her straight away. She had me out dancing and everything at the party, which isn't my scene at all, but she's just so bubbly and vivacious, always smiling, always in good form. Just like me, then. Actually, maybe not. Maybe that's why we get on so well, because we are so different. She's very good for me, and we're good together. We got engaged during the summer of 2006, and we're looking forward to getting married soon.

After Cheltenham's November meeting, the 2005/06 season didn't go to plan. A lot of the horses weren't running to form in the immediate aftermath. Martin couldn't explain it. He couldn't find anything wrong with them, but they just weren't getting home. Of the five winners he'd had at Cheltenham in November, none of them managed to win on their next outings, even though they were all well fancied. I had to pull Standin Obligation up five days later at Haydock, I pulled Getoutwhenyoucan up on his next outing at Sandown in early December, and I had to pull Our Vic up in the Robin Cook Memorial Gold Cup, run over the same course and distance as the Paddy Power, four weeks later. It was mystifying. They were just running lifelessly. Bannow Strand got beaten at odds-on in the revamped Edward Hanmer Chase at Haydock, and Not Left Yet got beaten at odds-on in an egg and spoon race at Market Rasen.

Actually, I'm not sure that Martin had his horses exactly where he wanted them to be at any stage that season. The stable star, Well Chief, was out for the season, which was a real pity as he had to have taken all the beating in all the top two-mile chases, including the Queen Mother Champion Chase at the Festival. There were a lot of rumours that Well Chief might be back in time for the Champion Chase, but he was undergoing stem cell treatment, with the result that he had to be kept in training. That was part of the treatment. The bookmakers had him in as short as 12–1 for the Champion Chase at one point, but he was never going to make it.

We did have a couple of good days during the season, though. I had a four-timer at Haydock in January, although only two of my winners were for David, Nous Voila and Don't Be Shy; the other two were Al Eile and Glasker Mill for John Queally and Henrietta Knight respectively. Still, any day you ride four winners is a good day. Riding Our Vic to win the Ascot Chase and Don't Be Shy to win the Game Spirit Chase at Lingfield in February was another good day. The Game Spirit was only a four-horse race and it was bottomless ground that day at Lingfield, but it was a decent performance from Don't Be Shy, a five-year-old, a novice, to beat hardened professionals like Armaturk (yes, again) and Mister McGoldrick. It all happened a little quickly for Don't Be Shy in the Arkle at Cheltenham and the Melling Chase at Aintree, but he would have been a serious prospect for 2006/07. Unfortunately, he had a fatal accident in his paddock during the summer.

The 2006 Cheltenham Festival could hardly have gone worse for us. Everything got beaten. When I finished third on Buena Vista in the opener, the Supreme Novices' Hurdle, I thought, 'That was close, not so bad.' I didn't think he was anything like my best chance of a winner, so I thought it could be a good festival. Turned out it was as close as I got the entire week. Don't Be Shy was well beaten in the Arkle, I pulled Korelo up in the William Hill Chase, and I pulled Commercial Flyer up in the SunAlliance Chase. Commercial Flyer was particularly disappointing as we thought he was our best chance of a winner at the meeting. Martin couldn't see him finishing outside the first three. Inch Pride in the Coral Cup, Celtic Son in the Jewson, Our Vic in the Ryanair, Westender in the World Hurdle, Bannow Strand in the *Racing Post* Plate, Standin Obligation in the Pertemps Final – they all got beaten, and most of them were well fancied. And then, finally, just to give me a good kick in the solar plexus as I lay on the ground, Celestial Gold unseated me in the Gold Cup. I was the one lying prostrate on the landing side of the third last fence so that the rest of the field had to be waved around the obstacle on the approach to the home turn.

That probably looked very bad for people watching because the medical people put the screens up around me. They usually don't put screens up around a horse or a jockey after a fall unless it's very bad. I wasn't that bad, but they decided to put the screens up because they didn't want the television cameras to see what they were doing. John

Francome had made some comments on the Tuesday about the way in which the racecourse medical staff looked after Andy Thornton after he had had a fall from A Glass in Thyne in the William Hill Chase. It was a bit of a misunderstanding, however, as Francome thought that Andy had injured his pelvis when actually it was his arm that was the focus of the medics' attention. Dr Disney, who headed up the medical team, was pretty annoyed about the whole affair actually, and he probably had every right to be. The medical teams at racecourses do a fantastic job and often don't get the credit they deserve. They threatened strike action at Cheltenham over Francome's comments if he didn't apologise, but he did, and the whole thing blew over. Anyway, that was why they had the screens up around me at the third last fence. It wasn't because things were bad for me, thank God, though I did suffer some bruising in my neck and had to give up the rest of my rides. It can be an awful place, Cheltenham, when things go against you.

It was the first time since 1988 that Martin Pipe didn't have a winner at the Cheltenham Festival. Nobody could explain it. The horses had all been tested before the meeting, as usual, and they were all fine. The final thump in the head was the fatal injury Basilea Star suffered when he fell four out when travelling well in the National Hunt Chase.

Even my outside rides were disappointing. Glasker Mill was well beaten in the SunAlliance Hurdle, Al Eile was fourth in the Champion Hurdle, and Wind Instrument, trained by Tom George, finished down the field in the bumper. There was one blinding ray of light at the festival for me, however. You're Special, the horse Brendan O'Rourke bought at the start of the 2005 season, because of the horse's name, in memory of his daughter Kate who died, won the Kim Muir at 33–1. That really was a bit special.

Still, in spite of our disappointing Cheltenham, it really wasn't a disastrous season. Though Martin had to relinquish his vice-like grasp on the trainers' title and give it, somewhat begrudgingly, to Paul Nicholls, he hadn't had an unsuccessful year by any standards. And David had his second best season ever as an owner, finishing a clear second to J. P.

McManus in the owners' championship. For my own part, I rode 87 winners and amassed £1.2 million in prize money, which wasn't too bad, given that I didn't even get close at Cheltenham.

But the biggest kick of the season for me from a professional point of view was when I was presented with the award for National Hunt jockey of the year at the Lesters in January. It meant a huge amount to me, as the Lesters are awarded on the basis of votes you receive from your peers, your weigh-room colleagues. It's like the Players' Player of the Year in football. It usually goes to the champion jockey – McCoy had won it for the previous nine years – so it was a great feeling when my name was called.

There was plenty of speculation in April about whether or not my agreement with David would be renewed for 2006/07. It's getting to be an annual occurrence at this stage, this speculation. David simply phoned me before Aintree.

'Same arrangement next year? I'm happy if you're happy.'

'I'm happy.'

So this was one of those rare racecourse rumours that had very little substance. We hadn't had as good a season as we'd had in 2004/05, and people seemed to want the agreement to end as a result. Perhaps the rumour was fuelled by the fact that I wasn't riding out for Martin so much, and wasn't riding for many of his other owners. I don't know. 'We had a few setbacks this season,' David told reporters, 'and some of our horses haven't been running as well as we would have liked. But some of our best horses have been out injured for the season. That's hardly Timmy's fault, now is it?'

CHAPTER EIGHTEEN

BLESSED

Things look good here in my back garden. I suppose things usually look good in the sunshine.

Sometimes you need to sit in your garden, take time out from the daily cycle and just think about what you have, how lucky you are. It is very easy to get caught up in running around, being busy, in living your life, without stopping to appreciate the things in it. I know I am luckier than most. There are few people in the world who have been given as many opportunities as I have to do things right, who fecked up as many promising situations as I have and who were still presented with one more. Don't think I don't appreciate that, because I do. Really I do.

Kay Hourigan says that I'm a jammy bastard, that things always seem to work out for me. She says I'm like a cat, that I always land on my feet. I'll tell you, there have been times when I didn't feel like I was on my feet, that's for sure. My knees, maybe, but certainly not my feet. Perhaps Kay is on to something though. Perhaps I have had about nine chances. I don't intend to blow this latest one.

Of course I regret a lot of the things I have done. I regret the hardship I have brought on the people closest to me, on my family, on Mam and Dad. I have no doubt that I dragged my Mam through hell and back. It is difficult to quantify the magnitude of the pain I must have caused her. To have a son convicted and sent to prison must be a really terrible thing. I can appreciate that now that I have a son of my own. And then to have him convicted of a sex offence and put on the sex offenders' register even if it was in error, and to have that information splashed all over the tabloid newspapers – I can't begin to imagine what that must have been like for her.

I didn't spend enough time getting to know my family when I was growing up. I didn't appreciate what Mam and Dad were trying to do for me. I was too busy trying to run away from them. They were just holding me back. I was going to make it as a jockey and they were just delaying me. As soon as I could move out of home I did, and when I did, I never felt that I could go back. It would have been a sign of weakness. Even when I was coming out of prison, I arranged to go to Hourigan's, not home. I figured that that was where I went through the least amount of shit in my life. Of course he had horses, but as well as that I knew I would feel safe there. It was, as I said, like going home.

I was never as close to my family as I should have been. Mam, Dad and Brian were always very close, but I suppose I was a bit of a black sheep. Every family has one. But my relationship with Mam and Dad is better now than it ever was. I used to think that going home was boring, so I didn't. Even when I was in Kildare, I wouldn't call out to the house. But since Shane has come along I do. Having your own children makes you realise how important home and family is. I was home for Ruby Walsh's wedding during the summer of 2006 and I spent two days with Mam and Dad. I know that they really enjoyed that, as did I. Dad hates flying, so he hasn't been over to see me as often as he would have liked. He hadn't been over to stay with me in ten years, but he came over with Mam during that same summer. I'm sure he thought he was safe when he landed in Heathrow, but I don't think he had reckoned on my driving skills! He came to Bangor with me the following day, and I'm sure the plane journey from Dublin to Heathrow was a lot easier for him than that two-and-a-half-hour car journey. I was going to Market Rasen the day after, and I asked him if he wanted to come with me, but he politely declined. It was great to have them over with me though, to stay with me, come racing with me and spend some time with Shane. My brother Brian comes over too. It used to be the case that I could only talk to my Mam when I was drunk, but now I find it easier. She sent me a text recently about something she was doing for me, and I texted her back: 'Mam, you're a great woman.' She replied to that with, 'Is it only now you're realising that?' 'Always did,' I came back, 'but didn't tell you often enough.' She still has those text messages saved on her phone.

Sometimes I regret that I didn't try harder at school, though I'm not fully sure about it. If I had tried harder I might not have put so much effort into riding. It's OK now because it has worked out for me, but it is probably not the wisest strategy to adopt, not so clever to put all your eggs into one precarious basket. Then again, I didn't do too many clever things in those days.

Strangely, I don't regret going to prison. In fact, looking back on it now, it was the making of me. Or rather, the aftermath was the making of me, and the aftermath couldn't have happened without the actual event. Don't get me wrong, I regret what I did and I regret the thorn bush through which I dragged my family and my friends. And at the time, I hated being inside. Absolutely abhorred it. But, as I have said before, I am a firm believer in the fact that things happen for a reason. Something had to happen for me to start to cop on to myself. What happened was fairly traumatic, as traumatic as it gets, but perhaps that was what was required in order for me to see sense. It made me appreciate life more. Appreciate living. It made me appreciate fresh air and space and the basic liberties we take for granted. Making decisions for yourself, going for a walk, having a cup of coffee. Strange thing to say, perhaps, but I think a spell in prison would do some people a lot of good.

Life's still not easy, of course. I have to work at it. And there are days when the red mist still descends. It's the little things that get me, like trying to change a wheel or getting stuck in traffic, always when I'm in a rush. It's the same when I'm racing. If I'm rushing to get there, often it doesn't happen. If I adopt a different frame of mind, though – let it happen, easy now – it's much better.

I am lucky to be surrounded by good people. Becky Ward, who sorts out my life, Chris Broad, Mark Pitman, Seanie Curran, David Johnson, Jim Old, Verity. And the lads in the weigh room, Graham Lee, Chocolate

Thornton, Paddy Brennan and Andy Thornton. Seanie Curran has started to train now and I ride for him whenever I can. In fact, my first ride for him was on Explosive Fox at Fontwell in May 2006, and we finished second to one of David Pipe's! I'll ride a winner for him soon. Michael Hourigan has been a rock to me. It didn't matter that I went to England, over to Kim Bailey's, without ever really telling him that I was going, after he'd made me champion novice rider on the point-to-point circuit and supplied the lion's share of the winners that allowed me to finish second in the championship. It didn't matter that I completely lost touch with him when I was in England. When I needed him he was there. He and his family.

Brendan O'Rourke, fantastic man who listened to me when I talked and was there for me when I didn't, and his wife Diane. They saw me through a really tough patch. Even now, Brendan records my races for Mam. She won't watch them live. She wouldn't enjoy them because she worries that something might happen to me, but she does want to see me ride. So Brendan records my races for her and brings the video down to her on Saturday evening. Mam sits on the sofa, has a glass of wine and watches me, knowing that I have come home safely. Adrian Maguire, too, has always been great to me, as have Norman Williamson and Mick Halford, who was a pleasure to work for and who sent me down to Hourigan's when I needed to go. Even today, Mick is a friend to whom I can turn whenever I need one. He understands what I go through sometimes.

I rarely feel like having a drink these days. I've learnt all the trigger points and I've learnt how to deal with them, thankfully. Sometimes if you're really thirsty it might come into your head: I'd love a cool beer now. But then you cop yourself on – 'Feck, what was I thinking?' – you have a glass of water or a Coke, and the thought goes. But I don't think any more when I'm out, 'I'm having a bad time here, I need a drink.' Now I think, 'I'm having a bad time here, I'm going home.' That's the way you deal with it. If you're having a bad time, it's probably because it's a bad night, not because you're not having a drink. Some of the other jockeys, my friends, don't drink either. Graham Lee doesn't drink, A. P. McCoy doesn't drink. That makes it even easier.

And you deal with the highs and the lows differently as well. It used to be the case that big high equals big celebration equals big drink, and big low equals big despair equals big drink. You learn how to deal with the two extremes in different ways. It doesn't have to be all about drink. I've never thought since, 'Fabulous day, let's go and get locked.' You can appreciate a fabulous day better when you're sober. Neither do I think these days, 'Bad day, I'm off to get pissed.' I know that in the morning the previous day will still have been bad and I'll just have to deal with a hangover as well. You just do something different. Ring somebody to whom you can talk, to whom you can give out. I usually ring Broady and give him a bollicking. Everybody should have a Broady in his life.

I'm proud of Shane. He is a great little fellow. Of all my achievements to date, he is the one of which I am most proud. The last couple of years haven't been easy for him, but he has done brilliantly. He's intelligent, he's articulate, he's athletic, he's great fun, and he's good at school. He enjoys school, which I didn't, so I'm delighted about that. I might be a little bit hard on him sometimes, making him do his homework and things, but it's only because I want what is best for him. Maybe there is a little bit of my mother in me after all.

Shane comes racing with me sometimes. During the summer I bring him with me a bit and he has great craic with the lads in the weigh room. Any bad words, though, and they get a smack of the whip, so there are usually a lot of slaps going around. I don't really push him with horses though. It's hard for a young fellow at school when all his mates are into football and nobody is into horses. Maybe we'll get him a pony if he's into it. We'll see.

Dawn is great with Shane. We are very lucky that we still get on so well and that we are living so close to each other. She has another man in her life now and I have Verity, and Shane gets on well with both of them, so from a situation that was less than ideal, things are working out fairly well. I wouldn't mind having more kids at some stage, all being well. I might be better prepared next time.

From a career point of view, things could hardly be better. My current job is one of those top jobs I craved when I was scratching around as a freelance, picking up scraps here and spares there. Of course, although I thought I was up to one of the top jobs, I knew it was highly unlikely I would ever get close. There are only a couple of those jobs in racing, and one of them, I thought, I definitely wouldn't get. If it came up, I probably wouldn't even apply for it.

David Johnson is a great person for whom to work. He understands how I ride. He realises that this is a long-term game. I speak to him most days in the car both on the way to the races and on the way home, even when he doesn't have runners. I can be straight up with David about his horses. He is not one of those owners who wants to hear that his horse wants a trip or better ground just because it's the thing to say. If I think it's useless, he wants me to say that I think it's useless. We are very similar in that way. And of course I get to ride good horses in good races, which was all I ever wanted to do. In short, I have never been happier riding for anyone, and, all things being equal, I would be delighted to ride for David Johnson until the day I retire.

Martin Pipe announced his retirement at the end of the 2005/06 season. People knew he couldn't go on indefinitely, but he did catch the racing world by surprise a little when he made the announcement on the last day of the season. He was an incredible trainer; he had unbelievable attention to detail. I don't think it is overstating the facts to say that he single-handedly revolutionised how National Hunt horses are trained. He was the first National Hunt trainer to embrace fully the concept of interval training, and you could see it in his horses. From the first winner Martin sent out – Hit Parade in a selling hurdle at Taunton in May 1975 – all of his horses were fit. It didn't matter if they were having their first run of the season or their ninth. That was why, in the early days, you often saw Peter Scudamore out in front on his horses, exploiting the fitness advantage he invariably enjoyed over his rivals. Gradually the others caught up, but not before Martin had trained the winners of almost 4,000 races, including a Grand National, two Champion Hurdles and just about every other big race on the calendar, and been champion trainer an incredible fifteen times.

Martin's son David has taken over the licence now. It is an exciting time for him. He is 33 years old and has been around his father long enough to have picked up one or two things. He will also have Martin in the background to help and advise him, and early signs are that there will be no let-up in the quality of horses being sent out from Pond House. From my own perspective, I don't think too much will change with David taking over. I have always had a good relationship with him, and I'm sure that will continue.

People have begun to ask me recently how long I think I will go on riding, which is probably a worrying sign. I was 32 in August 2006, and I guess my body will stop me riding by 40, so that leaves me seven or eight more seasons. A lot can happen in that length of time. I'm not sure yet what I'll do when I stop riding, but it will definitely be something to do with horses. It's all I know. It may be pre-training, it may be buying and selling a few, or it may be training. I wouldn't mind giving training a go. I have a couple of ideas that I've picked up along the way, and I think I would quite enjoy trying to implement them. They say that training horses is the easy part about being a racehorse trainer, so we will see. Who knows what the future holds?

For now, I am as happy as I ever have been. I am in the prime of my health, I have one of the best jobs in racing, a fiancée of whom I think the world, a son I adore, a few quid in the bank and great people around me. And as I said, I don't underestimate how lucky I have been. Not for a second. It wasn't that I was standing on the edge of an abyss staring down, it was more like I was actually halfway down it, on my way to perdition, and somehow I was hauled back out and taken to safety. You couldn't have thought four years ago that I would be where I am today, and I am forever grateful to the people who have been instrumental in getting me there. I couldn't have done it on my own, that's for sure.

I couldn't ride the storm alone. The demons are still there, on my back, on my shoulder, in my saddlebag. They will probably always be there, but for now, perhaps for ever, they are under control. Fortune has smiled down on me in spite of my best efforts.

That's me. Timmy Murphy. Blessed.

TIMMY MURPHY'S RACING RECORD

Statistics correct to 4 October 2006

POINT-TO-POINT WINNERS
1993

DATE	HORSE	COURSE
23 May	Gayloire	KILMUCKRIDGE

1994

20 March	For Kevin	CORRIN
20 March	Screen Printer	CORRIN
27 March	Mr Glynn	LISCARROLL
27 March	Fur N Money	LISCARROLL
20 April	Mrs Pegasus	KILLEADY
01 May	Mrs Pegasus	FARNANES
01 May	For Kevin	FARNANES
02 May	Connys Hope	DAWSTOWN
14 May	Fur N Money	MILLSTREET
15 May	Brother Hugh	KILLALOE
22 May	Brunswick Maid	DROMAHANE
22 May	Mrs Pegasus	DROMAHANE
25 May	The Griff	BALLINDENISK
25 May	Fur N Money	BALLINDENISK

1995

01 January	Ozeycazey	LISGOOLD
08 January	Ozeycazey	PATRICKSWELL
08 January	Grange Court	PATRICKSWELL
08 January	African Dante	PATRICKSWELL
15 January	River Unshion	KILLEAGH
04 February	Aoifes Boy	CARRIGTWOHILL
05 February	Pintex	TALLOW
06 February	Desperate Days	FAIRYHOUSE
12 February	Joe Begley	ASKEATON
12 February	An Spailpin Fanach	ASKEATON
11 March	Killisrew Abbey	SKIBBEREEN
12 March	Joe Begley	QUIN
12 March	Ask The Leader	QUIN
12 March	Misty Dew	QUIN
19 March	Cool Bandit	TIPPERARY
26 March	Carrolls Rock	LISCARROLL
26 March	JR-Kay	LISCARROLL
26 March	Burren Beauty	LISCARROLL
02 April	Goldenswift	BALLYNOE
16 April	Don't Waste It	DROMOLAND
23 April	Light Argument	FRIARSTOWN
14 May	Prize Lady	NENAGH

14 May	Brownroselad	NENAGH
14 May	Tell The Nipper	NENAGH
14 May	Hannies Girl	NENAGH
24 May	Halens Match	MALLOW
24 May	Yukon Gale	MALLOW
27 May	Hey Lad	KINSALE
31 May	Ideal Parner	BALLINGARRY

JUMPS WINNERS

1994

15 January	The Real Article	PUNCHESTOWN
10 February	Nine O Three	THURLES
17 March	Back To Black	LIMERICK
11 July	Mrs Pegasus	KILLARNEY
17 July	The Hearty Lady	KILLARNEY
25 July	May Gale	GALWAY
29 July	Very Adaptable	GALWAY
14 August	May Gale	TRAMORE
15 August	Lantern Luck	TRAMORE
26 August	Mrs Pegasus	TRALEE
20 September	Bless Me Sister	LISTOWEL
31 October	Bless Me Sister	GALWAY
09 November	Rosy Affair	DOWNPATRICK
09 November	Over The Stream	TOWCESTER
18 December	Icantelya	THURLES
29 December	Bless Me Sister	LEOPARDSTOWN

1995

18 March	Queen Of The Lakes	LIMERICK
03 May	Light Argument	TRAMORE
10 May	Trolly Dolly	KILLARNEY
10 May	Light Argument	KILLARNEY
15 May	Jenbro	LAYTOWN
25 May	Morning Dream	BALLINROBE
29 May	Light Argument	KILBEGGAN
05 June	It'snicetobenice	TRALEE
05 June	Morning Dream	TRALEE
12 June	Strategic Intent	ROSCOMMON
19 June	African Dante	KILBEGGAN
29 August	Quiet Amusement	UTTOXETER
11 October	Sprung Rhythm	EXETER
19 October	Far Senior	HEREFORD
25 October	Wilde Music	CHELTENHAM
26 October	Over The Stream	STRATFORD
28 October	Far Senior	WARWICK

23 November	Princethorpe	UTTOXETER
23 November	Stac-Pollaidh	UTTOXETER
08 December	Strong Medicine	CHELTENHAM
14 December	Walking Tall	SOUTHWELL

1996

04 January	Dominie	NOTTINGHAM
19 February	Price's Hill	FONTWELL
29 February	Dominie	NOTTINGHAM
04 March	Price's Hill	WINDSOR
04 March	Churchtown Port	WINDSOR
12 March	Andre Laval	WINDSOR
12 March	King Girseach	WINDSOR
13 March	Waterford Castle	HUNTINGDON
16 March	Celtic Park	LINGFIELD
16 March	Nathir	LINGFIELD
22 March	The Toiseach	NEWBURY
03 May	Its Grand	BANGOR-ON-DEE
04 May	Waterford Castle	HEREFORD
04 May	Mill O'The Rags	HEREFORD
22 May	Handy Lass	WORCESTER
29 June	Waterford Castle	WORCESTER
05 August	Kindergarten Boy	NEWTON ABBOT
09 August	Safety	PLUMPTON
17 August	Re Roi	STRATFORD
21 August	China Mail	HEREFORD
26 August	Maggots Green	NEWTON ABBOT
26 August	Re Roi	NEWTON ABBOT
28 August	China Mail	WORCESTER
29 September	SirteliMarch	NEWTON ABBOT
10 October	Drumcullen	WINCANTON
22 October	Capo Castanum	PLUMPTON
30 November	Rovestar	WARWICK
30 November	Fine Harvest	WARWICK
14 December	Naiysari	LINGFIELD

1997

16 January	Inch Emperor	LUDLOW
25 January	Forestal	CHELTENHAM
11 March	Red Branch	FONTWELL
12 March	Terao	CHELTENHAM
18 March	Red Branch	FONTWELL
21 March	Terao	NEWBURY
22 March	Red Branch	NEWBURY
09 April	Inch Emperor	LUDLOW
02 May	Red Branch	NEWTON ABBOT
03 May	Dubelle	HEREFORD

05 May	Ehtefaal	TOWCESTER
21 May	Stray Harmony	WORCESTER
26 May	Red Branch	FONTWELL
07 June	Rolled Gold	SOUTHWELL
11 June	Beck And Call	UTTOXETER
12 July	Caddy's First	SOUTHWELL
25 August	Mutual Agreement	NEWTON ABBOT
13 September	Rolled Gold	BANGOR-ON-DEE
15 September	Mutual Agreement	FONTWELL
23 September	Galatasori Januarye	STRATFORD
06 October	Ideal Partner	FONTWELL
09 October	Mutual Agreement	EXETER
13 October	Thursday Night	NEWTON ABBOT
17 October	Storm Run	HEREFORD
23 October	Mutual Agreement	WINCANTON
25 October	Strong Tarquin	WORCESTER
29 October	Galatasori Januarye	FONTWELL
05 November	Galatasori Januarye	NEWTON ABBOT
06 November	Fortunes Course	TOWCESTER
08 November	Dines	WINCANTON
10 November	Flaked Oats	FONTWELL
12 November	Miss Roberto	WORCESTER
14 November	Call Equiname	CHELTENHAM
18 November	Lake Kariba	NEWTON ABBOT
20 November	Mrs Em	WINCANTON
20 November	Sunley Bay	WINCANTON
22 November	Storm Run	AINTREE
25 November	Dancetillyoudrop	WORCESTER
25 November	Ottowa	WORCESTER
26 November	Lake Kariba	CHEPSTOW
26 November	Larry's Lord	CHEPSTOW
27 November	Gutteridge	TAUNTON
28 November	Strong Chairman	NEWBURY
06 December	See More Business	CHEPSTOW
08 December	Mr Strong Gale	LUDLOW
28 December	Young Mrs Kelly	LIMERICK

1998

17 January	With Impunity	WARWICK
19 January	Calling Wild	FONTWELL
22 January	Never In Debt	TAUNTON
24 January	Even Flow	KEMPTON
26 January	Storm Damage	WINDSOR
29 January	Bengers Moor	WINCANTON
29 January	Dines	WINCANTON
31 January	See More Business	CHELTENHAM
07 February	Calling Wild	UTTOXETER

07 February	Ottowa	UTTOXETER
13 February	Now We Know	BANGOR-ON-DEE
14 February	Court Melody	NEWBURY
19 February	Never In Debt	TAUNTON
21 February	Ottowa	CHEPSTOW
27 February	Nearly An Eye	KEMPTON
28 February	Even Flow	HAYDOCK
16 March	Merawang	TAUNTON
24 March	Gigi Beach	FONTWELL
26 March	Mrs Em	WINCANTON
06 April	Parahandy	FONTWELL
13 April	Lansdowne	CHEPSTOW
13 April	Mon Amie	CHEPSTOW
17 April	Lake Kariba	AYR
18 April	Lake Kariba	AYR
23 April	Gigi Beach	FONTWELL
24 April	Mr Strong Gale	LUDLOW
04 May	Mr Strong Gale	SOUTHWELL
04 May	Dines	SOUTHWELL
27 June	Marchine Society	NEWTON ABBOT
28 June	Little Joe	UTTOXETER
15 July	Flagship Therese	WORCESTER
30 July	Mrs Em	NEWTON ABBOT
07 August	French By Chance	KILBEGGAN
10 August	Queenofclubs	CORK
15 August	Change The Reign	STRATFORD
15 August	Mr Speculator	STRATFORD
16 August	Great Gusto	NEWTON ABBOT
16 August	Up The Tempo	NEWTON ABBOT
16 August	Churchstanton	NEWTON ABBOT
31 August	Great Gusto	NEWTON ABBOT
31 August	Lets Twist Again	NEWTON ABBOT
01 September	Mr Speculator	UTTOXETER
03 September	Mrs Em	FONTWELL
05 September	Change The Reign	STRATFORD
11 September	Mrs Em	WORCESTER
19 September	Mr Speculator	MARKET RASEN
01 October	Pride Of Pennker	TAUNTON
01 October	Mr Speculator	TAUNTON
03 October	Bluagale	CHEPSTOW
06 October	Via Del Quatro	FONTWELL
08 October	Little Joe	WINCANTON
10 October	Biya	BANGOR-ON-DEE
12 October	Dines	NEWTON ABBOT
17 October	Dines	KEMPTON
17 October	Bank Avenue	KEMPTON
17 October	More Dash Thancash	KEMPTON

25 October	Derrymore Mist	WINCANTON
29 October	Quistaquay	STRATFORD
05 November	The Eens	HAYDOCK
07 November	Chai-Yo	SANDOWN
07 November	Court Melody	SANDOWN
07 November	Mr Strong Gale	SANDOWN
07 November	Laredo	SANDOWN
10 November	Big Archie	HUNTINGDON
16 November	Burundi	LEICESTER
16 November	Church Law	LEICESTER
18 November	Mr Strong Gale	KEMPTON
19 November	Cool Gunner	WARWICK
20 November	Juyush	ASCOT
21 November	Kinnescash	AINTREE
23 November	Ferrufino	LUDLOW
27 November	Traluide	NEWBURY
02 December	Phar Less Hassle	PLUMPTON
18 December	Handy Lass	LINGFIELD
26 December	Pietro Bembo	WINCANTON
26 December	Three Farthings	WINCANTON

1999

06 January	Another Deadly	LINGFIELD
09 January	Flush	WARWICK
11 January	Dancetillyoudrop	FONTWELL
20 January	Collier Bay	HUNTINGDON
28 January	Devil's Advocate	HUNTINGDON
05 February	Park Royal	LINGFIELD
06 February	Clever ReMarchk	SANDOWN
17 February	Surprise Gunner	FOLKESTONE
18 February	Ashley Park	SANDOWN
19 February	Dawn Leader	SANDOWN
19 February	Around The Gale	SANDOWN
23 February	Ballysicyos	LUDLOW
25 February	Ambleside	WINCANTON
26 February	Wise King	KEMPTON
18 March	Sir Talbot	CHELTENHAM
19 March	Pietro Bembo	FOLKESTONE
26 March	El Freddie	NEWBURY
26 March	Motet	NEWBURY
27 March	Allgrit	NEWBURY
31 March	Sweet Lord	ASCOT
04 April	Genetic George	CORK
07 April	Wise King	ASCOT
10 April	Kinnescash	AINTREE
14 April	Allgrit	CHELTENHAM
05 May	Allgrit	CHEPSTOW

07 May	Dictum	STRATFORD
12 May	Colonel Blazer	EXETER
14 May	Albert Blake	AINTREE
07 June	Boots N All	TRALEE
07 June	Native Wit	TRALEE
16 June	Father Rector	WORCESTER
26 June	Ezanak	NEWTON ABBOT
11 July	Bungee Jumper	STRATFORD
12 July	Runaway Pete	WOLVERHAMPTON
02 August	Runaway Pete	NEWTON ABBOT
06 August	Art Prince	WORCESTER
31 August	Just Good Fun	UTTOXETER
02 October	Canasta	CHEPSTOW
02 October	Ever Blessed	CHEPSTOW
13 October	Klondike Charger	WETHERBY
14 October	Brave Dream	TAUNTON
16 October	Chai-Yo	KEMPTON
16 October	Bank Avenue	KEMPTON
20 October	Derrintogher Yank	CHEPSTOW
21 October	Macaw-Bay	WINCANTON
30 October	Romero	ASCOT
30 October	Nahthen Lad	ASCOT
02 November	Dictum	WARWICK
09 November	Count Campioni	NEWBURY
18 November	Sweet Lord	WARWICK
20 November	Romero	ASCOT
20 November	Catfish Keith	ASCOT
25 November	Talathath	TAUNTON
25 November	Bozo	TAUNTON
27 November	Ever Blessed	NEWBURY
30 November	Brave Dream	NEWTON ABBOT
08 December	Door To Door	LEICESTER
08 December	Belle Derriere	LEICESTER
09 December	Mite Equal	TAUNTON
09 December	Jason's Boy	TAUNTON

2000

10 January	Highland	FONTWELL
11 January	Forest Jump	HEREFORD
17 January	Reluckino	PLUMPTON
18 January	Browjoshy	FOLKESTONE
21 January	Just Good Fun	ASCOT
03 February	Outer Limit	TOWCESTER
05 February	Rockforce	SANDOWN
08 February	Tonka	WARWICK
10 February	The Land Agent	WINCANTON
11 February	Macaw-Bay	NEWBURY

16 February	Wain Mountain	LEICESTER
16 February	Crookedstone	LEICESTER
18 February	Canta Ke Brave	SANDOWN
18 February	Eltigri	SANDOWN
24 February	Kiss Me Kate	HUNTINGDON
25 February	Pietro Bembo	KEMPTON
07 March	Crookedstone	EXETER
08 March	Milligan	CATTERICK
11 March	In The Rough	CHEPSTOW
11 March	Brother Joe	CHEPSTOW
13 March	Kiss Me Kate	PLUMPTON
13 March	Danzig Island	PLUMPTON
17 March	Canta Ke Brave	FOLKESTONE
20 March	Funny Genie	FOLKESTONE
24 March	Dick McCarthy	NEWBURY
28 March	Indulge	SANDOWN
01 April	Romero	ASCOT
03 April	Motet	PLUMPTON
03 April	Mister Pickwick	PLUMPTON
13 April	Bozo	LUDLOW
22 April	Brave Dream	NEWTON ABBOT
24 April	Handy Lass	CHEPSTOW
25 April	Frank Byrne	UTTOXETER
27 April	Punchy	FONTWELL
01 May	Three Farthings	TOWCESTER
13 May	Captain Dee Cee	WARWICK
26 May	In The Rough	TOWCESTER
23 July	Taleca Son	SOUTHWELL
28 August	Taleca Son	SOUTHWELL
11 September	Storm Valley	PLUMPTON
19 September	Run For Paddy	FONTWELL
20 September	Mac's Supreme	LISTOWEL
30 September	Run For Paddy	UTTOXETER
30 September	Count Campioni	UTTOXETER
01 October	Luke Warm	FONTWELL
01 October	Monacle	FONTWELL
02 October	Strong Paladin	FOLKESTONE
13 October	Bright Novemberember	HEREFORD
24 October	Run For Paddy	CHELTENHAM
01 November	Bright Novemberember	KEMPTON
03 November	Kalisko	UTTOXETER
04 November	Royal Event	WINCANTON
04 November	Flaked Oats	WINCANTON
06 November	Sprig Muslin	FONTWELL
13 November	John The Greek	PLUMPTON
15 November	Bright Novemberember	KEMPTON
16 November	Mrs Wallace	WARWICK

16 November	Churchstanton	WARWICK
21 November	Dirk Cove	TOWCESTER
21 November	Dark Crusader	TOWCESTER
02 December	Luke Warm	TOWCESTER
02 December	Flying Trix	TOWCESTER
06 December	SMarchty	LEICESTER
07 December	Returning	TAUNTON
07 December	Dirk Cove	TAUNTON
07 December	Ludere	TAUNTON
18 December	Red Blazer	FAKENHAM
19 December	Dark Crusader	FOLKESTONE
20 December	Zaffre Noir	NEWBURY

2001

05 January	Spontaneity	LUDLOW
05 January	Dulas Bay	LUDLOW
06 January	Flying Trix	UTTOXETER
13 January	Browjoshy	WARWICK
25 January	Among Equals	WARWICK
26 January	The Leader	FOLKESTONE
29 January	Dulas Bay	KEMPTON
30 January	Thats All Folks	TAUNTON
16 February	Mitcheldean	FAKENHAM
17 February	Bright Novemberember	ASCOT
21 February	Platonic-My-Eye	LUDLOW
24 February	First Ballot	KEMPTON
12 March	Mouse Bird	PLUMPTON
20 March	Master Ride	FONTWELL
04 April	Mitcheldean	ASCOT
20 April	Vincent Van Gogh	TAUNTON
20 April	King Of The Castle	TAUNTON
20 April	Farmer Jack	TAUNTON
20 April	Broken Arrow	TAUNTON
21 April	City Venture	AYR
25 April	Davids Lad	FAIRYHOUSE
05 May	Khatani	HEREFORD
05 May	Cherokee Boy	HEREFORD
06 May	Davids Lad	FAIRYHOUSE
11 May	Cherokee Boy	WINCANTON
12 May	Punchy	WARWICK
15 May	Arlas	HEREFORD
18 May	Galapiat Du Mesnil	STRATFORD
18 May	Jentar Equilibra	STRATFORD
20 May	Davids Lad	NAVAN
03 June	Jackie C	SLIGO
04 June	Barba Papa	TRALEE
04 June	Get Along	TRALEE

11 June	General Claremont	NEWTON ABBOT
20 June	Torn Silk	WORCESTER
20 June	Suaverof	WORCESTER
30 June	Entertainer	WORCESTER
30 June	Suaverof	WORCESTER
21 July	Dorans Gold	MARKET RASEN
28 July	Arctic Burner	STRATFORD
29 July	Monty's Theme	NEWTON ABBOT
04 August	Comex Flyer	WORCESTER
27 August	Monty's Theme	FONTWELL
05 September	Punchy	NEWTON ABBOT
15 September	Hot Shots	WORCESTER
25 September	Comex Flyer	FONTWELL
06 October	Earthmover	CHEPSTOW
06 October	Valley Henry	CHEPSTOW
07 October	Comex Flyer	FONTWELL
08 October	Davids Lad	ROSCOMMON
09 October	Rainbows Aglitter	SOUTHWELL
11 October	Ballydonnelly	LUDLOW
12 October	Hotters	HUNTINGDON
12 October	Marchmaduke	HUNTINGDON
13 October	Hang'Em Out To Dry	BANGOR-ON-DEE
18 October	Il Capitano	TAUNTON
18 October	Torn Silk	TAUNTON
19 October	Colombian Green	HEREFORD
19 October	Sir Frosty	HEREFORD
20 October	Tonka	MARKET RASEN
20 October	Battle Royal	MARKET RASEN
22 October	Russian Court	PLUMPTON
22 October	Sir D'Orton	PLUMPTON
23 October	St Pirran	EXETER
24 October	Ivanoph	CHEPSTOW
24 October	Galapiat Du Mesnil	CHEPSTOW
24 October	Stennikov	CHEPSTOW
24 October	Percolator	CHEPSTOW
27 October	Armaturk	KEMPTON
28 October	Blackwater Brave	WINCANTON
05 November	Sir D'Orton	PLUMPTON
05 November	SMarchty	PLUMPTON
06 November	Cornish Gale	EXETER
10 November	Montifault	WINCANTON
10 November	Azertyuiop	WINCANTON
10 November	Phar From A Fiddle	WINCANTON
14 November	Gunnerblong	NEWBURY
15 November	Un Jour A Vassy	TAUNTON
16 November	Fireball MacnaMarcha	CHELTENHAM
17 November	Cornish Gale	CHELTENHAM

20 November	Ruby Gale	NEWTON ABBOT
20 November	Mattan	NEWTON ABBOT
28 November	Iverain	CHEPSTOW
28 November	Silence Reigns	CHEPSTOW
28 November	Extra Jack	CHEPSTOW
29 November	Knock Leader	TAUNTON
30 November	Le Roi Miguel	NEWBURY
30 November	Valley Henry	NEWBURY
04 December	Asador	NEWTON ABBOT
06 December	Satshoon	WINCANTON
08 December	Kates Charm	CHEPSTOW
10 December	Elegant Sprite	FOLKESTONE
18 December	Will Of The People	HEREFORD
19 December	Sterling Stewart	NEWBURY
20 December	Ruby Gale	EXETER
27 December	Jeannot De Beauchene	CHEPSTOW
27 December	Silence Reigns	CHEPSTOW
27 December	Extra Jack	CHEPSTOW
29 December	Armaturk	NEWBURY

2002

07 January	Bangor Erris	FONTWELL
10 January	Moving Earth	WINCANTON
16 January	Calldat Seventeen	HUNTINGDON
17 January	Sir Frosty	TAUNTON
04 February	Tommy Trooper	FONTWELL
07 February	Thisthatandtother	WINCANTON
11 February	Asador	PLUMPTON
16 February	Armaturk	WARWICK
18 February	Perange	FONTWELL
07 March	Candarli	WINCANTON
07 March	Santenay	WINCANTON
09 March	Galapiat Du Mesnil	CHEPSTOW
09 March	Saint Par	CHEPSTOW
11 March	Poliantas	TAUNTON
21 March	Kadarann	WINCANTON
21 March	Maybe The Business	WINCANTON
23 March	Cresswell Native	FONTWELL
23 March	Good Potential	FONTWELL
28 March	Valley Henry	EXETER
28 March	Ruby Gale	EXETER
01 April	Vol Solitaire	CHEPSTOW
02 April	Montayral	UTTOXETER
02 April	No Need For Alarm	UTTOXETER
02 April	Blue Dante	UTTOXETER
03 April	Julyie's Leader	LUDLOW
06 April	Armaturk	AINTREE

09 June	Torn Silk	WORCESTER
09 November	Santenay	WINCANTON
14 November	Zaffamore	LUDLOW
14 November	Soho Fields	LUDLOW
18 November	Briar	FOLKESTONE
19 November	Cresswell Quay	NEWTON ABBOT
26 November	Cresswell Quay	WARWICK
28 November	Misbehaviour	TAUNTON
29 November	Romero	NEWBURY
01 December	Greywell	CORK
05 December	Poliantas	WINCANTON
05 December	Bunratty Castle	WINCANTON
05 December	Hiers De Brouage	WINCANTON
06 December	Sir Frosty	EXETER
07 December	DuMarchan	WARWICK
10 December	Cresswell Quay	FONTWELL
14 December	Sackville	HAYDOCK
15 December	Beef Or Salmon	CORK
15 December	Satco Express	CORK
17 December	Dealer's Choice	FOLKESTONE
27 December	Bolt Action	CHEPSTOW
28 December	Hi Cloy	LEOPARDSTOWN
28 December	Beef Or Salmon	LEOPARDSTOWN
28 December	Be My Belle	LEOPARDSTOWN
29 December	Rathgar Beau	LIMERICK
31 December	Vol Solitaire	CHELTENHAM

2003

01 January	Sir Frosty	CHELTENHAM
12 January	Hi Cloy	LEOPARDSTOWN
14 January	Cresswell Quay	FOLKESTONE
17 January	Robbic Can Can	CHEPSTOW
18 January	Thisthatandtother	WINCANTON
19 January	Emmet	FAIRYHOUSE
23 January	Be My Belle	GOWRAN PARK
24 January	Be My Destiny	FOLKESTONE
25 January	Fireball MacnaMarcha	DONCASTER
02 February	Safe Route	PUNCHESTOWN
04 February	Lynrick Lady	CHEPSTOW
06 February	Armaturk	WINCANTON
09 February	Beef Or Salmon	LEOPARDSTOWN
10 February	Mercato	PLUMPTON
12 February	Physical Graffiti	LEICESTER
26 February	Burundi	WETHERBY
27 February	Miniature Rose	LUDLOW
01 March	Springfield Scally	DONCASTER
18 March	Hiers De Brouage	EXETER

19 March	Themanfromcarlisle	FONTWELL
19 March	King Of Mommur	FONTWELL
20 March	Hot Shots	WINCANTON
29 March	Keltic Heritage	MARKET RASEN
29 March	King Of Sparta	MARKET RASEN
02 April	Alvino	LUDLOW
16 April	Midnight Gunner	CHELTENHAM
17 April	Keltic Heritage	CHELTENHAM
20 April	Pay It Forward	FAIRYHOUSE
23 April	Toulon Rouge	PERTH
07 May	Tirley Storm	FAKENHAM
08 May	Central Billing	TIPPERARY
11 May	Black Church Lad	KILLARNEY
12 May	Dromhale Lady	KILLARNEY
15 May	Central Billing	GOWRAN PARK
18 May	Baranndee	CLONMEL
02 June	Central Billing	TRALEE
07 June	Captain Zinzan	WORCESTER
08 June	Achilles Spirit	LIMERICK
15 June	King Carew	CORK
18 June	Italian Counsel	WORCESTER
20 June	Gabidia	DOWN ROYAL
28 June	Captain Zinzan	WORCESTER
03 August	Central Billing	GALWAY
08 August	Central Billing	KILBEGGAN
09 August	Murghob	DOWNPATRICK
16 August	Conor's Pride	TRAMORE
31 August	Knockawad	BALLINROBE
07 September	Uncle Arthur	ROSCOMMON
12 September	Spin In The Wind	DOWNPATRICK
16 September	Central Billing	LISTOWEL
17 September	Native Performance	LISTOWEL
23 September	Gigs Gambit	FONTWELL
02 October	Dempsey	HEREFORD
09 October	Burning Truth	LUDLOW
15 October	Gigs Bounty	UTTOXETER
18 October	Step Quick	MARKET RASEN
18 October	Cork Harbour	MARKET RASEN
19 October	Spin In The Wind	CORK
23 October	Cassia Heights	HAYDOCK
24 October	Tirley Storm	FAKENHAM
30 October	Monte Cristo	STRATFORD
01 November	Hot Shots	ASCOT
03 November	Gigs Bounty	PLUMPTON
07 November	Another Club Royal	UTTOXETER
12 November	Goodtime George	NEWBURY
12 November	Secret Ploy	NEWBURY

16 November	Blue Away	CHELTENHAM
17 November	Dempsey	FOLKESTONE
22 November	Kildare	NAAS
26 November	Lynrick Lady	CHEPSTOW
01 December	Dempsey	FOLKESTONE
01 December	Kingsbay	FOLKESTONE
05 December	Premier Estate	EXETER
07 December	Beef Or Salmon	PUNCHESTOWN
10 December	Distant Prospect	NEWBURY
14 December	Beef Or Salmon	CORK
15 December	Cresswell Quay	PLUMPTON
15 December	Barton Nic	PLUMPTON
16 December	Bohemian Boy	FOLKESTONE
19 December	Master Trix	ASCOT
20 December	Easter Present	HEREFORD
21 December	Stacumny Bridge	THURLES
26 December	Hi Cloy	LIMERICK
26 December	Dyrick Daybreak	LIMERICK
30 December	Monte Cristo	STRATFORD

2004

01 January	Secret Ploy	CHELTENHAM
04 January	Kilbeggan Lad	NAAS
18 January	Vic Ville	CORK
19 January	Fabrezan	PLUMPTON
21 January	Harrycone Lewis	FAKENHAM
21 January	Monte Cristo	FAKENHAM
22 January	Kilbeggan Lad	GOWRAN PARK
01 February	The Parishioner	THURLES
07 February	Our Dream	CHEPSTOW
07 February	Bright Green	CHEPSTOW
07 February	Count Campioni	CHEPSTOW
08 February	Kilbeggan Lad	LEOPARDSTOWN
11 February	Dealer's Choice	LUDLOW
14 February	Be My Destiny	NEWBURY
14 February	Secret Ploy	NEWBURY
21 February	Our Vic	ASCOT
22 February	Starzaan	FONTWELL
23 February	Malek	CARLISLE
26 February	Rabble Run	LIMERICK
29 February	Hi Cloy	LEOPARDSTOWN
29 February	Point Barrow	LEOPARDSTOWN
07 March	Flying Trix	KEMPTON
08 March	Splash Out Again	FONTWELL
11 March	Hot Shots	WINCANTON
13 March	Perfect Fellow	SANDOWN
16 March	Creon	CHELTENHAM

17 March	Tikram	CHELTENHAM
21 March	A New Story	DOWNPATRICK
25 March	Master Rex	WINCANTON
01 April	Al Eile	AINTREE
04 April	Dempsey	WINCANTON
04 April	Annie Byers	WINCANTON
13 April	Hi Cloy	FAIRYHOUSE
14 April	Flying Trix	CHELTENHAM
15 April	Silver Charmer	CHELTENHAM
22 April	Flinders	FONTWELL
28 April	Beef Or Salmon	PUNCHESTOWN
01 May	Macs Joy	HAYDOCK
03 May	King Carew	LIMERICK
03 May	Sargon	LIMERICK
04 May	Sterling Dot Com	EXETER
06 May	Rambling Minster	WETHERBY
06 May	Up The Glen	WETHERBY
09 May	King Carew	KILLARNEY
11 May	Childer's Road	KILLARNEY
13 May	Brave Dane	LUDLOW
15 May	Montreal	BANGOR-ON-DEE
15 May	Polar Red	BANGOR-ON-DEE
06 June	Montreal	PERTH
08 June	Szeroki Bor	HUNTINGDON
10 June	Phase Eight Girl	UTTOXETER
13 June	Sargon	CORK
13 June	Sandy Owen	CORK
16 June	Punchy	WORCESTER
16 June	Vodka Bleu	WORCESTER
17 June	Dr Julyian	CLONMEL
18 June	The Screamer	DOWN ROYAL
20 June	Oyez	NAVAN
21 June	Por Chablis	KILBEGGAN
22 June	Vodka Bleu	NEWTON ABBOT
06 July	Leaveitso	ROSCOMMON
15 July	Almier	KILLARNEY
16 July	Sardagna	SOUTHWELL
21 July	Sardagna	WORCESTER
30 July	Sardagna	BANGOR-ON-DEE
06 August	Arabian Moon	WORCESTER
06 August	Made In France	WORCESTER
09 August	Johnny Grand	SOUTHWELL
10 August	Isard III	NEWTON ABBOT
10 August	Minibule	NEWTON ABBOT
15 August	Marcel	STRATFORD
21 August	Marcel	NEWTON ABBOT
25 September	Vodka Bleu	MARKET RASEN

25 September	Liberman	MARKET RASEN
28 September	Made In France	EXETER
02 October	Vodka Bleu	CHEPSTOW
02 October	Yourman	CHEPSTOW
03 October	Say What You See	UTTOXETER
03 October	Miss Cospector	UTTOXETER
05 October	Hot Shots	HUNTINGDON
07 October	Shining Lights	LUDLOW
09 October	Escompteur	BANGOR-ON-DEE
09 October	Comply Or Die	BANGOR-ON-DEE
12 October	Roll Along	FONTWELL
17 October	Flinders	HEREFORD
18 October	Acertack	PLUMPTON
18 October	Escompteur	PLUMPTON
18 October	Bubba Boy	PLUMPTON
19 October	SMarcht Mover	EXETER
20 October	Spring Pursuit	CHEPSTOW
21 October	Tizi Ouzou	LUDLOW
21 October	Donald	LUDLOW
23 October	Marcel	KEMPTON
01 November	Try Catch Paddy	PLUMPTON
06 November	Beef Or Salmon	DOWN ROYAL
10 November	Marchk Equal	NEWBURY
10 November	Candarli	NEWBURY
11 November	Regal Bandit	TAUNTON
11 November	Lutea	TAUNTON
12 November	Marcel	CHELTENHAM
12 November	Comply Or Die	CHELTENHAM
13 November	Over The Creek	CHELTENHAM
13 November	Vodka Bleu	CHELTENHAM
13 November	Celestial Gold	CHELTENHAM
13 November	Stormcz	CHELTENHAM
14 November	Team Tassel	CHELTENHAM
15 November	Forest Chief	LEICESTER
18 November	Liberman	MARKET RASEN
19 November	Best Mate	EXETER
21 November	Over The Creek	AINTREE
22 November	King Killone	LUDLOW
22 November	Deliceo	LUDLOW
27 November	Vodka Bleu	NEWBURY
27 November	Marcel	NEWBURY
27 November	Celestial Gold	NEWBURY
27 November	Distant Prospect	NEWBURY
28 November	Lutea	NEWBURY
30 November	Made In France	NEWTON ABBOT
30 November	Mioche D'Estruval	NEWTON ABBOT
01 December	Tanterari	PLUMPTON

03 December	Melford	SANDOWN
04 December	Contraband	SANDOWN
04 December	La Lambertine	SANDOWN
05 December	Church Island	PUNCHESTOWN
06 December	Hot Weld	NEWCASTLE
06 December	Brave Thought	NEWCASTLE
07 December	Royal Hector	FONTWELL
08 December	Lorient Express	LEICESTER
10 December	Therealbandit	CHELTENHAM
11 December	Lough Derg	CHELTENHAM
11 December	Control Man	CHELTENHAM
13 December	Royal Hector	PLUMPTON
13 December	Locksmith	PLUMPTON
15 December	Tanterari	BANGOR-ON-DEE
16 December	Maximize	EXETER
17 December	Royal Hector	WINDSOR
17 December	Marcel	WINDSOR
17 December	Lorient Express	WINDSOR
30 December	Royal Hector	HAYDOCK

2005

01 January	Korelo	CHELTENHAM
01 January	Westender	CHELTENHAM
02 January	Wee Robbie	PLUMPTON
08 January	Marcel	SANDOWN
10 January	Celtic Son	TAUNTON
15 January	Celtic Son	WARWICK
17 January	Figaro Du Rocher	DONCASTER
18 January	Visibility	TOWCESTER
19 January	Miss Academy	NEWCASTLE
20 January	Medison	TAUNTON
21 January	Sixo	CHEPSTOW
22 January	Headliner	UTTOXETER
23 January	Ulaan Baatar	LEOPARDSTOWN
24 January	Inch Pride	FONTWELL
27 January	It's Music	WARWICK
27 January	Figaro Du Rocher	WARWICK
29 January	Well Chief	CHELTENHAM
31 January	Field Roller	EXETER
02February	Captain Corelli	LEICESTER
02February	Spring Pursuit	LEICESTER
03February	Inch Pride	TOWCESTER
04February	Maldoun	FONTWELL
11February	Celtic Son	KEMPTON
12February	Over The Creek	NEWBURY
13February	Headliner	EXETER
14February	Calvic	PLUMPTON

16February	Galero	MUSSELBURGH
16February	Credit	MUSSELBURGH
17February	Tanterari	TAUNTON
17February	Alikat	TAUNTON
18February	Anatar	SANDOWN
19February	Mephisto	HAYDOCK
03 March	Medison	LUDLOW
05 March	Zeta's River	NEWBURY
07 March	Fortune Island	HEREFORD
12 March	Medison	SANDOWN
14 March	It's Music	PLUMPTON
15 March	Contraband	CHELTENHAM
18 March	Fontanesi	CHELTENHAM
19 March	Glen Warrior	UTTOXETER
26 March	Commercial Flyer	NEWTON ABBOT
27 March	Maswaly	FAIRYHOUSE
29 March	Joaaci	CHEPSTOW
30 March	Escompteur	EXETER
09 April	Al Eile	AINTREE
10 April	Inch Pride	NEWTON ABBOT
12 April	Standin Obligation	EXETER
12 April	Commercial Flyer	EXETER
14 April	Inch Pride	CHELTENHAM
14 April	Enhancer	CHELTENHAM
15 April	Locksmith	AYR
15 April	Joaaci	AYR
15 April	Commercial Flyer	AYR
16 April	Locksmith	AYR
21 April	Commercial Flyer	PERTH
23 April	Well Chief	SANDOWN
26 April	Forget The Past	PUNCHESTOWN
21 June	Time Bandit	NEWTON ABBOT
03 July	Enhancer	MARKET RASEN
10 July	Wardash	STRATFORD
11 July	Fontanesi	NEWTON ABBOT
11 July	Twelve Paces	NEWTON ABBOT
13 July	Lahinch Lad	WORCESTER
16 July	Sardagna	MARKET RASEN
20 July	Chase The Sunset	WORCESTER
21 July	Tonic Du Charmil	UTTOXETER
27 July	Getoutwhenyoucan	NEWTON ABBOT
27 July	Fontanesi	NEWTON ABBOT
01 August	Cantgeton	NEWTON ABBOT
21 August	Getoutwhenyoucan	NEWTON ABBOT
29 August	Mexican Pete	HUNTINGDON
31 August	Flying Spur	NEWTON ABBOT
04 September	Wembury Point	FONTWELL

09 September	Cantgeton	BANGOR-ON-DEE
11 September	Charango Star	STRATFORD
22 September	Yourman	FONTWELL
22 September	Scarrabus	FONTWELL
23 September	Noble Sham	WORCESTER
24 September	Whirling	MARKET RASEN
01 October	Flotta	FONTWELL
04 October	Mexican Pete	HUNTINGDON
05 October	Yourman	EXETER
12 October	Flotta	WETHERBY
13 October	Alikat	LUDLOW
20 October	Palace Walk	LUDLOW
21 October	Roll Along	FAKENHAM
22 October	Standin Obligation	CHEPSTOW
23 October	Impek	AINTREE
26 October	Itsmyboy	CHELTENHAM
31 October	Ask The Gatherer	PLUMPTON
01 November	Racing Demon	EXETER
03 November	Harris Bay	TOWCESTER
05 November	Iris Bleu	WINCANTON
05 November	Celtic Son	WINCANTON
10 November	Tuesday's Child	LUDLOW
12 November	Not Left Yet	CHELTENHAM
12 November	Standin Obligation	CHELTENHAM
12 November	Our Vic	CHELTENHAM
13 November	Bannow Strand	CHELTENHAM
14 November	Nous Voila	LEICESTER
16 November	He's A Leader	WINCANTON
19 November	Admiral	HAYDOCK
28 November	Muttley Maguire	FOLKESTONE
01 December	Nous Voila	LEICESTER
02 December	Harris Bay	SANDOWN
03 December	Racing Demon	SANDOWN
06 December	Tora Bora	FONTWELL
08 December	Cruising River	TAUNTON
16 December	Acambo	WINDSOR
20 December	Wenceslas	FONTWELL
21 December	Harringay	LUDLOW
22 December	D J Flippance	AYR
30 December	Neveesou	TAUNTON
31 December	Basilea Star	WARWICK

2006

01 January	Joaaci	CHELTENHAM
04 January	Boundary House	WINCANTON
09 January	Harringay	TAUNTON
12 January	Palua	LUDLOW

14 January	Roll Along	WARWICK
15 January	Patsy Hall	LEOPARDSTOWN
21 January	Glasker Mill	HAYDOCK
21 January	Nous Voila	HAYDOCK
21 January	Don't Be Shy	HAYDOCK
21 January	Al Eile	HAYDOCK
28 January	Korelo	CHEPSTOW
31 January	Doc Row	FOLKESTONE
12 February	Racing Demon	EXETER
14 February	Yes My Lord	FOLKESTONE
15 February	Harris Bay	LEICESTER
16 February	Commercial Flyer	TAUNTON
16 February	Lizzie Bathwick	TAUNTON
18 February	Our Vic	LINGFIELD
18 February	Don't Be Shy	LINGFIELD
25 February	Brave Thought	NEWCASTLE
26 February	Premier Rouge	NAAS
28 February	Yes My Lord	LEICESTER
10 March	Aztec Warrior	SANDOWN
12 March	Be My Destiny	WARWICK
13 March	Rowlands Dream	TAUNTON
25 March	Harringay	NEWBURY
01 April	Tora Bora	FONTWELL
06 April	Celestial Gold	AINTREE
16 April	Kilbeggan Lad	CORK
17 April	Patsy Hall	FAIRYHOUSE
19 April	Our Vic	CHELTENHAM
20 April	Standin Obligation	CHELTENHAM
24 April	Flotta	TAUNTON
28 April	Harris Bay	SANDOWN
05 May	Westmeath Flyer	SOUTHWELL
05 May	Enhancer	SOUTHWELL
09 May	Standin Obligation	KELSO
17 May	General Grey	EXETER
18 May	Zaffamore	LUDLOW
08 June	Bearaway	NEWTON ABBOT
14 June	Alikat	MARKET RASEN
18 June	Inch Pride	STRATFORD
22 June	Kivotos	SOUTHWELL
28 June	Didbrook	WORCESTER
07 August	Alikat	NEWTON ABBOT
11 August	Palace Walk	SEDGEFIELD
14 August	Kivotos	SOUTHWELL
19 August	Estate	BANGOR-ON-DEE
20 August	Kings Brook	NEWTON ABBOT
22 August	Lutea	PERTH
22 August	Andre Chenier	PERTH

22 August	Arresting	PERTH
22 September	Legal Glory	WORCESTER
23 September	Kings Brook	MARKET RASEN
24 September	Sunley Song	HUNTINGDON
28 September	Proprioception	HEREFORD
30 September	Tanterari	FONTWELL
30 September	Fairlight Express	FONTWELL
01 October	Cruising River	UTTOXETER
01 October	Weet A Head	UTTOXETER
01 October	Tora Bora	UTTOXETER
04 October	Harris Bay	TOWCESTER

FLAT WINNERS

2003

| 19 May | Teorban | WOLVERHAMPTON (A.W) |
| 15 August | Mexican Miss | TRAMORE |

2004

| 13 June | Step Back | CORK |

Point-to-point stats courtesy of www.p2p.ie
Racing stats courtesy of *Racing Post*

INDEX